Stephanie Williams

Hongkong Bank   The building of Norman Foster's masterpiece

Little, Brown and Company   Boston   Toronto   London

First US edition
Library of Congress
Catalog Card Number 89-80072

10 9 8 7 6 5 4 3 2 1

Designed by Pentagram

Phototypeset by Keyspools Ltd
Golborne Lancs England

Printed in Spain
by Graficas Estella SA

Contents

For Sarah and Sam

Norman Foster first asked me to write this book in the spring of 1984. What he wanted, he said, was a true account of how the new headquarters for the Hongkong and Shanghai Banking Corporation had been built. For him, and his office, it had been an extraordinary project; for the public, especially in Hong Kong from where I had recently returned to live in London, it was a source of high controversy. Early in 1985, Sir Michael Sandberg, then chairman of the Bank, endorsed the idea. He too was keen to see what he described as a 'warts and all' account of how the new Bank had been built.

For me, the opportunity was irresistible. Under the terms of my commission with the Bank and Foster Associates both parties agreed to open their files on the project and to instruct their staff, and the consultants and major sub-contractors on the project, to speak to me frankly; in return, Sir Michael Sandberg and Norman Foster retained a veto over statements that they believed would unfairly damage the reputation of the Bank or Foster Associates. In the event, neither has exercised it, and the views expressed in this book are my own.

My aim was to be objective. Wherever possible, I have relied upon letters, reports, minutes of meetings and other immediately contemporary sources to confirm and round out what I have learnt in interviews. The manuscript has been read by Sir Michael Sandberg, Roy Munden, John Strickland and Ray Guy of the Hongkong Bank; and Norman Foster, Gordon Graham, Spencer de Grey, David Nelson, Ken Shuttleworth, Graham Phillips and Chris Seddon of Foster Associates. In addition, it has been read by Trevor Bedford and Norman Thompson, as members of both the board of the Bank at the time and of the Project Policy Co-ordination Committee which oversaw the construction of the building; and also by Ron Mead, the project co-ordinator; Jack Zunz and Mike Glover from Ove Arup & Partners; Frank Archer of John Lok/Wimpey, and Dennis Levett and Gifford Carey of Levett & Bailey. In each case, these people have checked facts, and attempted to amplify, rather than to inhibit, statements in my book. For all their time and their patience, their efforts in helping me to get the story right, while, at the same time allowing me to draw my own conclusions and write it as I saw fit, I cannot adequately begin to thank them.

It has been impossible to tell it all. The development of the building, by hundreds of people, in locations around the world, over a period of nearly eight years, was extraordinarily complex. Even as I write, I continue to learn about many new things that happened during the course of the project. Many problems and issues which once coloured days and even weeks of the project with worry, bitterness and dissension were put aside long before it was finished, and are forgotten now. Some of these I have included; others have been put aside in an attempt to put on record those things that made this project remarkable. Every person who came near this project has his own version of what happened; each of us would write this story differently.

In a very important sense, however, it does not matter that what follows is the story of the Hongkong Bank. What is revealed here – possibly for the first time – is the true nature of the long, painful and extremely difficult process of realising any major building. Most building projects, from the smallest house conversion to the completion of a major headquarters like this one, are fraught with conflict and difficulty; many involve bungling and misjudgment, are open to bad publicity and lawsuits. Provided that he has the confidence of his client, the architect is like a choreographer: he can set the dance in motion, but he depends upon a whole corps of other specialists, and contractors, to bring off the performance. The legal, practical and technical obstacles standing in the way of any building are formidable; when that building purports to be something more, they are frequently overwhelming.

This is one reason why an account like this is, as far as I know, without precedent. Few would have the courage to let it be told. The other is that, without the co-operation I have had, such an account would be almost impossible to compile. On site especially, events move fast. Problems are extremely complex, frequently dangerous, and have to be resolved with speed. Afterwards, people remember that there were difficulties, but memory of their details is shortlived. As soon as a project is complete, the design team, the consultants and sub-contractors disperse; files and papers are weeded out and destroyed, reduced to microfilm or stored in an obscure location. At the end of the day, all that stands is the creation itself; of the process that put it there, there remain some drawings, a model or two, and the fallible memories of those who helped realise it.

In all of this, the Hongkong Bank was no exception – except, perhaps, in terms of its scale. During the course of its construction, it became the focus of international press attention. Dubbed the world's most expensive building, in early 1983 the project was reported to be running wildly out of control. What was really happening was scarcely appreciated even by those at the heart of the events at the time.

I do not know if the Bank is the world's most expensive building; at over £500 million it is undeniably extremely costly. I suspect, however, that the only fair comparison might be with buildings from other ages, or other products of enlightened patronage in our time. It was not intended that this building should be just like any other. This was a project that went beyond creating a conventional building of aesthetic merit: here was an attempt to fabricate a building in a way that had never been tried before, using standards of perfection previously confined to the realms of defence or nuclear construction. Yet in spite of these ambitious goals, in spite of the enormous tasks of researching, developing and co-ordinating products from markets from around the world; despite the personal conflicts, the physical difficulties, the sheer hard work; and most of all against the implacable deadlines of the timescale: they brought it off. What follows in this book is the story of the building of a masterpiece by one of the foremost architects of the twentieth century.

If it had been Norman's idea in the first place, without Sir Michael's enthusiasm this book would never have happened. More importantly, without the sustained support and practical encouragement of Gordon Graham at Foster Associates, and, until his retirement from the Bank in late 1985, of Roy Munden, my task would have been impossible. They gave me the resources, laid the necessary papers before me and provided the introductions which allowed me to get to the heart of the story of the building of the Bank.

Many others, usually extremely busy, and much preoccupied with the actual business of getting the building up, took valuable time to brief me well and provide me with yet more papers, introductions and leads to information. In particular, I must thank Frank Archer, project director of the John Lok/Wimpey consortium for the thoroughness he applied to my queries, and his offer to put the papers of the management contractor at my disposal; Gifford Carey of Levett & Bailey for his clear explanation of the cost picture of the project; and Mike Glover and Tony Fitzpatrick of Ove Arup & Partners for their patience with my seemingly endless questions about the structure.

In addition, I am grateful to Phil Bonzon, of Cupples Products, for one of the most lucid explanations of how a designer sets about his work; and to Ray Guy of the Hongkong Bank for his invigorating tours of the building under construction.

To Foster Associates, I am deeply indebted. Foster himself has overseen the design of this book, and provided the illustrations. Many members of staff, in both London and Hong Kong, helped me put together the details of this story. I am especially grateful to David Nelson, Graham Phillips, Chris Seddon and Ken Shuttleworth for their initial scepticism, their patient explanations, and finally their real enthusiasm for my project.

Katie Harris has spent many hours helping me track my way through the vast Foster archive of illustrative material; Janet Procter has fielded much of my communication with Hong Kong. My grateful thanks are also due to George Cardona of the Hongkong Bank, to Frances Kelly, agent for this book, to the Reverend Carl Smith for background research on the Hong Kong economy, to Gareth Davies of Simmons & Simmons for legal advice and to Robyn McLean, formerly of the Hong Kong Public Records Office, for her long support of my research into the urban history of Hong Kong. Wholehearted thanks are also due to the entire team of editors, designers and production staff at Jonathan Cape who worked so tirelessly on this book's behalf, and to Alan Fletcher and Debbie Martindale at Pentagram for their painstaking care over the design.

During my research trips to Hong Kong many friends looked after me. In particular I must thank Peter and Ruth Willoughby and Tim and Hilary Bridgman and their children. In London I could not have done without the cheerful help of Maureen Molloy, and the enthusiasm of Tanja Betterman and Silvia Sekora. Finally, to my husband, William Knight, my most constructive and long-suffering critic, who believed in this book from the first moment that Norman suggested it, my most grateful thanks.

Stephanie Williams
London, 1988

A case of modern patronage

Symbols of the Hongkong and Shanghai Bank: one of two bronze lions, copies of ones which were made for the Shanghai branch in 1923, which traditionally guard the entrance of the Bank facing the harbour.

The *fung-shui* man stands quite still. The twenty staff from International Corporate Accounts are silent, watching intently, as a patient will watch while being examined by a doctor, for the least expression that all may not be well. Small, almost dapper in his brown suit and mustard tie, his face wizened like a walnut, Mr Lai exudes an air of seeing things that other people cannot see. Originally, it had been the department's two young secretaries who had asked to consult him. Their new desks are aligned directly beneath a great metal beam. It is a cardinal rule of Chinese geomancy that such a feature will bring them ill health and bad fortune. The manager of the department, who happened to be German, thought – and the rest of the staff agreed – that a geomancer ought to be asked to guide them on how to ward off these and other evil influences in the vicinity. Everyone joked about it, but it was better to be safe than sorry, and the manager had called in Mr Lai.

The staff had moved into their offices in the new headquarters of the Hongkong and Shanghai Banking Corporation two days earlier, on a warm and sunny November day in 1985. They were right to be concerned. During the course of its construction many stories had been told about this strange new building. It stood on the site of the Bank's old headquarters, a building which had been regarded in the popular mind as a symbol of prosperity and stability for the whole community of Hong Kong. After that building had been demolished, a chain of events had been unleashed that threatened to undermine the entire welfare of the colony: negotiations between the British and the Chinese authorities had been opened over the issue of the future of the territory, when the lease of the New Territories expired in July 1997. Gradually, as this new building had risen from the ground, the panic with which the early negotiations between Britain and China had been greeted had subsided. By now, the political future had been settled for nearly a year. With consequences that could only be guessed at, the whole of the territory was to be returned to China in 1997. For most of those who were now to work in this new building, brave new symbol of Hong Kong's well-being, the future in the long term was dangerously uncertain. It behoved the staff to take advice on the environment that they were to inhabit, to take what precautions they could to safeguard their welfare.

13

In any case, this building was quite unlike any other they had ever inhabited before. To begin with, it did not sit on the ground, but was raised on a series of steel columns. It was made almost entirely of glass and steel, and was full of escalators moving up and down. Inside, it looked a bit like a set for *Star Wars*. On the thirtieth floor where they were standing now, there was an uncanny sense of being, in fact, much closer to the ground. On either side of a wide, open floor were vast windows, stretching the whole length of the building. The views, through full-height panes of glass, were stunning: on one side of the building lush tropical greenery tumbled down the hillside of the Peak, on the other the brilliant blue of the harbour and a haze of Kowloon were spread wide. They provided in fact a classic recipe for excellent health and good fortune according to the basic precepts of *fung-shui* (literally 'wind and water'), the ancient Chinese method of interpreting the effect which the surrounding landscape and predominant physical features might have on the fortunes of those who lived in the vicinity. With a mountain at the back of the Bank to shelter it from strong winds and evil influences, and wide, open views over water to welcome the good in the front, the excellence of the overall position of the building went a long way towards making up for any shortcomings in the way the furniture was arranged.

Mr Lai reassured the staff. A wastebasket rearranged here, a desk moved a few inches there, and the secretaries had been moved beyond the evil influences of the beam above their heads. A bank of elegant matt-black filing cabinets, which to several of the staff looked too much like coffins to bring good luck to anyone, was discounted. One accountant, who sat with her back towards an escalator, was disturbed by the sense of constant movement, like a tiger, threatening her desk. If she turned it to put the tiger to her left, she would face all the beneficial effects coming in from the harbour. But that would throw out the orderly symmetry of the lines of desks in the open office. A more practical solution was required. A vase of fresh flowers, or a plant, symbols of life and beauty, placed at the head of the escalator, would ward off the tiger. After two hours, Mr Lai had inspected each desk and room in the department. A mirror had been prescribed for this position, a plant for that, a chair moved here. Overall, his diagnosis was excellent. The *fung-shui* was almost unrivalled in Hong Kong. Whether the staff really believed him or not, they could rest easy. They had taken out their insurance.

The Hongkong Bank is an extraordinary institution, the product of an unusual history in a unusual place. It has a personality which goes far beyond the conventional, western notion of a bank. It was among the first British overseas banks to be opened in the Far East. The Hongkong Bank owed nothing to a head office or financial backing in Europe, America or India. It had been founded in 1865 by the merchants of the young colony of Hong Kong, to finance their trade in China, Japan and the Philippines and did so with great success. Indeed, the affairs of the Hongkong Bank reveal a major facet of the involvement of the west

Worshippers at Wong Tai Sin temple, Kowloon, 1986.

with China. The Bank managed consortia which financed a series of Chinese Imperial Government loans, including the money to cover Japanese demands for war reparations following the Sino-Japanese war of 1894–5; it became the main instrument in the supply of capital for much of the Chinese railway system; it supported several of the viceroys and in 1913 organised a £25 million international loan to the supporters of Yuan Shih-k'ai – Sun Yat Sen's opponent.[1] At the same time as its doors opened for business in Hong Kong, the Bank opened a branch in Shanghai and an agency in London. It also appointed an agent in Bangkok, the first bank of any description to do so. The Bank was one of the first five foreign banks to open in Japan in 1866 (three of them soon failed). Before long, offices in the other Chinese Treaty Ports – Amoy, Foochow, Hankow, Tientsin – had been opened. Calcutta and Bombay, Saigon, Haiphong, and Singapore; Jakarta, Surabaya, Manila, Penang: within fifteen years the Bank had spread a network across much of Asia. In 1875, it opened a branch in San Francisco – the focal point of the American trade with Canton – and in 1880, still on the back of the China Trade, it became the first British bank to open in New York. By the turn of the century, it was the leading foreign bank in Asia, and, by the outbreak of the Second World War, by virtue of its intimate local connections and a determined policy of developing close ties, 'the most powerful banking organisation of foreign interests in China'.[2]

Meanwhile, in Hong Kong itself, the Bank had developed into a quasi central bank. There is an old saying, not to be discounted, that 'Hong Kong is ruled by the Bank, the Jockey Club and the Governor – in that order'. For well over 100 years the Bank has been the principal banker to the government of Hong Kong. It acts for the government in the foreign exchange and money markets, and issues 80 per cent of the local currency notes. It helps to steer the territory through financial crises, organises corporate rescues, and – as part of the Hong Kong Association of Banks – plays a part in setting interest rates.

It is this role, together with the Chinese connection, the intimate meshing of common British and Chinese interests, which goes a long way towards explaining the unique character of the Hongkong Bank today. It is very powerful, fiercely independent, immensely profitable, and very careful of its public relations. Its banking principles and its most senior management remain British. Fuelled by the most up-to-date technology the West can offer, its banking methods are among the most advanced in the world. Nominally, its ownership rests, however, largely in Hong Kong, where the efforts and hard work of the local Chinese population have been responsible for much of its profitability.[3] Between 1949 and the late 1970s, while China remained closed to the West, the Bank concentrated on the recovery and development of Hong Kong itself after the traumas of the Second World War and the Communist Revolution. It became fantastically profitable. Between 1949 and 1986, its profits rose from HK$17.8 million to HK$2.49 billion, a compounded growth rate of approximately 15 per cent per

Symbols of the Bank:

香港上海滙豐銀行

信譽保証 安全可靠

1979 Hongkong and Shanghai Bank logo.

$100 note showing the 1935 Hong Kong headquarters, issued 24 September 1959.

year. In 1965, it purchased a controlling interest in Hong Kong's second largest bank, the Hang Seng, and rescued it when rumours caused a run on its funds after a slump in the property market. According to the *Far Eastern Economic Review*,[4] the Hongkong Bank now controls 60 per cent of the deposits in Hong Kong's banking system. An important source of these deposits for both the Bank and the Hang Seng, with its entirely Chinese management, is the Hong Kong factory worker, who puts a fixed amount of his income every month into his savings account: a simple, easy, reliable operation taken care of by a name the workers have come to know and trust.[5] Between 1960 and 1984 the Bank's local retail branches grew from seven to 288. By the late 1970s, the Hongkong Bank had come to fulfil a unique function in the consciousness of the local population. It was involved in merchant banking, stockbroking, investment management, insurance, shipping; it owned portions of the local airline, Cathay Pacific, and the main English-language newspaper, the *South China Morning Post*. In a society which was extremely money-conscious, the image of the Bank had become highly prominent; expanding television advertising accompanying the advent of auto-pay systems and cash-card machines at the end of the 1970s, only served to make it more so.

Visually, that image was based on the façade of the Bank's headquarters, which had been completed back in 1935. The profile of the building was used everywhere as the trademark of the Bank's business: on the back of its banknotes, as a logo on its publications, on the signs over the door of every one of its branches in the colony. Mention 'the Bank' and the vision of a commercial organisation of rock-solid substance rose before the eyes. The Bank's headquarters was a building of monumental massing, with severely vertical lines and expressionist decoration redolent of the eclecticism of the 1930s. For much of its life, it had dominated the foreshore of Hong Kong and dwarfed its neighbours. It was the symbol of all that the Bank stood for.

There is little doubt that among the largely illiterate population of Hong Kong of the immediate post-war period, this building, with its mighty symbolism and dominating presence, assumed a powerful, almost mythological character. Long before it was conceived, however, the Bank had adopted the practice of inscribing the reverse of its notes with a picture of its Hong Kong or Shanghai headquarters, to indicate clearly the source of the notes it was issuing. Every town in China had a large number of private banks or 'money shops', many of them backed only with small capital, and perhaps operating only within a street or neighbourhood, each with its own device for issuing notes. The Chinese characters chosen by the Bank to represent its name, pronounced 'Wayfoong' in English, translate as 'abundance of remittances'. A name only, of course, but in Hong Kong the building with which it later became associated also housed the government's treasury. Here was the source of most of the colony's currency. Was it merely because its massive steel vaults provided a ready-made bomb-proof bunker that the Japanese army of occupation made this building

Entrance of the Hongkong and Shanghai Bank, designed by Palmer and Turner, in Queen's Road, Hong Kong, 1886.

'Spare no expense but dominate the Bund.' Perspective by Cyril Fairey for Palmer and Turner to illustrate their proposals for the Shanghai branch of the Hongkong and Shanghai Banking Corporation, completed 1923.

Octagonal hall inside the Shanghai branch completed in 1923, with mosaic ceiling details by a Russian, Podgoursky, who would later prepare similar designs for the Hong Kong headquarters.

its headquarters in 1941? It was said that customers in search of a secure and lasting burial ground interred ashes of their cremated dead in its vaults. As happened to families known to be wealthy, unwanted babies were placed on its doorstep. At every Chinese New Year, every Christmas season, armies of amateur photographers took pictures of the Bank with its special seasonal decorations. In front of the Bank's main entrance crouched two magnificent bronze lions; by the late 1970s their paws had been rubbed to a high polish by the hands of passers-by hoping that some of the prosperity of the Bank might be transferred.

Was the Bank conscious of how powerful the potential was for evoking superstitious trust when it first built its early buildings in China? It is doubtful. But the Bank was certainly aware of the value of building well, and of using architecture to convey a message. Its first headquarters was completed in 1886 on the present site in Hong Kong. The result of a competition between three local firms of architects, the new building was designed by Clement Palmer, a young architect fresh out from England. It was a remarkable building. The half which faced the harbour was little more than a late-Victorian version of its neighbours, the Italianate arcaded buildings common on the China coast. But the half that looked back towards Victoria Peak, and faced the colony's main street, Queen's Road, was a magnificent baroque domed bank which owed everything to the seeds Sir John Soane had planted in his designs for the Bank of England, and which had now sprouted a whole breed of new conventions for bank building in Europe and America: glazed domes, clerestory lighting, splendid marble banking halls and monumental stone façades.[6]

It was Palmer's firm, Palmer & Turner, which carried out most of the Bank's subsequent architectural commissions, in remarkably eclectic styles throughout Asia. In Shanghai, the redevelopment of the Bank's branch was completed in 1923 by GL 'Tug' Wilson, then the senior partner of the practice. The result was one of the most lavish exercises in British colonial architecture of the twentieth century. Wilson's brief from the Bank seems to have been fairly unequivocal. When he applied for permission to make improvements that would add another million dollars to the cost of the building, the instructions from head office came back: 'Spare no expense but dominate the Bund.'[7] The magnificence of the resulting building, crowned by a massive dome, and the lavishness of its internal decoration were without compare. Two splendid bronze lions, predecessors of the Hong Kong lions that would later become symbols of the corporation, flanked the flight of steps leading to the main entrance. The building's unrivalled grandeur was popularly acknowledged; today, that building is the headquarters of the Shanghai municipal government, and the local headquarters of the Communist party.

The success of the Shanghai headquarters made Wilson the logical choice of architect when, together with the board, the chief manager of the Bank, Sir Vandeleur Grayburn decided in the early 1930s that the

'Progress through the Ages in
Transport, Trade and Industry in the
Western and Eastern Hemispheres':
details of the mosaic ceiling from the
1935 headquarters.

'Men of Vision': granite piers on the façade of the 1935 Hong Kong headquarters.

19 September 1934: the steel frame of the 1935 building under construction; 150 tons of steel had been erected in the previous week.

Bank ought to take advantage of the depression to build itself a new head office in Hong Kong. The Bank purchased City Hall next door. Now the site was more than double that of the existing, 1886, building. If anything, Wilson had to outshine his performance in Shanghai.

He took his inspiration for the new headquarters from the latest skyscrapers of New York, with their neo-classical massing and eclectic range of details culled from the art deco of the Vienna Secessionists, the German Expressionists and the fashionable 'Egyptian' style. But Wilson also repeated many of his decorative ideas from Shanghai. Details like the lamp fittings, the staircases and balustrades, the domed mosaic ceilings and the two lions at the entrance were almost identical. The Hong Kong building was constructed on a frame of high-tensile steel, a material not previously used outside North America. It was prefabricated and shipped out to Hong Kong from England, together with a range of special equipment, concrete mixers, steel scaffolding (the first ever used in Hong Kong), furnishings and plumbing, bronze and other materials, and marbles from Devon, Italy, Belgium and Sweden. Only the granite used to clad the building was local, cut from a quarry specially opened for the project.

The building, completed in 1935, was put up in record time – less than two years – and designed to be as forward-thinking and efficient as possible. Like the Shanghai headquarters, which had the first system in Asia, the new Hong Kong building was fully air-conditioned. It had high-speed lifts and specially commissioned furnishings and filing systems by Roneo. Not only the structure, but also the plate glass in the windows were designed to withstand the winds of a 130 mph typhoon. There were cavities left behind the walls of the manager's office to take the kind of wiring anticipated by the likely advent of telex communications, and the roof was specially loaded to take autogyros. It was a building that at the time would have been noteworthy in New York or London. News of its completion was reported around the world. To have built such a building in a distant colony was regarded as an astonishing achievement.[8]

Inside, the banking hall covered an acre. It was crowned by a vast mosaic barrel-vaulted ceiling where 'Progress through the Ages in Transport, Trade and Industry in the Western and Eastern Hemispheres' centred on a great allegorical group featuring Helios, the Sun God, driving his chariot of light across the sky. Ornamentation throughout the building was heavily symbolic. Figureheads depicting 'Men of Vision' surmounted massive piers on the towers; besides these, lions' heads represented 'Strength'. The main entrance in Queen's Road was through a pair of magnificent bronze gates beneath a grille and three Norman figures in armour, the whole a sort of medieval portcullis. Then there were the famous lions couchant, copied from those which guarded the Shanghai headquarters. Flanking the main entrance to the Bank from the harbour, they would soon become almost as powerful a symbol of the Bank's existence as the building itself.

'Men of Vision' – that sunburst in the dome of the banking hall – the Bank as a beacon beaming light to the masses. The portcullis, the bronze lamp standards, the marble walls and floors and massive black marble pillars all combined to suggest an impregnable institution of iron stability. By comparison with Shanghai in 1935, Hong Kong was a backwater, but the message of the severe and monumental lines of the new Bank headquarters left passers-by in no doubt that this was an organisation of substance, with its eyes on the future.

But in 1978, when this story begins, the Bank had outgrown this headquarters. It would require a massive renovation to bring it up to date, to take account of the modern advances in fire precautions and equip it for the latest systems of telecommunication. Departments were now scattered piecemeal into offices all over central Hong Kong, in space that amounted to almost a third again of what the headquarters building offered. Conservative estimates suggested that the Bank would grow at least as rapidly over the next five or ten years as it had during the 1970s. Within five years, it was judged that the Bank would require at least another 4,185 square metres (45,000 square feet) of working space. This *ad hoc* way of dispersing offices and staff could not continue much longer.[9] The issue of any redevelopment would have to be handled carefully, however. In the hard-won prosperity and stability of post-war Hong Kong, the Bank's headquarters stood out, a well-loved monument to good fortune.

Even if most people in Hong Kong today dismiss *fung-shui* as mere superstition, belief in its tenets is still sufficiently powerful for it to be considered a valid reason for compensation or a change of design when villagers in the outlying areas claim that a new road or housing development will destroy their good *fung-shui*. Furthermore, the whole character of Hong Kong as a city had changed almost beyond recognition since the completion of the old headquarters in 1935. Any attempt to create a new building with the same capacity to dominate its surroundings and capture the popular imagination in this new context promised to be unusually difficult.

Physically, Hong Kong is unique. *Fung-shui* was a far cry from the more practical issues which concerned the building of the new Hongkong Bank. Norman Foster is fond of saying that the Bank that he designed is a unique response to time and place; that it could have been built nowhere else but Hong Kong, and conceived at no other time than at the very end of the 1970s. The Hong Kong he is talking about is high-rise, high-density, a mixture of Chinese and European influences, a city where things happen fast and the past is quickly forgotten. In building, Hong Kong is a place where above all two things count: the ability to get the maximum floorspace out of a site, and to build at remarkable speed. The wider context was profoundly influential.

Hong Kong's urban areas combine the world's highest concentrations of people with one of the fastest rates of development in the world. The

1981 census showed that the *average* density of urban Hong Kong, Kowloon and the neighbouring new town of Tsuen Wan was 28,479 persons per square kilometre (10,995 per square mile), two and a half times Tokyo's comparable figures.[10] With a population of 5,500,000 Hong Kong is small; as a British colony, isolated, and curiously provincial. Yet because of its position on the borders of China and South-East Asia, its concentrated wealth, free political system and a sophisticated Western expertise, it is immensely powerful. A free port in the south of China, the territory today supports the world's second largest container port, and the fourth most important financial centre after London, New York and Tokyo. In 1979, the issue of 1997 and the future of the territory as a British colony was no more than a froth of cloud on a distant horizon. Instead, local business interest was concentrated on a rising stock market, and an expanding property boom, the third of its kind since 1945.

For Hong Kong is exclusively a post-war city. Scarcely any pre-war buildings survive. Even in the New Territories, a brief hinterland between the highly urbanised areas of Kowloon and Hong Kong and the Chinese border, few examples of Chinese vernacular building remain. Some parts of Hong Kong have been redeveloped not once but twice and, in the case of one celebrated site in Central district, three times since the war. In 1970, 95 per cent of all buildings in the city were less than twenty-five years old and the majority of these had been constructed between 1955 and 1968.[11]

The reason why Hong Kong is so new, and has become so densely crowded, is that since 1945 it has been subjected to huge migrations of people from China. The colony has been a haven for Chinese refugees through most of the troubled points of recent Chinese history, ever since the outbreak of the Tai Ping Rebellion in the 1850s. The outbreak of war with the Japanese in 1937 brought 750,000 immigrants to the colony over the following three years. During the Second World War and the occupation of Hong Kong by the Japanese, more than one million people returned to China. When it was over people came back to Hong Kong, at first at the rate of 100,000 per week. By the end of 1947, the population had trebled from 600,000 at the end of the war, to over 1,800,000. Then, in October 1949, the Communist Revolution succeeded. By May 1950, 750,000 refugees had crossed the 17-mile border with China to the north.

Before the move to high-rise building. Western District, Hong Kong Island, 1953.

At this time Hong Kong was a city only four or five storeys tall. It had accommodation and livelihood for perhaps 1,200,000. It was concentrated in a small area on the north shore of Hong Kong Island where the first settlement, Victoria, was founded in 1841. Because of the steeply mountainous nature of the island, the built-up areas had been limited to land which had been progressively reclaimed along the coastline. The city stretched along the north coast of the island from Kennedy Town in the west to Wanchai, development thinning towards Causeway Bay and becoming completely rural at the fishing village of

Shaukiwan in the east. There was a road that completely circled the island, but the south side of the island was almost entirely unpopulated except for the fishing village of Aberdeen. Across the harbour, where the Kowloon peninsula had been acquired in 1860, building was loosely developed, mainly around the terminus of the Kowloon-Canton railway. The New Territories were entirely rural.

Outside a small section of Hong Kong's Central district devoted to western business and where the Bank had its headquarters, most of the colony's buildings were a standard type of Chinese tenement block. The European parts of the town were marked by spacious planning, and large, classically detailed buildings built of granite. By contrast the Chinese districts were much more intensively planned and developed, with narrower streets paved with granite, lined with rows of tenement houses. These tenements were higher and deeper descendants of the common shop-house that had first been built in Hong Kong and which remained traditional elsewhere in China. They were normally 5 metres (15 feet) wide, the average length of a China fir beam, and three or four storeys high, but stretched back deeply 20–30 metres (60–90 feet) from the street. On the ground floor was a shop or a workshop. Each of the floors above, however, was arranged as one long room from front to back, with a single toilet, and a room for cooking at the rear. Commonly each 'tenement floor' was let to one tenant who sub-divided it with partitions into cubicles, which he sub-let to others. In turn, the tenant of a cubicle might sub-let a bedspace to someone else. This was the basic theory, which was refined and extended whenever pressure for accommodation became more acute.

Thus, with the vast influx of refugees at the end of the war, the floors of the urban tenements were infinitely divided and sub-divided into cubicles, and sitting spaces, store spaces, business spaces, 'cocklofts' (ranging in size from a shelf to a mini-mezzanine), and bedspaces – which might be let in slots of eight hours each. Each building became home to extraordinary numbers, sometimes hundreds, of people. At the same time, squatter settlements – with no roads, no mains water, sanitation or electricity – grew up wherever they could find a foothold on Hong Kong Island. In just two years in the early 1950s the numbers of squatters rose from 30,000 to an estimated 300,000 people. In Kowloon, vast tracks of shacks, sheltering an average of 4,900 people to the hectare (2,000 to the acre) in flimsy, single-storey huts, gradually expanded until, by 1954, the normal expansion of Kowloon had been brought to a halt because all the land suitable for building had been covered by squatters. On Christmas night 1953, a fire in a squatter area in northern Kowloon took hold. Within hours, more than 50,000 people – the equivalent then of the city of Chester – had lost their rudimentary homes. The sheer numbers of homeless prompted the government to take effective steps towards a full-scale public housing programme. Then, on 1 January 1956, a new building ordinance which permitted high-rise building came into effect. It was the start of an astonishing ten-year building boom.

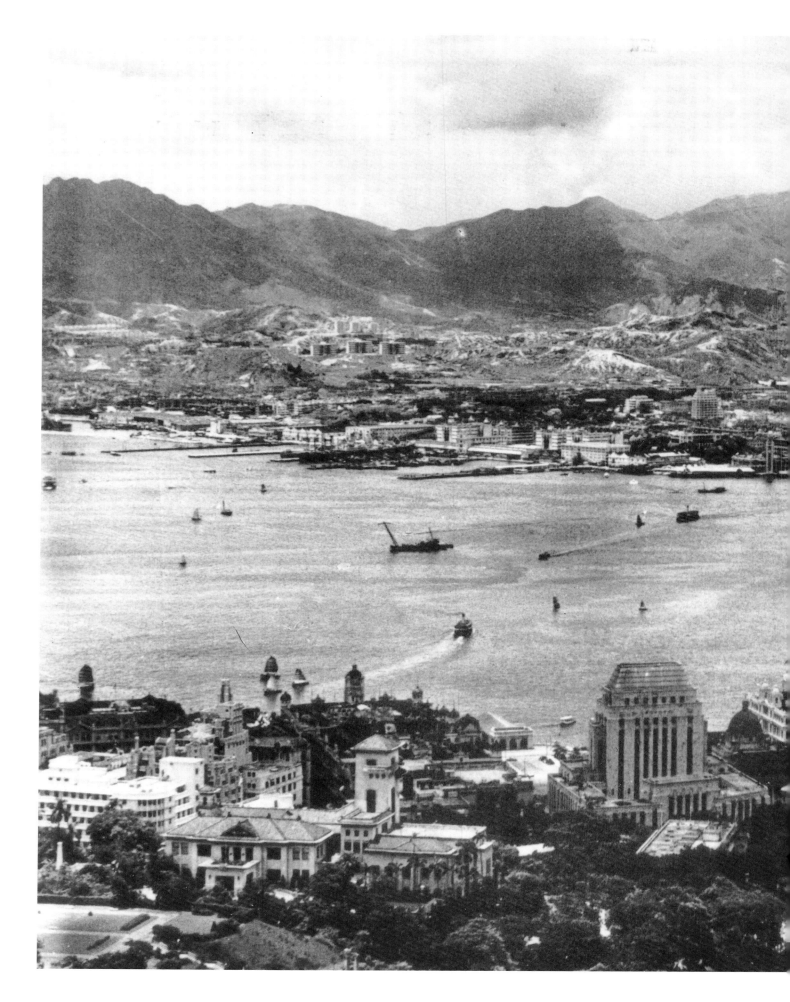

Given the demand for more space and the opportunity to provide it, those who owned property leapt at the chance to redevelop. There was a great surplus of labour among the refugee population, and no shortage of funds or experience. Between 1946 and 1948 275 Shanghai companies had transferred their registration from Shanghai to Hong Kong. As Joe England has pointed out,[12] *Fortune* magazine estimated that as much as US$50 million of Chinese wealth had taken refuge in Hong Kong by October 1947. The Shanghainese in particular 'injected comparatively more capital, more skilled labour, more knowledge of markets, more entrepreneurial flair, and more sheer industrial expertise than probably any non-industrial state has received in modern times, including Israel'.

As soon as it was announced that the building ordinances were to be changed, Hong Kong rapidly assimilated the principles of high-rise building. With the arrival on the market of cheap, relatively high-speed lifts, contractors in the colony began to construct buildings that were little more than items of equipment: four-square concrete shelters in which flats, open tenement floors, self-contained apartments and shops, offices and factories could be stacked up. All of these could be let profitably to the burgeoning population. For the first time factory floors were mounted one on top of the other in high-rise buildings. During this period, unqualified draughtsmen, 'teahouse designers', churned out drawings produced from the geometrical calculations required to meet the building regulations. Some of the towers were built singly, where one narrow tenement had stood before. Others were the product of several landlords joining forces to create sites filling entire city blocks. The standards of building were generally poor. Universally, concrete, the only locally obtainable building material, was used. Inside finishes were rudimentary: concrete floors and, often, concrete block walls. Extras like plastering, extended plumbing, hot water supplies and air-conditioning were the responsibility of the tenants. Many high-rise blocks of flats were built without garbage chutes, and if a building was less than eight storeys high it frequently did not have a lift. The speed of construction, normally under two years from submission of plans to completion of a high-rise block fifteen storeys high, set new records in Asia. The amount of money spent on construction had never been seen in the colony before: private investment in housing alone amounted to 4 per cent of GNP between 1963 and 1968.[13]

View east over Causeway Bay, 1979.

This building boom did far more than change the Hong Kong skyline. The social and economic effects were widespread, but they remain largely uncharted. Certainly it was clear by the early 1960s that while crowding within separate contained flats had improved, net site densities of 12,350 people per hectare (5,000 per acre) were becoming normal in the built-up areas, while it was by no means uncommon to find individual building blocks where the density rate exceeded a rate of 24,700 per hectare (10,000 per acre).[14] Moreover, the new brand of high-rise building had simply been imposed on a street pattern that in

Causeway Bay.

North Point, Hong Kong, 1980.

some parts of the colony had remained little changed from what it had been at the end of the nineteenth century. A huge new post-war population had taken root, in many areas where it was too late to change the roads. The building regulations were changed again, with effect from 1966, to prevent the worst excesses of overbuilding. This is why most of the apartments, office blocks and hotels built during the next building boom, which began in 1972, stand on top of a five-storey podium containing shops and restaurants.

If the Chinese architectural tradition had proved incapable of the mass-production and adaptation to the huge variety of new uses which life in post-war industrial Hong Kong required, the character of this new, high-rise city was very much defined by the way the Chinese had lived previously. The congestion of people carrying on a multitude of activities in the same small place intensified. The Chinese tradition of a rich and varied street-life proliferated and now began to be carried on vertically, on different floors, up into the buildings. High-rise buildings provided space for all manner of means of making a living, including all but the heaviest and most noxious of manufacturing. Today it is common to go shopping for clothes, or jewellery, to visit a travel agent, go to a clinic or out to lunch in suites located on different floors in a series of tower blocks. Efficient vertical transportation rapidly assumed even more importance than that along the ground; most people could find anything they needed within a short walk of home or workplace, but baulked at carrying heavy loads up more than a few storeys. Because of the great concentrations of population within very small areas, banks and chains of supermarkets, Chinese department stores, restaurants and chemists built dense networks of outlets. The congestion at ground level encouraged pedestrians to take comparatively longer journeys across high-level walkways, through buildings and across man-made plazas to avoid the discomfort at ground level and to take the opportunity to escape out of the heat and humidity, or drenching downpours, into the cool of air-conditioning. In the same way great interior public spaces – like indoor shopping centres, which are air-conditioned and cool – take the place of the large central parks to be found in London or New York.

The story of post-war housing in Hong Kong, however sketchy, is important because it gives some indication of the extreme pressure on space in the colony. Furthermore, the conventions which applied to the building of housing applied equally to building commercially. Before the end of 1957, less than two years after the 1956 building ordinance had come into effect, articles in the newspapers on subjects like 'The changing face of Hong Kong' were calling attention to the new orthodoxy in building – in the following example, as it affected the expatriate Englishman: '. . . soon the old porticoed, heavily pillared building with its high ceilings, fans and broad verandahs would be as out of date as the pith helmet'.[15] The new trend was towards 'functional architecture' in both the commercial and the domestic sphere. In the city, maximum use was being made of a site; elsewhere, apartment blocks were replacing villas and former lawns and gardens were being turned into sites for garages and car parks.

The post-war building regulations were specifically intended to permit the kind of multi-storey reinforced concrete frame construction associated with the international style of architecture then becoming fashionable in America. The 1956 regulations said that a building could be built to be twice as high as the width of the street it faced; above that point the main walls were required to be set back within an angle of 76 degrees with the horizontal. Subject to these limitations the height of a building was only restricted by its permitted volume, calculated by multiplying the width of the street by the area of the site by an arbitrary factor, 'F', the plot ratio. Factor 'F' increased where a building was on a corner site, and again if it abutted on to three or more streets. Designing a building became little more than a question of doing a few sums, drawing straight lines, and submitting plans and elevations for building ordinance approval; that, in most cases was what was done.

It is worth noting that the art of architecture and the role of the architect as it is understood in the West was an alien concept not just in Hong Kong, but in all of China. By the advent of the twentieth century the same kind of buildings, erected by craftsmen, had been built in China of the same materials, to the same designs, for more than 2,000 years. The layout and appearance of buildings were dictated not so much by a concern for aesthetics as by an imperial building code and an all-pervasive code of ethics. These decreed, for example, that the hall built for an emperor was to have ten columns and be divided into nine bays, that of a prince was permitted to have eight, a mandarin six and an ordinary person four columns, or three sections to his house. Details of decoration were also according to rank. Most buildings of any significance were regarded as a sort of stage-set for ritualised behaviour. It was not their design, or appearance – the architecture – that were important, but the precepts that gave rise to them. Thus, when a building's useful life was over it could either crumble away or be rebuilt all over again in the same way as in the past.[16] In a significant way, Hong Kong's building regulations, with their detailed rules on heights, setbacks of façades, the sizing and spacing of windows and specifications for services, took the place of the imperial building code.

Similarly, because most buildings in Hong Kong were traditionally designed and erected by craftsmen, the notion of a professional architect was also strange. To be permitted to design or oversee the construction of a building in Hong Kong you must be registered as an 'authorised person'; that is, as an architect, engineer or surveyor or, until the early 1970s, an experienced draughtsman who has been examined on the contents of the building ordinances. The whole system ensures very little variation in appearance. Under the ordinances it is only in special circumstances, and on payment of prescribed fees, that a new building may differ 'in height, design, type or intended use from buildings in the intended neighbourhood or

The mass production of façades does not cease. The Island eastern corridor, North Point, Hong Kong, 1986.

previously existing on the site'.[17] Developers, anxious for speedy clearance of plans through the Building Ordinance Office (these can be considered for not more than 60 days), select their designers on the basis of their ability to get as much and more as the letter of the building regulations permit on a site, and to clear these plans with no problems. In the 1970s, large architectural practices often offered clients a selection of façades from a plan chest: behind these façades the internal layout of the apartment or office block would be sufficiently standardised around a central structural core of lifts to permit speedy clearance through the Building Ordinance Office.

As long as a building complied with the letter of the building ordinances, architectural appearance was not an issue. From the mid-1950s the concept of designing a purpose-built building – a house, an office or even a factory – became a thing of the past: housing and commercial property built to this high-rise scale had to be let not only to finance the construction, but to cover the cost of the site: which was invariably several times more costly than the construction. Buildings had become no more than agglomerations of lettable space. Because of the weight of investment required, developers spent the minimum on buildings, constructing them as little more than concrete shells for incoming tenants to fit out – whether they were designed as apartments, offices or factories. The pressure to build quickly, to hasten the time for returns on investment, was enormous. Even today, after nearly thirty-five years of record production, and having built housing for almost half the population, the public housing programme has yet to catch up with the numbers still squatting. Work takes place six and a half days a week, and on special projects twenty-four hours a day. During the property boom of the late 1970s, it was common for developers to contract to sell space in a new building as soon as plans had been approved, almost before the foundations had been cut. In new office development, developers asked tenants to occupy space at the bottom of a tower while the top was still being built. By this time buildings were seldom designed to be less than twenty-five storeys high, and went up in under three years from receipt of first brief to occupation.

Even in buildings of the highest quality, the standard of workmanship and finishes remained poor. During the boom skilled labour was in acutely short supply and contractors commonly employed peasant men and women, newly arrived from China, to work on site. Anyone who was any good could set himself up as a contractor overnight.

With a few honourable exceptions, by the end of the 1970s, Hong Kong high-rises were highly uniform, slightly tacky and beginning to look, from an international point of view, ever-so-slightly old fashioned. Property and construction were looked upon as a cornerstone of the Hong Kong economy. In 1977/78 and 1979/80 income from land sales and their associated taxes and revenues alone supplied the government with 20 per cent of its money for expenditure.[18] Two years later, less than one per cent of buildings would be more than thirty-five years

Squatter settlements in northern Kowloon, 1979.

old.[19] As there were few building materials held in stock in the colony, anything out of the ordinary – from structural steel to decent doorknobs – had to be ordered far in advance and imported from Europe, America, Australia or Japan. There had been no time, nor indeed much inclination, on the part of architects to innovate or investigate new processes. Given the economics of property in Hong Kong, the preservation of old buildings, so fashionable in the West, was virtually ignored. More surprising, in a climate that requires air-conditioning from March to November and relies largely on imported fuel for electricity, ideas for saving energy in buildings had not yet been investigated or applied in new construction.

At the same time Hong Kong land values were reckoned to be the highest in the world. The cost of a site so far outweighed the cost of construction on a major commercial project that, by the close of 1980, land normally accounted for 70 per cent of the total value of a completed property.[20] Rents for office space in the Central business district had trebled since 1977; they were now higher than comparable space in London or New York. This combination of factors meant that any commercial building which did not make the most of its potential space, or was poorly planned, was regarded as economically obsolete.

For the Hongkong Bank, setting out to build a new headquarters building, the implications of these factors were manifold. The existing bank was a classic example of a building that no longer made economic sense. In valuers' language, 1 Queen's Road Central, site of the head-quarters built in 1935, represented *prime* real estate, in the economic and political heart of the colony. What was once the tallest building between Cairo and San Francisco now represented potential for a new building with more than three times its current floor space. It was also highly visible real estate.

In a city where there are scarcely any landmarks familiar to the entire population, the Bank's headquarters was one of which the ordinary public – who also constituted the vast majority of the Bank's customers – were more than usually conscious. As has been seen, the building was a powerful symbol of the colony's prosperity, beloved by the common people and those who worked in it; but there could be no denying that it was also beginning to look old fashioned. If the Bank was to take the step of redeveloping it was honour bound to abide by Hong Kong conventions. It must exploit its site to the fullest; it must also build just as quickly as anyone else developing a Central site. But by commissioning a building for its own use, it would also be doing something exceptional. If this was not to be a speculative venture, producing an office block that was no more than a shell, such an exercise would nevertheless be the yardstick by which it would be judged. As will be seen, once the Bank took the decision to redevelop and selected an architect, more than any other influence it was the Hong Kong conventions of building which were to govern its attitude towards the construction.

The Bank in festive dress: Chinese New Year 1980.

On 27 April 1979, John Scott from PA Management Consultants went to see Courtenay Blackmore, the man at Lloyd's who was in charge of overseeing their new building in the City of London. It was being designed by Richard Rogers, architect of the legendary Pompidou Centre in Paris. Scott was there on behalf of the Hongkong Bank to find out how Lloyd's had organised the selection of its architect.

In the past, when the Bank had decided to build, getting on with the job had not been too difficult. On the 1935 headquarters, 'Tug' Wilson had worked directly for the chief manager, Sir Vandeleur Grayburn. In October 1935, less than two years after the site had been assembled, the job had been accomplished. By early 1978, however, when the Bank seriously began to consider the future of its 1935 headquarters in detail, the question of such straightforward redevelopment was considerably more complicated. The chairman of the Bank, Michael Sandberg, had not the time required to oversee the construction of a new headquarters personally. The Bank was now a far larger institution, on the verge of major international expansion. Nor was the issue politically straight-forward. The value of the image of the north tower of that 1935 building was impossible to quantify. The building's character was a significant element in the *fung-shui* of the whole colony: tearing down the Bank would appear to threaten its stability and prosperity, and, in turn, the well-being of Hong Kong. It was a well-loved landmark, a feature on every postcard of the Hong Kong waterfront which in the increasingly sterile environment of high-rise Hong Kong stood apart, a reassuring symbol that some fundamentals in life never change.

Apart from these, two practical problems arose from tearing down the existing building. The first was to find alternative space in Central District into which the Bank could move its headquarters while redevelopment took place. Given the extreme shortage of good office space in the tiny area, a mere few blocks, which made up the international business heart of Hong Kong in the late 1970s, this was a major problem. The second, at least as difficult, was to find a good architect.

Roy Munden was the assistant general manager (of the Bank's management services) whom Sandberg had asked to take charge of these problems. Munden looked like every Englishman's idea of a

The north tower of the Hongkong and Shanghai Banking Corporation headquarters, Hong Kong, designed by Palmer and Turner, completed 1935.

branch bank manager. Slight, with thinning hair, behind the thin rims of his glasses his green eyes missed little. He had a wry sense of humour. Munden had spent all his working life with the Bank, serving in remote parts of Borneo and as manager in Bombay before joining head office in 1970. He was shrewd, canny and cautious of first impressions. He had an eye for detail. One of his favourite tactics before taking a decision was to play devil's advocate – pursuing an issue from every angle and arguing, sometimes fiercely, against an idea before deciding to accept it. It kept people on their mettle.

The first hurdle to be crossed was the short-term consideration of finding suitable accommodation in Central for at least five years while redevelopment took place. Munden enlisted PA Management Consultants, who were already familiar with the Bank's operations, to refine space calculations and to help sort out a temporary headquarters. They considered all manner of options: building underneath Statue Square in front of the Bank, renting temporary space in dozens of different buildings, even exchanging the Bank's 1 Queen's Road site for another, Central District, site. Altogether they looked at thirty-eight possible locations. In each case a temporary move seemed to make the redevelopment period even longer than necessary – nearly nine years – and the whole idea too disruptive. As for a permanent move, Munden and PA could find no other site that, in their opinion, was the equal of the one the Bank already possessed. For, at heart, no one at the Bank wanted to give up its existing site. Statue Square, which it owned, was dedicated to public use, and gave the Bank a unique open and civic space in front of the building. Not only did this space in front of it enhance the Bank's visibility and 'presence' in the heart of Hong Kong; its *fung-shui* was too good to give up. In the end, the impossibility of finding temporary accommodation (it had to include a prestige banking hall and appropriate vault space) seemed so total, that from this point on it was to have a fundamental effect on the Bank's approach to redevelopment, the brief to the architect and, ultimately, the design and method of construction of the new building itself.

The conclusion of the unsuccessful search for temporary space was to see if the existing site could be developed in phases. PA thought that the north tower of the existing bank could stand on its own to a remarkable degree. Together with an annexe, built in 1966, it looked as if the north tower could provide enough space for the Bank to operate from the site, while the rest of the building could be demolished and a new high-rise tower could be erected behind it. PA's report was 220 pages long. Its conclusion was for 'phased redevelopment' of the site. In November 1978 the board gave its blessing to a three-month, £100,000 (HK$1.2 million) feasibility study, using a full range of building consultants, to find out whether a tall 'south tower' could be married 'aesthetically and practically with the lower north tower'.[1] Afterwards, it was felt likely that an international competition would be held to find a bolder, more imaginative and effective scheme.[2] PA were to serve as co-ordinators and project managers.

Roy Munden

The board had stressed that only specialists of the highest international qualifications were to be employed. 'Ove Arup & Partners', PA told Munden in a report on potential structural engineers, 'can almost certainly claim to have the most outstanding structural engineering reputation in the world'.[3] They were willing to be appointed. Levett & Bailey were a large and highly successful firm of quantity surveyors who had begun practice in Hong Kong in 1962. Their local expertise was regarded as crucial; they too agreed to join the exercise. Finally, J Roger Preston & Partners, the Hong Kong office of a London firm and Hong Kong's leading building services engineers, were appointed to advise on the building services. The Bank wanted to appoint an architect 'with an international reputation for outstanding quality of design' at this point. But they also felt that the need for an architect with good local knowledge and experience was probably more important at this stage. It was natural for the Bank to approach Palmer & Turner, who had continued as architects to the Bank, to join the feasibility exercise.[4]

The feasibility study started in mid-January 1979. A month later, nearly fifty different variations had been produced showing different ways of arranging the Bank's requirements for accommodation within some parts of its existing headquarters while demolishing others; and of massing new buildings on parts of the site which in future might – or might not – be joined by further redevelopment. The task was not proving simple: after a meeting of the feasibility study group in late February Munden records that the most attractive of the Palmer & Turner schemes would take too long – until early 1985 – and the others were not attractive enough.

Early in April, two main options for the future use of the site were presented to the Bank's board. One was to retain the north tower of the existing Bank, to demolish the southern part of the building and to build a new, much taller building, a 'south tower', on that portion of the site. The second option was to redevelop the site totally, but in phases: first, by converting the north tower for working purposes, then demolishing the rest of the building and building new accommodation on the south side; when this was complete the north tower itself could be demolished and the new building completed in this area. It was estimated that this second option would take six and a half years – that is, until the end of 1986 – and cost HK$600 million at 1979 prices.

The board decided that it wanted still more investigations of these options performed, this time with 'additional creative contributions ... from several firms of architects of international repute'. In the meantime, the Bank should take up any suitable alternative office accommodation 'to allow both possibilities to go forward'.[5] It is clear that at this point the Bank felt committed to nothing, that it still had its options for building, or not building, wide open. In fact, something more subtle had happened. The Bank had now closed the door on complete demolition and redevelopment, in one process, on the site.

With the feasibility study ended, and its conclusions accepted, one important path had been closed: the Bank no longer believed that it could move off the site during the construction; it had now become essential to be there during the entire period. The architects were briefed accordingly.

From the beginning the 'approach to the aesthetic problem' had been seen as fundamental. PA described it as crucial. But it was not easy for the Bank to decide how best to set about finding an architect. Given the nature of the building's past it was essential that any new replacement must be capable of the same powerful symbolism. 'Whatever it looks like, it must look like a bank – whatever that is,' Peter Williams, then deputy chairman of the Bank, was heard to say. But here they were, some of the world's most powerful men, in a small colony not noted for the quality of its buildings, thousands of miles from the major centres of the West where distinguished architects could be found. Large corporations do not build themselves new headquarters on the same site very often and by the time they come to do so those who oversaw the birth of the previous building were likely to be dead, or at least retired. There was no one to fall back on for advice.

The difficulty was to resolve the apparent contradiction between selecting an architect who could handle the limitations and complexities of the Hong Kong construction scene while providing the Bank with a bold and imaginative building. The question of holding some form of competition had been raised the previous autumn. But who should take part? At least equal in importance to innovative design ability was a mastery of the local building regulations 'and the ability to persuade government to show flexibility'.[6] The suggestion that a local firm and a 'big name' might team up for the project did not appeal, because of the dangers of divided responsibility and poor motivation. Despite the long and successful association with Palmer & Turner in the past, the Bank was anxious to commission an architect with 'an international reputation for outstanding design'.[7]

But besides this international reputation, whoever was to get the job had to have proven experience of building a tower, preferably a bank. He must have experience of running a job from the other side of the world, and be able to deploy the staff resources necessary to get on with the job. By the time the feasibility study had been concluded at the end of March, dozens of names had been considered. A final shortlist of possible candidates was being refined. With one exception they were all good mainstream corporation architects with branches in Hong Kong. Besides Palmer & Turner the other firms being considered for the shortlist were Skidmore, Owings & Merrill (SOM), the Chicago-based group that had pioneered the characteristically American team approach to architecture; their British equivalent, Gollins, Melvin & Ward; and the lesser-known Australians Yuncken Freeman. All had branches in Hong Kong. The fifth candidate was IM Pei, but he was reported to be worried about his workload.

Gordon Graham

It was at this point that John Scott from PA Management went to visit Lloyd's. Here Richard Rogers had been selected at the end of a unique competition between six architects. The six – who included IM Pei (USA), Webb Zerafa (Canada), Norman Foster, Arup Associates (Lloyd's' architects in the past) and Serete (France) – were briefed together by Lloyd's and then sent away to prepare a package that would convince Lloyd's to appoint them. Four months later each returned not with a design or a concept, but with a description of the approach they would take to the problems Lloyd's faced. On the basis of a written submission, live presentations, and lunch afterwards, Rogers – who had put forward seventeen different ways of tackling the issues – was appointed. The man who had guided Lloyd's down this apparently successful path of selecting an architect was Gordon Graham, then president of the Royal Institute of British Architects.

A few days later, Scott met Graham at the RIBA in Portland Place. In his smoke-filled office, Graham had about him the air of a man used to running things. His instincts were those of a politician and a businessman first, of an architect second. He was the founding partner of Architects Design Group, a Midlands-based practice with a good reputation for industrial buildings. Over the past eight years, however, Graham had been drawn more and more closely into the affairs of the RIBA. He had acted as second-in-command to his predecessor in office, Eric Lyons. Together, they had established a formal lobby to bring the interests of the architectural profession to the attention of the government. The role of the RIBA president is, after all, chiefly to promote the profession of architecture and the building of fine buildings. This suited Graham's passion for architectural excellence. He was positive, honest, and tough.

Scott was relieved to find Graham well briefed, and willing to act as an assessor in a competition for the Bank. His term as RIBA president would be up in July. A month later Munden flew over to see him with a mandate to appoint him as the Bank's architectural adviser. The idea was that Graham would help prepare the terms of reference for the architects, comment on their suitability, and help assess the aesthetic and practical aspects of each scheme put forward.

None of the standard types of competition recommended by the RIBA appeared to suit the Bank, who really wanted to find an effective way to select an architect from an international field. An open international competition would take time. Nor would the Bank retain as much control as it would like over the development of the design. Graham advised Munden to take a leaf from Lloyd's book and devise a 'request for proposals' from a limited number of architects. He also recommended that Norman Foster's firm, Foster Associates, should be one of the names they ought to select from a further shortlist the Bank had now drawn up. Besides Foster it included Minoru Yamasaki, Harry Seidler, Oscar Niemeyer and Webb Zerafa), architects the Bank considered might contribute original, even wild, ideas to it's dilemma.

In June the board sanctioned the request for proposals idea suggested by Graham and the final shortlist of architects. The information presented to the board, which included a list of recent banks, and other buildings 'of special relevance' and their height, appears below:[8]

USA:
Skidmore, Owings & Merrill (Chicago)

Chase Manhattan, New York	1960	60 storeys
Bank of America HQ, San Francisco	1969	52 storeys
Sears Tower, Chicago	1974	110 storeys
John Hancock, Chicago	1970	100 storeys
Hong Kong experience		

Hugh Stubbins & Associates Inc. (Boston)

Citicorp Center, New York	1977	59 storeys
Federal Reserve Bank, Boston	1977	33 storeys

Australia:
Harry Seidler & Associates (Sydney)

MLC Centre, Sydney	1978	58 storeys
Australia Square, Sydney	1967	50 storeys
Australian Embassy, Paris	1978	
Conzinc Riotinto HQ, Melbourne	1975	50 storeys

Yuncken Freeman Pty Ltd (Melbourne)

BHP HQ, Melbourne		40 storeys
Hong Kong experience		

Britain:
Gollins, Melvin & Ward Partnership (London)

P & O Building, London	1969	14 storeys
Commercial Union, London	1969	26 storeys
Banque Belge, London	1978	15? storeys
Barings Bank, London	In progress	
Hong Kong experience		

Foster Associates (London)

Sainsbury Centre for Visual Arts, Norwich	1978	3 awards
Willis Faber HQ, Ipswich	1976	3 awards
IBM Office, Cosham	1971	2 awards

Hongkong:
Palmer & Turner

Reserves:
Minoru Yamasaki (USA)

World Trade Center, New York	1974	100 + storeys

Yorke Rosenberg Mardall (London)
Hong Kong experience

Top, left to right:

John Hancock Building, Chicago; architects Skidmore, Owings & Merrill.

Citicorp Center, New York; architects Hugh Stubbins and Associates, Inc.

MLC Centre, Sydney; architects Harry Seidler & Associates.

Centre, left to right:

BHP House, Melbourne; architects Yuncken Freeman.

Commercial Union Assurance Company headquarters, London; architects Gollins, Melvin & Ward.

Sainsbury Centre for Visual Arts, Norwich; architects Foster Associates.

Bottom, left to right:

Connaught Centre, Hong Kong; architects Palmer & Turner.

World Trade Center, New York; architect Minoru Yamasaki.

London offices for their own use; architects Yorke Rosenberg Mardall.

The final list was almost ultra-safe. The request for proposals ought to result in a good-looking, but hardly revolutionary, international style corporate headquarters. The members of the board might have been expected to be personally familiar with several of the buildings noted in the list: certainly those of Palmer & Turner, and of Skidmore, Owings & Merrill, the 'corporate architects for corporate clients' who had made the whole international style famous. Hugh Stubbins, whose work was largely based in the college campuses of the north-eastern USA, had recently completed the highly acclaimed Citicorp Center, the new headquarters for Citibank in New York. On the reserve list, Minoru Yamasaki, was sixty-seven, a Japanese American from Seattle, and the designer of the remarkable, but not uncriticised, creation of the twin towers of the World Trade Center, New York.

The other candidates were also in the glass and steel international style mainstream. SOM's British equivalents were Yorke Rosenberg Mardall, and Gollins, Melvin & Ward – designers of Britain's best-looking high-rise building, the Commercial Union in London. At fifty-six, Harry Seidler, one-time student of Gropius at Harvard and assistant to Marcel Breuer and Oscar Niemeyer, was without doubt 'the best Australian', as someone from the Bank pencilled beside his name. He specialised in a brand of smoothly sculptured and beautifully engineered white concrete buildings. By contrast, the other Australian team, Yuncken Freeman, was scarcely known outside the sub-continent, but there it had a sound track record reaching back to 1933, with several recent good-looking high-rise towers to its credit. It had had an office in Hong Kong since 1975.

It was Foster Associates who stood apart, an unpredictable element, from the other firms in the list. They failed all the Bank's most basic criteria for selection: they had built nothing over four storeys, had never designed a bank and had no Hong Kong experience. Indeed, the outsides of their buildings, which usually ended up looking like beautifully elegant sheds, tended to baffle the public. Nevertheless, at forty-four, Norman Foster was a man reputed in international architectural circles to have one of the cleverest and most innovative minds in the business. One-time partner of Richard Rogers, author of the extraordinary Centre Pompidou in Paris, Foster ran a small, young office. He differed from the other 'corporate' architects on the list; his whole approach to building was unconventional, based on being as flexible as possible. His briefings took the form of exhaustive questioning of clients' requirements, working from these to suggest a number of possible design solutions that would eventually be refined, at the last possible moment, into a final design.

On 14 June 1979, the Bank wrote to the seven selected firms. The architects were invited to take part in a three-month exercise to help the Bank decide the best way to tackle its problems, and to select an architect. Pleading pressure of work Gollins, Melvin & Ward withdrew at once. In their place, the second-string British firm, Yorke

Rosenberg Mardall, came in. All were to attend a joint briefing on 11 July in Hong Kong and submit their proposals by 6 October. Following this they might be asked back to give a live presentation of their ideas. Each firm would be paid a fee of HK$150,000, which the selected architect would set against his final account.

The Bank might not be allowed to call the exercise a 'competition', but few tests have been devised to award an architectural commission that have been as tough. Most architectural competitions are held in search of inspiration, a good design; who the architect might be is of secondary consideration. The brief is kept as open as possible. Here the chief aim was to find the best architect for the job – a person with whom those at the Bank felt it could work and whom it could confidently expect to come up with the kind of building it wanted. As a second object, was the opportunity for clever concepts to emerge. The possibility that the Bank might obtain a design suitable to be put forward for Building Ordinance Office approval was reckoned at less than one per cent. But the architects involved did not know this.

In order of importance, the aims of the request for proposals set out by the Bank were:[9]

'To help the Bank decide on an approach to solving the problems of whether a full phased scheme or a south tower scheme is better.

To help the Bank decide whether the best scheme is better than doing nothing.

To select and appoint an architect.'

At the same time the Bank did 'not wish to define closely how far architects should go in providing solutions to the problem during this exercise'. The Bank's intention was to give the architects a free hand, to let them get on with the job in their own way. Thus, apart from the dry configuration of the problems set by the request for proposals, and a single day's briefing in Hong Kong, when no one was allowed to ask questions which were not heard by the others, there was no input from the Bank, no way of telling what kind of organisation the Bank was or what it was really looking for. The contestants were told that important criteria for judgment would lie in the way in which they showed an appreciation of the Bank's problems and local conditions and clarified the issues on which the Bank's decision depended. Most of them felt that preparing the schemes was like firing a shot in the dark.

As the Bank had already invested nearly a year in investigations and feasibility studies to figure out the best way to redevelop its site, the brief in the request for proposals was detailed and hedged round with requirements. The most stringent was the need to keep the Bank in operation from the site throughout the redevelopment period. The architects were to examine the two options for dealing with the Bank's problems that had come out of the feasibility study. Option one was to redevelop the site in phases. The feasibility study had recommended converting the north tower first, to enable it to operate as an independent building. Following the conversion, the south part of the building would be demolished. Then the first part of a new building, providing a minimum of 15,000 square metres (162,000 square feet) of usable floor space, would be erected. The Bank would move into this new building and, subsequently, the north tower would be demolished. Then a second part, phase two, of the new building would be put up.

The site was just over an acre in size. The challenge was to design a complete new building that would provide as much space as the building ordinances would allow – in two separate phases, while the Bank continued to operate its headquarters from the site in the meantime. It had to be constructed with the minimum of disturbance – from noise, vibration, dust, blocked access and interrupted views. More importantly, it also had to make a significant visual impact. The same criteria applied to a new banking hall to be built inside. As the heart of the building, lying at its centre, it would have to be done in two parts. The phase one section must work perfectly, look striking. When joined to phase two, it must all be smoothly integrated, and look terrific too. But the Bank wanted to keep its options open: the designers were warned that it might decide to halt development after only phase one had been completed, and retain the north tower of the existing building.

The second option the architects were asked to consider was to demolish the south-west corner of the existing building, and put up a tall building on that part of the site alone. The north tower would be retained permanently; and the barrel-vaulted ceiling, complete with Helios, chariot and sunburst, was to be neatly, and ingeniously, knitted into a new banking hall that successfully married the old with the new. The new tower should provide the maximum space under the building regulations (a plot ratio of 15). Again, what it all would look like was of primary importance. Here also all the construction must be achieved with the least possible noise and disruption: the banking hall would be expected to function throughout the redevelopment period.

Lastly, the Bank invited the architects to put forward any other schemes which might meet its needs. All the proposals had to give due consideration to the requirements of the Building Ordinance Office, and the planning regulations, and the fact that almost all the surrounding buildings would be torn down and redeveloped before long. The Bank required no detailed proposals for structural engineering, foundations, building services, construction methods, costs and programme, but the underlying suggestion was that they ought to be considered – and would be assessed – if necessary by representatives of the consultants retained for the feasibility study (structural engineers Ove Arup, mechanical and electrical engineers J Roger Preston and Levett & Bailey, quantity surveyors). The Bank proposed that these consultants should be used on the eventual construction. 'Despite the constraints inherent in such schemes,' the Bank's formal document concluded, 'the Bank is determined that the building should be one of considerable architectural merit.'[10]

Monday, 3 September 1979: Melbourne, Australia. Munden is at the beginning of a round-the-world trip to meet the candidates on their home ground and then tour some of their buildings in the company of the client who had commissioned them. It is of course invaluable. Not only does it enable him to look at buildings at first hand, to see their merits and their faults, but it means that he can talk over ideas for construction management that have yet to be successfully tried in Hong Kong. In Yuncken Freeman's offices he sees 'some excellent, imaginative ideas for 1 QRC' but two of the buildings he goes to visit with clients have had bad leaks. Two days later in Canberra, he is impressed by Seidler and gets good reports of almost every aspect of his practice. He decides it is not necessarily a bad thing that 'you always know a Seidler building when you see it'.

To England next, to see Yorke Rosenberg Mardall and the Scandinavian Bank building, with which he is not impressed. At IBM's offices at Greenford, however, Norman Foster comes in for high praise from his client, Richard Watts: 'If he had to name one characteristic of Foster Associates which stands out,' Munden recorded in his notes of the trip, 'it would be their ability to present alternative solutions to a building problem and to respond quickly to change.' None the less, Munden does not like the style of IBM's buildings ('They are all steel frame with the structural members left exposed. Even the lift shafts are merely covered in glass'). But: 'the design is a brilliant solution to the problem of many diverse users'.

'*Tuesday, 18 September 1979: London,* An exhausting day with Foster. He talks and talks and talks. His strengths are a brilliant and innovative mind, painstaking research and careful planning. He and his team are impressive . . . Much will depend on the concept. We would certainly obtain from Foster the benefit of the latest technology and good supervision.

'*Thursday, 20 September 1979: Ipswich,* By train to Ipswich. The Willis, Faber Dumas building presents an extraordinary appearance with its tinted glass walls with no supports. In my opinion it is quite unsuitable to the town . . . The building itself has several serious defects. Blinds have had to be installed to make it inhabitable in sunlight (there were none proposed in the original design) and the air-conditioning is still inadequate. The ground floor is largely wasted and the placing of a swimming pool on that floor is crazy. The pool is hardly used.

Conclusions: If we use Foster we shall have to be tough. The benefit of his brilliance and good management could be outweighed by the lack of practicality of his designs.

43

A case of modern patronage

Top, left:

Hugh Stubbins and Associates, Inc.: Hugh Stubbins firmly rejected the south tower options proposed by the Bank. His firm had investigated three possibilities and considered them neither 'comfortable, rational nor attractive'. Instead he recommended full phased redevelopment, beginning with the demolition of the south block of the Bank, and the construction of a curved tower that would embrace a low banking hall providing 'in excess of 300 linear feet of teller stations' beneath a central rotunda.

Top, centre and right:

Harry Seidler & Associates: Although Seidler prepared a south tower scheme he believed it unconvincing. Instead he proposed redevelopment in two phases. The first, set behind the north tower, could remain complete by building a high atrium over the existing banking hall to bridge between the old and the new structures. But to exploit the site to the full, Seidler recommended completion of phase 2, a powerfully expressive concrete structure in place of the north tower.

Bottom, left and centre:

Palmer & Turner: using their early experience in preparing the feasibility studies for the Bank, Palmer & Turner favoured partial redevelopment of the site. They proposed placing a high tower on the southern portion of the site to maximise the plot ratio. At the time, it would have become the highest building in Central Hong Kong.

At a later date, they suggested, the North Tower of the Bank and the banking hall could be demolished to produce a new podium and hall.

Bottom, right:

Yuncken Freeman: Yuncken Freeman recommended full phased redevelopment to be carried out in six stages. The first, and most dramatic, step was to build a megastructure of four columns which would pierce through the existing banking hall and support 15,000 to 20,000 m² of usable space in a tower above the Bank. Banking business could continue on the site while construction took place, and subsequently, if the Bank wished, redevelopment could continue using the megastructure as the basis to support a large new tower.

'*Tuesday, 25 September: New York,* Morning and lunch with Marine Midland . . . The core of 140 Broadway [designed by SOM] is enormous and this leaves a ribbon of space around the outside. Many fittings are non-standard thus causing heavy maintenance expense. The main banking hall has thousands of recessed incandescent down-lights – a maintenance nightmare. Also on this floor are solid marble floors – inflexible. Not a good advert for SOM but it was designed more than a decade ago . . . Afternoon with Citibank . . .' and later in Boston at dinner with Stubbins, Munden is subjected to widely conflicting accounts of Citicorp's construction: 'It must have been a jolly few years!'

On Monday, 1 October, he is in Chicago to visit SOM:

'Today has been a revelation but must be careful not to be overwhelmed by clever salesmanship . . . Toured a building under construction and discussed the relative merits of steel and concrete in Hong Kong. It is clear that steel should not be dismissed out of hand because the calculation must include many more factors than just the initial cost.

Toured Hancock and Sears towers. Their knowledge and experience of really high-rise buildings must be unsurpassed in the world. The way these enormous buildings work so efficiently makes [a well-known tower on the Hong Kong waterfront] look like a major disaster.'

Later, in San Francisco, Munden continues to be impressed with what he is told about SOM by their clients, Bank of America, California First Bank and Crocker National Bank. 'The more I listen, the more I like the "feel" of SOM.' But the trip has been invaluable in other ways. It clears his mind on how the project should be managed, presenting strong arguments for using a management contractor to organise the job, a concept that had scarcely ever been applied in Hong Kong. It teaches him caution about sanctioning 'clever, unproven items' in the new building, and confirms his instinct to avoid space planning, hard floors that cannot take underfloor servicing, and any other unnecessary constraints. 'I think we should concentrate on flexibility,' he records as he leaves San Francisco. 'Perhaps we should look at our total space needs including residential. We might build apartments on the top of the new building but they would have to be convertible to office floors in the future.'[11]

Munden got back to Hong Kong on 6 October. Two days later, the submissions were opened. The material each candidate judged it appropriate to send varied. Some accompanied written submissions with large mounted drawings. Foster and Palmer & Turner also submitted models to illustrate their proposals. Munden, Gordon Graham and David Thornburrow, a partner with the Hong Kong architectural firm Spence Robinson, sat down to judge the material sent by the candidates. They were assisted by five others from PA

Management and the Bank. PA had prepared a checklist of basic items for the five 'non-architectural' assessors to examine, to see whether government building regulations had been complied with, how each scheme met broad user requirements for space, and details of site coverage and plot ratios. Schemes which were shortlisted were to be assessed by the consultants in charge of structure, servicing and cost.

At the end of two days' work, however, there was no real doubt as to the most impressive presentation. Yuncken Freeman, SOM and Foster Associates all proposed radical improvements on the straight phased redevelopment that the Bank had initially envisaged. But Foster had stolen the field. His written submission was judged to be of extraordinarily high quality. 'The amount of work that has gone into it is enormous,' recorded Munden. 'The general theme of "flexibility" is exactly what we need and repeats what IBM said about Foster':[12]

'Some of Foster's thoughts mirror ideas of my own which had not developed when I saw him, eg: we must design the building as though we are going to occupy all of it; all floors must be as totally flexible as possible; use computer heat to warm the building in winter; consider apartments on upper floors. The whole concept feels right.'

On 11 October, Roy Munden rang Gordon Graham at the Mandarin Hotel. 'Come and have lunch,' he said. 'I want to know if we have to have all the competitors back.'

At lunch Munden showed Graham the draft of a letter he wanted to send to the competitors. It told them they would not be required to return to Hong Kong to present their schemes in person. Graham was taken aback. Then Munden said the letter was to go to all except Foster. It was the first Graham knew of Munden's decision.

'We agreed,' Graham recalls. 'It just stuck out like a sore thumb. Foster's submission was in a league of its own.' Munden telephoned Michael Sandberg who was on holiday in the south of France. He agreed with Munden's recommendation. The next day a special circular to the directors of the Bank would tell them that all the options would be placed before the Board in November; in the meantime further talks would take place with Foster.

Later that day, Graham wrote to Munden, recording these events:[13]

'I had no hesitation at all in giving my unqualified support to your proposition that you should immediately approach your Chairman . . . I applaud his decisive approach and it is now plain to me that with varying degrees of surprise and breathlessness so do all the other people who have taken part in the study and appraisals.'

A month later, on 13 November, after delivering a presentation of his proposals to the board, Foster was appointed.

News of Foster's probable appointment had already appeared in the press. But no designs or details of his firm's concept were published. The other competitors, who had received telexes as soon as the assessment was complete, saw their treatment as cavalier; several doubted that proper consideration had even been given to their submissions. In spite of appearances, however, the board's decision to commission Foster Associates to design its new headquarters was not quite the foregone conclusion it seemed to outsiders. Norman Foster was invited to meet the Bank's board on 13 November 1979. The meeting began at 4 pm.

Roy Munden and Gordon Graham, as the Bank's architectural adviser, were asked to go in first. Foster was invited to wait in a small anteroom, empty except for a few chairs. Meanwhile, the board went into session. The old boardroom of the Hongkong Bank was rich and sombre. The walls were panelled with rare woods from all parts of the Far East and hung with fine pictures by Chinnery and other nineteenth-century painters of the China Sea Trade. The heavy doors of beaten bronze closed silently; the windows were sealed and the blinds half drawn. Around the table sat several of the most powerful men in the Far East. That day, besides representatives from each of the major 'Hongs' – like David Newbigging, taipan of Jardines, and John Bremridge (later to become financial secretary to the Hong Kong government) from Swires – the list included shipping magnate YK Pao, and QW Lee, then chief executive of the Hang Seng Bank. Also present was Norman Thompson, tough, vigorous and uncompromising, who was about to oversee the completion, on time and under budget, of the first stage of Hong Kong's Mass Transit Railway (the MTR, its underground network), the largest civil engineering project yet undertaken in the territory. Together these men held sway over the direction of the Hong Kong economy. Some of them were in competition with one another, as well as being important customers of the Bank. Thus certain issues of Bank business were never brought into this forum, but were dealt with by the executive directors of the Bank. That day Munden was confident of a quick hearing. He had planned a Chinese banquet for Foster and his team at 7.30 that evening. 'It will either be a celebration or a wake,' he had said drily.
But the board meeting went on for nearly three hours, discussing the other architects' presentations, and Foster's qualifications. The session

Norman Foster, 1984.

was detailed and intense. Munden and Graham were conscious that they were going to be very late for dinner. Meanwhile, Foster was imprisoned in the anteroom. There was nothing to read, nothing to distract him. Clearly what was going on in the boardroom was going very wrong. Just after seven he was invited into the boardroom, and seated between Munden and Graham. Graham had no time to let him know that all was all right, he had got the job, before the meeting adjourned for a drink. Only after everyone had been served did the chairman offer Foster his congratulations.

Norman Foster had been in practice as an architect for just over sixteen years. During that time in Britain, he had come to be regarded by his colleagues with a mixture of scepticism and envy. Few knew him well. He was an elusive personality, operating outside the bounds of the architectural establishment. He rarely lunched his clients or went to professional dinners. In his spare time, he flew gliders. He was not at home in the gentlemanly world of British architecture.

Journalists found him difficult to talk to: he used a language laced with puzzling technical terms and neat phrases which skirted, seemingly endlessly, round the heart of an issue. He looked to the aircraft industry and the space programme for inspiration for his buildings. 'Achieve more with less' was one of his favourite catch-phrases. Other architects were suspicious of his affection for the inanimate world of advanced technology and use of industrial materials in his buildings. He was nervy, fast-talking, sensitive, disarmingly intelligent. People reported that they could talk to him all evening, but learn nothing of the man himself. He seemed to exist solely in the dimensions of architecture.

In the mid-1970s, when nearly everyone else in the field was talking about making their buildings 'respond to a human scale', and applying pitched roofs, using 'appropriate' materials (bricks, not concrete) and going into anguish about where the modern movement had gone wrong, Foster was obsessed with numbers, with making things fit, and with precision and technology. His approach to design took the form of relentless, punishing examination of all the possibilities before him, before deciding on a course of action. This earned him a reputation for flexibility. He was ruthless in refining his designs to make them as simple as possible, and manipulating a budget to get the best materials his client could afford for a job. He did not talk in the rather doctrinaire way that others did about architecture in relation to people. His arguments stressed the rational, the functional, and the practicalities of getting value for money. He rarely talked about architecture as something that should give people pleasure, as a function of the spirit. To him it was obvious.

In this his approach to architecture differed from that of many of his colleagues. Foster used his pragmatic arguments, like getting value for money and what the building would cost in use, to persuade his clients that providing a better working environment need not cost them any more, but would cheer people up. He wanted equality of standards in the workplace. Why should carpets and fine finishes be confined to reception areas and management offices? Was it appropriate to demarcate the shop floor with ugly utilitarian surroundings? 'There is no question of a reaction against fine finishes, it's merely how you define priorities and reflect them in the allocation of fixed resources (ie money)', he wrote after the completion of the headquarters for Willis Faber & Dumas, the insurance brokers.[1] The secret ingredient which Foster attempted to add to all the dry, numerical practicalities of any brief was joy.

Among his early clients were a handful of individualistic companies who either wanted industrial buildings or inexpensive offices that could be built cheaply and fast. It is significant that one of them was IBM, for whom Foster built a pilot head office in Hampshire in 1971. The building attracted immediate attention and an RIBA architectural award. It looked like little more than a line of glass on the horizon, 'a mere fence of glass reflecting sky and trees, like the equivocal gesture of a conceptual artist,' wrote Robert Maxwell in an essay revealingly entitled 'Purity and danger – the Foster method'.[2] Reyner Banham added: 'The walls of that IBM building, consist of sheets of glass over twelve feet high, held in place by almost nothing; just aluminium glazing bars about an inch wide.'[3] This kind of simplicity in detailing provoked immediate controversy in the architectural press. How could Foster get away with it? What about problems like condensation? How could it possibly work?

News of his buildings spread steadily in Europe – to France, Germany and Italy – and then to Japan. In 1976 the American Institute of Architects awarded him one of America's most prestigious architectural prizes, the RS Reynolds Memorial Award, for his first major commission, the Willis Faber headquarters in the market town of Ipswich in Suffolk. Three years later, he was given the Reynolds prize again for his next job, the Sainsbury Centre for the Arts, an art gallery for the University of East Anglia. Neither building looked like any other small town office block or art gallery that had ever been produced. Yet the consistency in the handling, the 'intensity of control' as Maxwell described it,[4] allied these buildings to the more modest projects Foster had handled before, and marked them with an instantly recognisable stamp.

These things commanded his colleagues' admiration. His buildings were unconventional, frequently baffling. But, apparently effortlessly, Foster's buildings achieved what so many architects who had adopted the tenets of the modern movement had been aiming for, for nearly fifty years. They were lean and elegant, honed down to the absolute essentials of structure and an outside skin. They looked superbly refined, ordered and finished. Spare, shiny, clean, efficient, and – stunning. The difference with a Foster building was that to go inside was usually to take your breath away. His designs had a purity, a ruthless clarity of perception, which made the hairs on the back of the neck stand up in pleasure. Where so much of the best of what was being built in Britain at the time could at most be described as 'worthy', each new building to come out of that office was a surprise. Foster himself, nervy, mercurial, complex and unpredictable, was more than obviously competent. If the man himself remained enigmatic, what he did possess, as Banham said when IBM was first completed, was sheer nerve in making buildings. He was a kind of *wunderkind*, a high-tech wizard whose every building seemed to go straight to the front cover of the architectural glossies and pick up the latest architectural award.

Norman Foster was born in 1935, in Manchester. His childhood, spent in the back streets of that city, was devoid of any influences that might have suggested a career in architecture. He succeeded in doing well in his O-levels, and armed with these attainments, left school at sixteen for a clerical career in the city treasurer's department at the town hall. For two years he was trained in the rudiments of commercial law, bookkeeping and accountancy. Then came National Service in the RAF, with training in technical radar and electronics. It was during National Service that Foster first became aware that there might be other possibilities than a lifetime spent in Manchester town hall.

He had first come across architecture and design in the formal sense through reading an introductory history of architecture by Frederick Gibberd while preparing for O-level art. In his spare time, he had begun to investigate the work of Le Corbusier and Frank Lloyd Wright through the shelves of the public library. Pictures of Wright's Johnson's Wax building fired his imagination. He discovered Henry Russell Hitchcock's *The Nature of Materials*, and more. The architecture and furniture of the twentieth century became a secret, private passion, which he fuelled from books in his room at home. For a boy from Manchester just after the war, these were arcane tastes. There was no one he could talk to about them, or who could advise him on how to pursue them. But by the time he had finished National Service, he had made up his mind to try and get a job in the design field.

He applied to a number of furniture manufacturers, without success. Then, on the basis of his training in the town hall, he got a job in the contracts administration section of a large firm of architects, John Beardshaw & Partners. By now, he was nearly twenty-one. For the first time he was working surrounded by drawings, and, more importantly, architectural magazines. A client gave him a stack of old *Architectural Reviews*. He discovered Reyner Banham, the Smithsons, Cullen and Ian Nairn. By now it was no longer a question of whether he would study architecture, just of where and when.

There were two choices before him: the Manchester School of Art, which was a recognised school of architecture and for which he could immediately obtain a grant, and the University of Manchester. The research he had done had shown him that the university course was of a higher standard than that at the school of art. He decided he would go to the university, but he would have to work his way through.

Foster's days as a student developed a pattern. In between the lectures and tutorials were jobs selling furniture or ice-cream, commissions for architectural perspectives, and being paid double time on Sunday nights for acting as a bouncer in the local cinema, patching up the seats with copydex after the gangs had been in. The summers found him working in a cold store until the news arrived that he had won an RIBA Silver Medal for measured drawings, or a Manchester Society of Architecture Award, or a Builders Association Travelling Fellowship. With the £100 or so from an award he would be off, to Scandinavia or Italy. In Denmark he became aware of Utzon, his house and his housing, and the work of Kay Fisker. He catalogued the work of Arne Jacobsen and his white, stripped style. The slides he took as a student of Siena, Tuscan hill towns and the Galleria of Milan still feature as illustrations in his work today.

In his final year at Manchester Foster applied for a Fulbright and a Henry Fellowship to study in the United States. He was offered both, but turned down the Fulbright. Under its terms he could not apply for an immigrant visa to work in the States. The Henry Fellowship was tenable at Harvard or Yale; Foster chose Yale.

If Foster had felt that studying architecture in Manchester had been a first stage towards liberation, and self-discovery, Yale was a revelation. It was not just the quality of the teaching, it was the general sense of freedom and opportunity in America that enthralled him. He once told Frank Thistlethwaite, vice-chancellor of the University of East Anglia, how fortunate he had been to have made up his mind about what he wanted to do by the time he went to university. It seemed to him an incredible luxury to be studying architecture in the Yale of the early 1960s.

'I found myself among an unusual combination of teachers,' he told an interviewer, in 1975,[5]

'. . . three of whom in particular were positive creative influences: Paul Rudolph, Vincent Scully and Serge Chermayeff. Rudolph for his professionalism, for the way he demonstrated how a project could be explored three dimensionally through drawings and models, for the emphasis he placed on the fact that it was never too late to alter a concept, even at the eleventh hour.

Then there was Chermayeff who was not at all concerned with how the thing looked, but was very much more concerned with questioning the need for a particular building, and equally influential. Vincent Scully, who was then running the history of architecture course and the first person I'd come across who managed to make history of any kind come alive . . .'

While at Yale, he used his town planning training from Manchester to work part-time for an architectural firm at New Haven. Urban renewal was just getting off the ground in the USA, and planning skills were in demand. The project was for Westover at Chickapee, Massachusetts. Chickapee was sited next to a federal airbase for Strategic Air Command. In a display of the kind of lateral thinking that would characterise his later projects, Foster turned the legal arguments designed to supply impacted aid for poverty traps in Kentucky to gain both federal and state aid for Chickapee.

Yale was important for another reason. Foster had first met Richard Rogers, his leg in plaster from a skiing accident, for a fleeting moment at a Fulbright reception in London early in 1961. At Yale, they discovered a rare rapport. They shared the same reactions to buildings, the same enthusiasms about architecture. They collaborated on several projects, and, at the end of the year, together with Richard's wife Su, and another friend, Carl Abbott, went to look at Frank Lloyd Wright's buildings and then west to California.

It was a fairly well-trodden route of monuments. But it was accompanied by considerable speculation about a pioneering project based at Stanford's School of Education and Berkeley's Department of Architecture. While Foster was at Yale, demand for school places had surged in southern California. In the Los Angeles area alone, elementary schools were being built at the rate of one a week.[6] The method of approving and building one new school at a time was politically complicated, time-consuming and expensive. The School Construction Systems Development (or SCSD project, as it became known) was set up to develop a component system for building high schools. Its theoretical base had been developed from a study of British post-war efforts in system building, particularly those used in building schools.

The novelty of SCSD was that the architects of the system intended to design each of the components with the manufacturers who would make them. Tenders for each component would be invited not on a basis of detailed specification, but in terms of their required performance, and each bid submitted by the manufacturers would be accompanied by drawings of what they considered to be the solution to the architects' problems. Against common expectation, in the late summer of 1963, manufacturers flocked to bid for contracts to make the SCSD components. At the time SCSD was regarded as a bold and radical experiment. Its theories were to have profound influence on Foster's own work.

Foster returned to England in 1963. He and Richard Rogers had decided to go into practice together, along with two sisters, Georgie Wolton and Wendy Cheeseman. They set up shop in Wendy's flat and did everything – the telephoning, the typing, working drawings, and site meetings – themselves. But four years later, after the completion of several houses and the start of work on an electronics factory for

Norman and Wendy Foster, 1969.

Reliance Controls in Wiltshire, Foster and Rogers agreed to dissolve the partnership that had been known as Team 4. Their workload, which had always been precarious, had nearly dried up. Though they remained close friends, and shared many of the same ideas, they also found it difficult to work together. They were developing in different directions. During their partnership, Foster had married Wendy Cheeseman. Together, they now set up Foster Associates.

Foster has always acknowledged a deep debt to the time he spent in the United States. He remains a frequent visitor. Two attitudes acquired in America have become keys to his architectural approach. First is a deep scepticism that anything can be as simple as it first appears. His first step is thoroughly to question a client's requirements, study his business and his style of operation. His aim is to prepare an analysis of the client's 'range of options' in order to discuss various ways of solving his problems, and, in the process, to encourage his client to think flexibly about what he might need in the future. Once the client's needs have been established, these hard, objective requirements become the starting point for the design.

Foster remains obsessed with flexibility. He is deeply reluctant to commit himself to a design until he is entirely satisfied that it is right. 'There are few things that you can guarantee about a building,' he told the University of East Anglia in 1978; 'what you can guarantee is that it won't be perfect.'[7] Perfection, nevertheless, is what he is striving for. The way is paved with trial and error, doubt, arguments, work all night and baskets of waste paper. Here, his wife Wendy remains a powerful influence; she is his toughest critic, and will spend hours with him working on and debating the details of a design. According to Foster, she is far more ruthless and less subject to compromise than he is, and will encourage him to insist on last-minute changes to improve a building even when everyone else is declaring that the job has gone too far down the line. While it remains possible to reach the right solution, no effort must be spared to erase any imperfections.

The second important hangover from America is his belief that buildings being built today should be constructed using the materials and methods of our time – materials like aluminium, glass and steel that have been developed to 'achieve more with less', to give high performance, to be more easily maintained, and to save energy. In appearance, these new materials should celebrate their manufactured origins: be light, shiny, and orderly. Foster is an unashamed optimist; his faith is in the future. What he admires most in other people is their skill in doing things well. He treasures fine craftsmanship; he also believes it is increasingly difficult – especially on a large scale – to achieve it using conventional wet trades, such as plastering, rendering and screeding.

In the office, the quest for the best solution is tough. Foster likes, as he says, to put 'a little grit' in the managerial wheels. As the possibilities for a certain building begin to shake down, Foster often runs two, even three, groups of architects in parallel, each developing different approaches to a design, until one of them emerges as a clear winner. Numerous solutions to problems are roughed out, frequently in three dimensions. Before any proposal is finalised Foster Associates have prepared dozens of rough models showing a range of configurations and different massings of a building on a site. By the time they had started work on Willis Faber in 1970, they had devoted a large part of their office space to full-scale tests and mock-ups of cladding systems, components, furniture, and other untried things which they wanted to use in a building. In 1972 they incorporated a model shop into their offices. During the initial designs for the Hongkong Bank, a gigantic red diagonal beam was made of polystyrene and mounted across the office to see what it would be like to work with a section of cross-bracing running through a portion of office floor.

The prototype for the SCSD system, California, 1965.

Meanwhile, the research into new products, new methods of manufacture, is constant. Significantly, shows of new aircraft, not building exhibitions, have proved to be the source of several Foster innovations. Reading contemporary accounts of the SCSD experiment reveals just how important an influence the project had on Foster. Because SCSD was conceived to meet the requirements of dozens of different school boards, it was essential that the system should be highly flexible. Consequently, it developed long-span structures, so that the space inside could be arranged in a multitude of ways – using lightweight, movable partitions. The services for the building were to be located in the space between the ceiling and the roof in what was called a 'service sandwich'. Each part of this sandwich was to serve as many functions as possible: the top of the sandwich was the roof deck; the light fixtures provided heat; the underside of the sandwich was a ceiling – and, incidentally, a reflecting surface for the lights, and one from which to hang the demountable partitions.

Developing these components crossed all the building disciplines: the architects worked with specialist engineers and manufacturers to develop them. The components were designed to be easily transported, assembled and rapidly erected. And analysis of the final costs of the SCSD components showed savings of 18 per cent over conventional building methods.[8]

Foster's own approach has been uncannily similar. On each of his buildings, he has worked with industry and collaborated with specialist consultants to rationalise the components in a design and devise systems of relatively few, repetitive, elements. His aim has been to prefabricate a few elements – like a kit of parts – that can be delivered to a site and assembled, rapidly and easily, in a number of ways. Foster Associates adopted SCSD's radical approach to devising tenders for a job. After investigating the kinds of companies capable of manufacturing a particular component, prospective manufacturers are asked to base their price for the job on a 'performance specification';

that is, a detailed description of what the designers want the component to do, and perhaps an outline sketch. With the contracts agreed, Fosters work with the manufacturer to produce the particular components they need. These principles were to form the basis of their approach for the Bank.

In the interests of rapidly assembling a building, and remaining flexible, Foster's practice became one of the first architectural firms in Britain to introduce the principles of fast-track construction, and, in the process, to make effective use of a management contractor. Instead of drawing up a brief with the client, going away and designing a building in its entirety, and then beginning construction, in fast-tracking an outline design is produced and construction commences; design then continues on most of the details of a building only a few paces ahead of the construction. The advantages of the process are that the detailed design and construction processes can be telescoped into one and project time dramatically reduced, saving not only time, but money. It is possible also to postpone certain design decisions to a late stage, while taking advantage of an early start on site. Although the jobs which Foster had done before were substantial, they were small in comparison with the Bank. With perhaps thirty sub-contracts to be co-ordinated and managed, the main risks lay in failing to meet the deadlines of the programme. But on the Bank the 199 sub-contract packages that were later to make up the project each involved such a degree of custom design that their co-ordination was to become a nightmare. It was not just the greater number of sub-contract packages, but the scale and complexity of each one that meant that the managerial function would assume a scale no one could even dream of.

For Fosters in their early work there was an added piquancy in trying to beat the deadlines. Each time they approached a commission they also attempted to improve, even revolutionise, conventional components and methods of construction. They added extra stages of modelling, prototyping and testing to programmes that, in terms of time, were already pared to the bone.

Foster's unconventional method of approaching design and construction involved an attitude to the economics of building which few other architects applied. It went beyond counting the actual cost of making a new building, to take into account what that new building would cost to use. 'It's not what it costs you to build it, it's what it costs you to run it,' was one of his favourite phrases. The cost of cleaning and maintaining a building, rearranging it to accommodate changes in staff and methods of working, Foster argued, must all be taken into account when weighing up the estimated cost of a new building. This point of view made sense to his clients. It also made both parties, client and architect, think hard about how their new building was to be used.

Frequently at this point in a discussion of his approach to architecture, Foster reverts to comparisons between buildings and aeroplanes, his

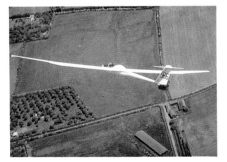

Norman Foster in his glider.

other abiding passion. He took a joy-ride in a glider after a picnic on Dunstable Downs one day in 1973, then started gliding in his spare time. Now flying is almost as important to him as architecture. He used to say he flew 'for speed for maximum distance'; and his favourite image was that of a glider. As objects they fascinate him: technologically they are simple, in operation highly efficient, and, to look at, extremely beautiful.

Foster's emphasis on speed, on analysing the long-term cost implications of designs, and above all, on flexibility, succeeded in gaining the practice early commissions in the field of low-cost, fast building. It was a world of warehouses, dock buildings and cheap factories, dominated by builders and package dealers, and one where architects were usually scorned. Their clients wanted cost-effective, inexpensive buildings, fast. 'We never talked about architecture – it was a word that just wasn't used,' Foster told $A + U$ magazine in 1975:[9]

'We were able to muscle in on that non-architectural field by demonstrating that not only could we build at the same cost, but that we could operate, if anything, faster, by using techniques of prefabrication, by introducing design concepts of flexibility and by recognising that for most of our commercial clients the only constant was change itself.'

It was a fine, pragmatic and radical approach. The added extra, not talked about, was the Foster eye, the extraordinary capacity to see a single taut and faultless line through a building, from the minutest level of the way in which the metal for a handrail might be rolled, to the final shape of the building in its site. It was this unmentionable ingredient which alone translated these practical and unassuming buildings into the realms of architecture.

Foster first demonstrated this approach in the designs he produced with Richard Rogers for Reliance Controls's electronics factory in Wiltshire, completed in 1967. It was built in nine months, cost £110,000 and was designed to provide the maximum flexibility for change and growth. The building looks extremely simple, a long, single-storey shed, with single cross braces expressing structure. It was his first attempt to combine the functions of the services, structure and skin of a building. Overhead lighting was set into the profile of the metal decking used for the roof, so that besides having a structural function the metal decking acted as a lighting reflector. By contrast, the partitions within the building had nothing to do with the structure, and were designed to be moved. Instead of designing a conventional factory, with a management box in the front and a workers' shed in the back, 'with its implications of "we and they", "clean and dirty", "posh and scruffy",' as Foster wrote later,[10] this building accommodated production, warehouse space and office uses under a single roof. The amount of space devoted to one purpose could be easily changed to another. When the client suddenly had to expand his production line he was able

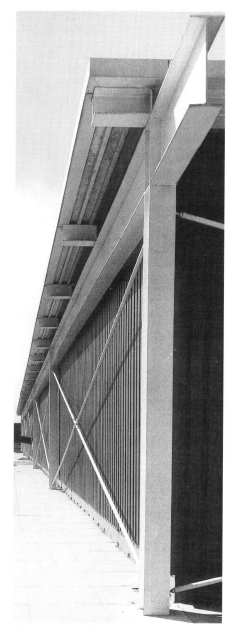

Factory for Reliance Controls, Swindon, Wiltshire, 1968.

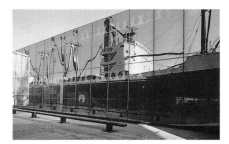

Fred Olsen Amenity Centre, Millwall Docks, 1971.

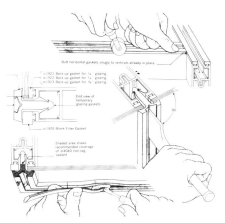

Details of the gasket system for the glazing at the Fred Olsen Amenity Centre, 1969.

Overleaf:

IBM Advance Head Office, Cosham, Portsmouth, Hampshire, 1972.

to convert a third of the rest of the accommodation, without builders, over a weekend. Reliance was the first in a series of steps Foster would take in providing flexibility in a building – a process which would be taken to a much more sophisticated level in the case of the Bank.

Next, the Fred Olsen Centre in the London docks: built to provide facilities for the dockworkers and port administration of a Norwegian shipping line. Completed in 1969, it is now the headquarters of the London Docklands Development Corporation. Today Foster might say that this project was more socially than technologically influential to his work, because it made him aware of standards in the workplace. But the story of the design of this two-storey building, wedged and supported between two neighbouring sheds, introduces several themes that will become familiar in his work for the Bank. Like Reliance, the Olsen building was designed and built fast: in twelve months. Piling for the foundations started only six weeks after design work started. The final scheme evolved from comparative studies of six alternative designs. Full-height glass walls dominate either end of a large open office space. Ideas for flexible servicing are culled from the California SCSD work: castellated steel beams which span 27.5 metres at roof level and 13.7 metres at first floor (90 feet and 45 feet) provide the structure as well as the frame for the services for the building. Air-conditioning is supplied from packaged units through a system of fixed and flexible ducts.

Writing after that building had been finished, Foster revelled in the quest for the best solution, in the skilled workmanship and technological achievement which for him the job had represented:

'The relation between the external glazing, internal comfort, and cooling loads was considered in some detail. Various alternatives such as external louvres, heat absorbing glasses, blinds and drapes were investigated and a case finally established for the use of a heat and light reflecting 'mirror' glass so far unused in this country.'

The best of three types that were available, technically and from the point of view of delivery times and assembly, was American. 'The full size details were finalised at the manufacturer's plant in Indiana. The wall was installed ahead of schedule with $\pm\frac{1}{16}$ inch tolerances over 30 feet between pre-cut glass panels and components.'[11]

Foster's requirements for tolerances of a mere 1.5 millimetres over 9 metres (0.06 inch over 30 feet) for fitting the glazing at Olsen correspond with tolerances on the Bank of less than 50 millimetres in 183 metres (2 inches over 600 feet) on the cladding of the steel masts. In the principles behind the use of packaged air-conditioning units at Olsen, lay the kind of thinking that would provide the inspiration for the modules at the Bank. Long steel spans, deep-plan offices, full-height glass walls, speed and accuracy of construction, developing new details in conjunction with those who would manufacture them after

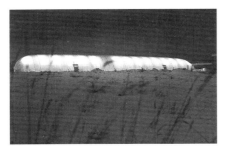

Air-inflated office built to provide temporary accommodation for Computer Technology while they redeveloped their permanent offices, 1970.

Air-inflated office, interior.

Willis Faber headquarters, Ipswich, Suffolk, 1974.

'extensive tendering with performance specifications'; all these characteristics of a building, and methods used to custom-make them, would be echoed in the work on the Bank.

Foster took the notions of flexibility explored in Reliance and Olsen a step further with his next commission, to design an advance head office for IBM. The brief was to select a series of prefabricated buildings and link them together to house a variety of activities: large computers, offices, canteens, and a communications centre. The schedule was so tight (less than a year for design and construction) that IBM had assumed that 'off the shelf' timber buildings would be the only answer, and had budgeted accordingly. 'It seemed, in the spirit, if you like, of the Reliance project, much more logical to put them under one umbrella, all under one roof, in such a way that the activities could change,' Foster said later.[12] Instead of buying-in ready-made buildings, therefore, his team devised a set of components that could be erected, clipped on and bolted together: simple steel frame, walls of solar glass, concrete screed floor, and a steel roof deck. Air-conditioning, lighting, electric and telephone trunk lines, were housed and distributed from the ceiling. The building ended up as an elegant streamlined glass box in the landscape.

'These two impressions of the IBM building sum up the Foster method,' wrote Robert Maxwell, 'a technological competence which is adventurous and experimental, but assured: and a firm grasp of a pure architectural order derived from regular structure and kept within the bounds of convenience.'[13] Inside that building, the canteen alone has now changed its location twelve times.

Three years later, upon the completion of the Willis Faber headquarters in 1974, the technical themes which absorbed Foster had been refined and developed; and further characteristics of the Bank are foreshadowed. The headquarters for Willis Faber is set on the scruffy edge of the centre of the market town of Ipswich. It is remarkable for its striking façade that consists of nothing but a curving wall of black reflecting glass, rising four storeys high, and following the edges of a 1 hectare (2.4 acre) site, roughly the shape of a giant grand piano.

The black glass wall consists of huge glass sheets, hung from the roof with neoprene joints. There is nothing between them but a kind of thick translucent silicone glue (new technology at the time), and almost nothing, it appears, just a glass fin at right angles, to support them. The wall was an ingenious – and controversial – solution to several problems: the curving shape of the site; keeping the building low in order to set it more sympathetically into the historic mesh of Ipswich; and making it large enough to be commercially viable. The problem with such a low, deep building was to introduce daylight into the middle and to let people working in the building see outside. The solution, as Foster saw it, was to incorporate large roof lights above a central well, and to put as much glass as possible around the walls.

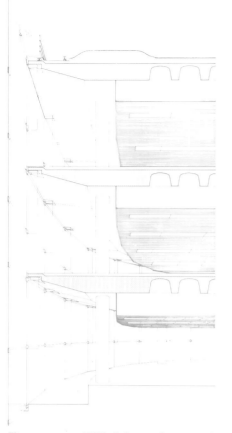

The system at Willis Faber: columns and floor slabs of concrete; walls of black glass hung from the roof and supported by fins.

Foster Associates began to investigate systems for glass curtain walls in Belgium, Germany, France and the United States, but the kind of wall they wanted was not available off the shelf. They decided to test two systems that would produce a sheer glass wall in parallel: one, a conventional glass curtain wall using steel mullions; and a second, which they designed, assembled completely from glass. This system was based on the principle of using glass in tension with glass fins to absorb wind loads. 'Everybody said that we were crazy . . . it was not technically feasible,' Foster said afterwards:[14]

'So we did the calculations. We did the shop drawings. Eventually enough numbers and technical details emerged to convince Pilkington Brothers that the idea was not only viable but very attractive costwise, which was hardly surprising since it reduced elements to just glass and glue.

At this point we made a trade-off. We had two choices. We could either go into the glass-wall business and probably ensure that every building we would do from here onward would wear the same glass curtain. Or, we could decide that we were more interested in being architects than in marketing glass walls, and that we were more likely to keep sharp if we had some kind of incentive to continue what was an attempt at a progression between projects.'

Which is what they did. In exchange for the design rights on this system, Fosters persuaded Pilkingtons to take responsibility for the design, should the wall fall down.

During construction the floorslabs and columns of the structure, which were made of concrete, were fabricated on site. The remaining parts of the building were manufactured elsewhere in factories, for quality control and cost, and also, as Foster later confessed, out of 'a belief and delight in the materials of the age'. When finished, parts of the building were to be assembled cleanly, neatly on site. On Willis Faber, the main contractor was expressly forbidden to become involved in *construction* work. His job was to oversee the work of sub-contractors and the assembly of components on site. On this project, Foster Associates took another step closer to the stage they would realise on the Bank; that of an architecture which is 'shop built and site assembled'. As Kenneth Frampton later wrote of Willis Faber, 'here all the emphasis has been placed on the elegance of the production itself'.[15]

Willis Faber provides important clues to the kind of building the Hongkong Bank might one day become. The first is in the approach to the job itself, and in Foster's attempts to reassess conventions on the ways offices work and should be designed. A brief analysis from Fosters for Willis Faber on the advantages and disadvantages of a high-rise/cellular planned office block weighed against those of a low-rise/open-plan block showed the low-rise building, with its much deeper, open spaces, to be much more efficient and pleasant to work in.

65

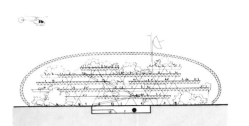

The 'Climatroffice' was a theoretical proposal for a totally enclosed office environment developed with Buckminster Fuller while early design work on the Willis Faber headquarters was in progress.

Working with Buckminster Fuller, 1971. Left to right: Fuller, Michael Hopkins, Tony Hunt, John Walker, Norman Foster.

Judged by Foster's performance on Willis Faber, if the Bank were to be a high-rise building, large untrammelled open spaces within it would be a priority.

Second, at Willis Faber people are not transported up the building in banks of elevators, but up a central moving staircase of escalators lit by daylight from skylights in the roof overhead. This large light well serves the double purpose of bringing light down into the centre of the building, while focusing attention on the modern equal of a grand staircase, a concept that had its source in the idea that it is more fun to go up escalators than to be boxed up in a lift. As if to reinforce this idea, the working parts of the escalators are exposed behind glass; pots of palm trees are planted at the landings, where their green is picked up in the colour of the carpet. The pleasurable effect of the whole, the light, space, movement and colour, together with its efficiency (studies showed that the escalators were more efficient at moving people up a building than conventional lifts), captured critics' imagination. At the Bank the extensive use of escalators, and a sunscoop to pull sunlight into the heart of the building, would be essential ingredients of the design.

On Willis Faber, Foster overturned the convention of using expensive finishes in the entrance to the building while keeping standards in the offices to the minimum. The entrance at Willis Faber is furnished in as functional a manner as the plant rooms, with painted concrete columns and studded rubber flooring. By contrast, on the open office floors there is carpet, the ceilings were custom designed and there is a lighting system specially developed to reduce glare and energy consumption. 'There is no question of a reaction against fine finishes,' Foster wrote in *Architectural Design* in 1977:[16]

'It's merely how you define priorities and reflect them in the allocation of fixed resources (ie money). Usually the workspace is 'out of sight and out of mind', bypassed by the grim anonymity of elevator cars and the drab monotony of corridors – orientation in the typical office building is the elevator floor button you push, the number on the door. Here the reverse is everywhere apparent.'

In a similar vein, the roof is turfed and planted as a garden; it is pleasurable, while functioning as an insulating, energy-saving, quilt. It was part of an approach that deliberately set out to reconcile the art of architecture with the business of putting up buildings. As Foster put it, 'to put all those dry objective pieces of the jigsaw (research, statistics, cost plan, site analysis, structural options – the check list is endless) together in the spirit of a celebration'.[17]

At the Sainsbury Centre for the Arts, completed in 1978, the general characteristics of Foster's approach are further developed. Here, in one long, low, and supremely elegant aluminium- and glass-walled shed are to be found an art gallery, seminar rooms and conservation areas,

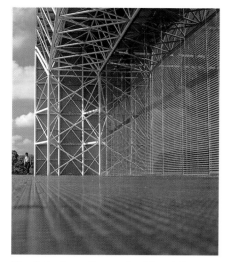

The Sainsbury Centre for Visual Arts, 1978.

The Sainsbury Centre for Visual Arts, interior.

faculty offices, a restaurant and a senior common room. Early talk about the designs for the Sainsbury Centre focused on the technical features: the innovation of creating a unique system of panels to clad the outside of the building, the novel way in which natural light was introduced into the gallery using mechanical controls, and the highly skilful integration of services, structure and skin.

Those panels, manufactured specially for the building, were moulded of superplastic aluminium, in a manner developed from methods used in the aircraft industry. They came in four versions: solid, grilled, curved and glazed – and were designed to be bolted by two men on to the welded steel frame of the building in just five minutes. The idea was that they should be completely interchangeable, so that areas of glazing in the walls or roof could be changed, depending on the needs of those inside. Neoprene gaskets sealing the panels double as rainwater channels, and drain the roof into grilles at the base of the building.

Once more Foster used a steel frame, this time of welded tubing, to create a clear span of thirty-five metres (115 feet) over the building. Inside, the space is entirely unbroken by columns or structural walls. A lining, made of perforated white louvred blinds, is suspended from the inner edge of the steel frame. The lining dampens sound and controls the amount of daylight entering the building. The louvres open and shut according to the commands of a computer, which monitors and adjusts the amount of natural and artificial light required in the gallery.

Sandwiched between the outer skin of panels, and the inner lining of the louvres is a 2.4 metre (7.8 foot)-wide zone for servicing the building. Here are to be found the extraneous, but necessary, rooms and equipment required in a building: the lavatories, darkrooms, cloakrooms, store and plant rooms and pipework. Overhead the space is used for maintenance. At either end of the building are magnificent full-height glass walls, framing views of a lake at one end, and woods at the other.

Technically, the Sainsbury Centre provides a feast of details, from the immaculate full-height glass walls, a refinement from Willis Faber, and the engineering of the aluminium wall panels, to the fastidious ordering of the catwalks, ladders and louvres overhead. The Sainsbury Centre was essentially produced in factories as a kit of parts: aluminium panels, structural steel, internal linings, lighting, end glazing. But the lasting impression here is of the control of light, filtering into a vast, uncluttered space from above. At either end of this immense long gallery clear glass walls open to the green of trees and blue of lake and sky. Cool and serene, fastidious and spacious, the inside of the Sainsbury Centre has that special quality reserved for great cathedrals, this time translated into a vast, whitened and silvered gallery.

The story of the work of Foster Associates is not entirely glorious. People have frequently criticised the exteriors of their buildings,

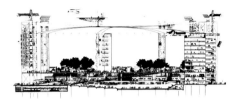

The Foster proposal for a transport interchange at Hammersmith, West London, 1979.

Spencer de Grey

particularly the black façade of Willis Faber, as being insensitive to their surroundings. This remains a matter of personal taste. But sheer nerve in making buildings, skating along the boundaries of the possible, is bound to bring one close to the edge at times. On the Sainsbury Centre, one-third of the aluminium panels had to be replaced because they did not meet Foster's specifications. One early housing scheme at Milton Keynes not only appears uncomfortably industrial to look at, but the system used to build it leaked and caused claims of £3 million to be levied against the main contractor, the roofing and cladding sub-contractor and the architect.

The Sainsbury Centre was the last building of any size completed by Foster Associates before they won the commission to build the Bank headquarters. Ironically, almost on the day that they received the request for proposals from the Bank, design work was halted on the job that they had hoped would be their next major project: to build a major transport interchange at Hammersmith in west London. Newspapers reported that the client, London Transport, had begun to lose its nerve over such an ambitious project, and was worried about raising the funds to cover it. Fosters had always maintained a policy in the office of never taking on more work than they could handle and do well. With the prospect of Hammersmith before them, they had turned down commissions for a hospital and an industrial estate. The Sainsbury Centre and their latest project for IBM were in the final run-off periods. When Fosters were approached by the Bank to see if they would be willing to participate in the request for proposals exercise, they had no other major commission on the horizon. They were determined to win it.

In the few weeks between receiving the request for proposals and leaving for Hong Kong to attend the one-day briefing by the Bank on 11 July, Foster put the office to work gathering as much information as possible about Hong Kong, and the Bank. Soon after he had read through it, Foster put the 'Request for proposals' to three of his architects: Roy Fleetwood, Ken Shuttleworth and David Morley. 'See what you can make of this,' he said.

By the time he, Wendy and Spencer de Grey (the associate Foster had nominated to come along as his right-hand man) left London, they had a comprehensive list of what they wanted to achieve in Hong Kong. In his pocket Foster had a rough photomontage of a building which Fleetwood, Morley and Shuttleworth had outlined – with services on either side of large open offices, spanning the site. He also had fifty detailed questions arising from the request for proposals: about the Bank's requirements for car parking and staff restaurant facilities, its views on the use of steel construction, the legal restraints on the use of basements, the sizes of office most in demand in Central District. These questions for the Bank would form almost three-quarters of the questions asked by the competing architects responding to the request for proposals. Like some of the other competitors from overseas, Foster

Street Market, 1979.

Shrine to local street god, Western District.

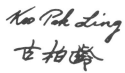

Koo Pak Ling's first sketch, showing the most fortuitous alignment of the entrance to the new bank, at an angle to the harbour front. The arrangement was to influence the angling of the entrance escalator in the new building.

planned to spend as short a time as possible in Hong Kong, and to capitalise on the distance he had travelled to tour other places in the Far East.

But, once there, Foster jettisoned these plans. All three of them were captivated by the crowds and what Foster called the sheer vibrancy and dynamic of the place. In contrast to the complacency of the UK, Hong Kong was large-scale, entrepreneurial, full of drive. The energy and confidence were infectious. The meeting of the architects with the Bank took the form of a day spent discussing the background to the Bank's redevelopment plans and touring the existing building. In the evening they were entertained on a junk in the harbour. While others waterskied and chatted to their hosts, Norman and Wendy sat at the back of the boat and observed their competitors.

Then: 'We decided that we wanted to see how the banking hall worked in the Bank. We wanted to do more research. We said we'd like to see what makes the banking process tick,' Foster recalls. They went to visit the banking hall again:[18]

'We asked all sorts of questions – about everything except the architecture. We were probing out a series of preconceptions, testing, seeing to what extent you could shrink the backup to a banking hall. Asking: what were the essential things that had to be public? What things could be more remote? What sort of things could be relocated? What sort of things were even relevant? What sort of things would change over time?'

They made a detailed analysis of the site. The Bank stood between its two local rivals: the Standard & Chartered Bank to the west, and the Bank of China to the east. It lay directly below the government's offices on the slopes of Victoria Peak, and opposite the Star Ferry terminal, the historic crossing point from the island to Kowloon. The views out from the Bank at high level were magnificent, straight out to the harbour and the hills of Kowloon beyond. The views were safeguarded because the Bank owned Statue Square on the ground below, and permitted its use by the public in return for their preservation.

In 1979 Statue Square was a messy, quirky, unco-ordinated space, Hong Kong's sole significant civic square. It took its name from the time when it had been a formal English square, centred on a large memorial of Queen Victoria and a statue of Edward VII that was demolished during the Japanese occupation. When Foster first viewed it, it featured landscaping in raised beds, some Festival of Britainish canopies and fountains, a broad and scruffy pedestrian underpass to the Star Ferry, and, to the eastern end, a lonely, unshaded war memorial. It was bounded north and south by roads.

Both the Bank of China (1950) and the Chartered Bank (1959) had been designed by Palmer & Turner in styles that were very similar to the

Bank's own 1935 building. Most of the other surrounding buildings were also by Palmer & Turner: across Queen's Road, the Hilton Hotel (1962), and on the western side of Statue Square the massive Princes Building (1963). The clock tower and terminus of the Star Ferry conveyed little more than functional charm. Along the eastern edge of Statue Square, however, the most distinguished official building from Hong Kong's pre-war colonial era survived: the Supreme Court designed by Sir Aston Webb, architect of the Victoria and Albert Museum, in 1904. This building, with its central dome, its Chinese clay-tiled hipped roofs, its classical pediments and substantial granite columns supporting a surrounding arcade is today the Legislative Chamber. Near by also was the old Hong Kong Club building, a blue-and-white confection built by Palmer & Turner back in 1897. Here too could be read the signs of a Hong Kong style of building that preceded the advent of air-conditioning, one that depended on shading and shuttering, downdraughts and the cooling effects of plants and trees and running water, characteristics that Foster would wish to return to in his ideas for the new design.

They sketched and photographed, and surveyed so that they could reconstruct a model of central Hong Kong when they got back to London. The Bank was already preparing a context model into which competitors could slot a model of their proposed building, but Foster wanted to be sure it would work. At the briefing, the Bank had told the competitors not to worry about investigating *fung-shui* at this stage. The geomantic intricacies could be absorbed later. Foster, however, sought out a geomancer so that they could understand for themselves what *fung-shui* was all about. Koo Pak Ling explained. His first sketch for the most fortuitous location of the entrance of the Bank influenced the way the escalators from the plaza underneath the building would be arranged in the final design. They also took a hard look at Hong Kong's other buildings. They studied the way the inhabitants of high-rise buildings had adapted them to deal with the heat and humidity of the climate, by adding on individual awnings and balconies, filling them with pot plants. They looked at the indigenous Chinese architecture of the New Territories.

In the end, they stayed nearly two weeks. They made contacts with local architects, some of whom helped advise them on local practice. One drew up a typical 'Hong Kong' solution to the Bank's exercise, based purely on the building regulations and plot ratio considerations. They visited the Building Ordinance Office, commissioned accountants to estimate the cost of full-phased redevelopment of the site, and met the local consultants who had worked on the feasibility studies.

The Bank had already decided that apart from the architects Palmer & Turner, the consultants who had already served on the feasibility study – Ove Arup & Partners, the structural engineers; Levett & Bailey, the quantity surveyors; and J Roger Preston & Partners, mechanical and electrical engineers – ought to be commissioned to work on the final

Contextual influences:

Battery Path, Hong Kong, 1979.

Giant television screen at Shatin Racecourse, 1980.

Waterfall at Paley Place, New York.

building; whoever the architect might be, he would be expected to work with them. During the request for proposals exercise, the architects were permitted to work on their schemes with the consulting firms, as long as they did not have contact with the individual consultant who had been retained by the Bank. Before leaving London, Foster had invited Jack Zunz, senior partner of Ove Arup in London, to be the structural engineering consultant on the Foster submission. Zunz was an eminent figure. Full of integrity, talented and creative, he was a true architect's engineer. He believed passionately that buildings ought to be conceived to delight. It was no accident that he had been responsible for the design of the structure of Sydney Opera House; he had worked closely with Jørn Utzon and had come away from the experience convinced that Utzon was one of the finest architects of the century.

Foster left Hong Kong having come to several conclusions about the kind of building he believed they should design. It had to be 'banklike'. It had, as he put it, 'to respond to the grain of Hong Kong' and to the climate. He knew the building had to be high-rise, but he wanted it to work in more than two dimensions; not just from front to back and up and down, but axially in space. He wanted to break down spaces within the building socially as well as technically. He also wanted to keep everyone's options open.

From Foster's point of view the surrounding buildings were far less important features of the site than its place in the transport mesh of the city. The existing building seemed to block a natural north-south pedestrian route that ran from the Star Ferry, up across Statue Square to Des Voeux Road, and then somehow wound its way around the Bank or through the vast banking hall, to Battery Path, a lush and shady route up to the Cathedral, the government offices, the city's Botanic Gardens and the terminus of the Peak tram. In an important way the Bank was marooned, cut off from the network of walkways above the roads and the shopping malls underground that was becoming extended within Central District. One of the first things Foster planned to do was to see how the Bank could be incorporated into this network.

On a more personal level, Norman Foster wanted to get away from the traditional notions of a high-rise building. Was there another way to do it? This was not to be a frivolous rewriting of a style for the sake of it. He wanted to go back to first principles. The building he proposed to design would have a clear identity, be more expressive and less simplistic than other high-rise towers, particularly in Hong Kong. Within it, he wanted to effect a breakdown in scale, and create a sense of progressing through vertical spaces, linked by the eye – in the same way that architects through the ages have invited people to move along a path on the ground, with a view through an arch, into a courtyard, beneath a portico, into a hallway beyond. It was a traditional idea but one which had not been applied in high-rise building before.

Movement through the building would be more efficient than in other towers, not just constrained to a central core of elevators. He wanted people to be able to see through the walls of the building from outside to inside.

To get the freedom to create such a building while at the same time solving the Bank's fundamental problem – how to keep the existing banking hall in operation – they would have to build up and over that banking hall. The first question Foster put to Jack Zunz at Ove Arup when he got back to London was: 'Is it possible?'

Hong Kong Club, 1980.

Preparing the competition hand-in, Hong Kong, October 1979.

Zunz told him it was. Together they directed a small team from Ove Arup, and a dozen architects from Fosters. They succeeded in devising a method of building up and over the Bank's existing banking hall. The solution that Foster Associates presented to the Bank's request for proposals was obvious, convincing and ingeniously simple.[1] Bridge the existing banking hall, and build a new headquarters on top of it. Stay in business on the same spot in the meantime. The scheme that Foster proposed offered the Bank the opportunity to combine a new building with parts of its old one. The system of construction the team had conceived meant not only that the present banking hall could easily be retained, but so could the north tower. The whole emphasis of the submission was on different options, and on flexibility. Foster called the solution he and his team recommended 'phased regeneration'. It was a gentler way of redeveloping the site, he said, than in the several phases of demolition and reconstruction that the Bank's feasibility study had recommended. The attraction for the Bank was that Foster's approach made it possible for it to have its cake, and eat it too.

Fosters began their report by disposing of the two courses of action that the Bank's feasibility exercise had identified. They defeated the argument that the Bank should demolish part of its headquarters, and construct a tall, thin south tower in one corner of the site, by the simple graphic device of cropping a photograph of the inside of the banking hall to show how that impressive interior would have to be cut in half, crudely destroying its proportions, in order to accommodate a new building in one corner of the ground floor. They built and photographed a model that showed that, even if it might be possible to save the barrel-vaulted ceiling inside the banking hall, and retain the north tower, from the waterfront a tall tower lined up on an asymmetrical line with the north tower would look hopelessly crude. It would destroy the Bank's prominence on Statue Square, obliterate its Queen's Road façade, and dominate the north tower in a way that would only detract from the appearance of the Bank's headquarters. In Foster's view, not only was the site too small to accommodate two such disparate buildings, but a tall, thin south tower was likely to be inefficient and poor value for money.

Next they attacked the Bank's alternative proposal for redevelopment of the site. This involved moving the main banking operation into the

The interior of the 1935 banking hall.

Overleaf:

Demolishing the south tower argument.

is this the
building site ?!

north tower, demolishing the remainder of the headquarters, and erecting a new building on the rest of the site. Phased redevelopment, as the Bank envisaged it, would, in Fosters' view, be too disruptive. Again, the architects' approach in the report was simple, and graphic. A series of diagrams showed that, in order to accommodate new construction, phased redevelopment would involve moving the contents of the banking hall alone three times. 'It's not only what it costs you to build it. It's what it costs you to run it,' was the message. 'Can you really afford the disruption factor of continually moving banking halls?'

Instead, Foster recommended a new approach to the Bank's problem. His so-called 'phased regeneration' would provide a new building – and minimise disruption. It would retain the existing banking hall until it was time for a direct move into a new one. The basis of his proposal was a radical new structural system which provided a revolutionary degree of flexibility not only in the sequence by which it could be erected, but also in the way floors and services could be arranged within the building. Furthermore, far from being compromised by the Bank's requirements, the architectural appearance of the building Foster outlined held real promise.

On either side of the 1935 Bank building Foster proposed to construct a line of reinforced concrete lift and staircase towers, which would provide the main vertical supports for the new building. In the first phase of construction, these six structural towers, three on either side of the site, would be built up to a level just above the roof of the banking hall. A deck would then be erected above the roof, using props supported on the existing columns of the banking hall, to protect the building below. Next, five huge steel trusses, the equivalent of two storeys each in height and forty-eight metres (157 feet) long, would be spanned between the core towers, horizontally across the building. Once this first level of trusses had been constructed, and a permanent steel and concrete floor deck built on top of them, the protective deck below could be demolished. Then construction would continue on the core walls to the point where a second level of steel trusses could be mounted.

The floors in the building were to be suspended, hung down from the trusses on a series of steel hangers like a stack of roads from a suspension bridge. During construction, the main steelwork beams for the floors would be erected, using temporary props and the steel for the hangers as supports for them, until the next truss levels could be completed. Once the trusses were in place at the second level, hangers to support the floors below could be connected, the secondary steel beams and decking for the floors beneath lifted into position, and concrete topping pumped into place. In the meantime, construction of the core walls would continue up to roof level, thirty-two levels above the banking hall, followed by the steelwork for the upper floors and the final top trusses.

View of phase one.

In this way, the first phase of the building would be completed, and stand behind the north tower. The occupants of the north tower could then be evacuated into the new building, the north tower demolished (or not, if the Bank did not wish redevelopment to continue) and a similar construction sequence involving four structural cores could then be repeated. This time, a shallow basement would be dug, and a new banking hall would be established in the lower levels of the building. When this second phase was completed, the third phase of the redevelopment could begin, if desired, with the demolition of the 1935 banking hall.

The drama of the steel trusses, and the massive concrete columns at the edge of the structure, gave the building Foster proposed a powerful and dominating personality. Clear glass walls gave the impression of being able to see through the building from Statue Square at the front to the green slopes of the Peak at the back and revealed Foster's characteristic lightness of touch. It was a striking contrast to the ordinary, stolid-looking Hong Kong buildings which surrounded the Bank. On the west side, the steel cross bracing that would be required to give the structure rigidity was distinctive; on the east side, the elevation, which had to be heavily indented around the escape staircases to meet the Building Ordinance Office's regulations regarding the shadow the building would cast, was equally expressive. The building was designed to cover 65 per cent of the site; it was deep and wide rather than tall. Its massing – four-square at the head of Statue Square, Hong Kong's most important civic space – echoed that of the 1935·building. Its geometry was clearly expressed, and symmetrically organised. Architecturally, the concept Foster proposed was strange to look at, but it was also imposing. Once one got used to it, it might even look like a bank.

The appeal of Foster's whole approach to the Bank's problems lay in its flexibility. He did not tell them what to do, he merely set new possibilities before them. The proposal he envisaged was only an example of his thinking. By choosing a structural form that could be suspended he suggested to the Bank the possibility of retaining almost everything, particularly the existing banking hall, intact, at ground level. Foster proposed to 'cocoon' the centre of the banking hall, both its entrances and the north tower so that the banking hall could continue to operate, with its supporting administration in the north tower, while construction took place. The attraction of this 'phased regeneration' was that it could be halted after each stage. The Bank could decide, almost as it went along, whether it wanted to keep the north tower, whether to retain the banking hall, or whether it wanted an entirely new building. The scheme could be 'complete' at any stage, even though Foster recommended that it would be wise to complete the redevelopment. For an organisation that had yet to make up its mind as to what it wanted in a new building, Foster's suggestive and pliant approach held much appeal.

A case of modern patronage

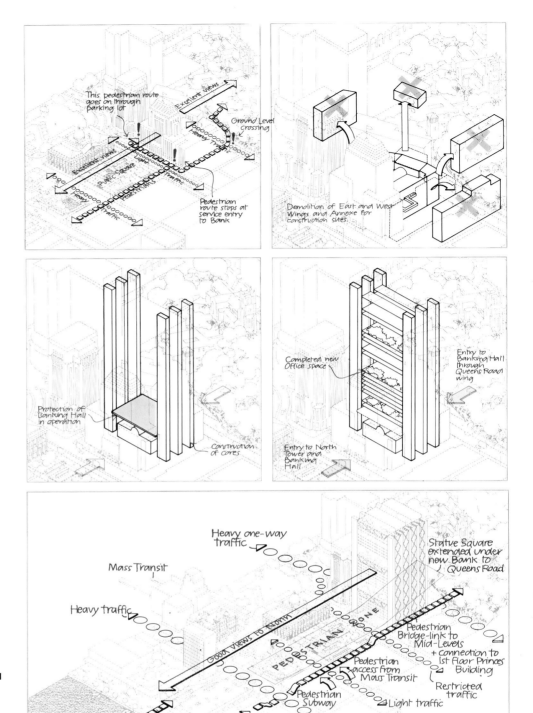

Top, left to right:

Fosters' analysis of the site context of the existing building.

After demolishing the east and west wings and the Annexe of the Bank . . .

Centre, left to right:

Two rows of concrete towers, to contain lifts and staircases, and a platform over the banking hall, would be constructed.

Then the structural towers, interspersed with three great pairs of steel trusses, are extended to their full height, 32 floors above the new banking-hall level. Floors are suspended from the trusses on hangers. Meanwhile, banking continues in the banking hall below.

Bottom:

Fosters' proposals for exploiting the site.

Far right:

Foster's sketches for pages 24 and 25 of the report in answer to the Bank's 'Request for Proposals'. 'Existing banking hall continues operations. New banking hall under . . . Use, build, remove'

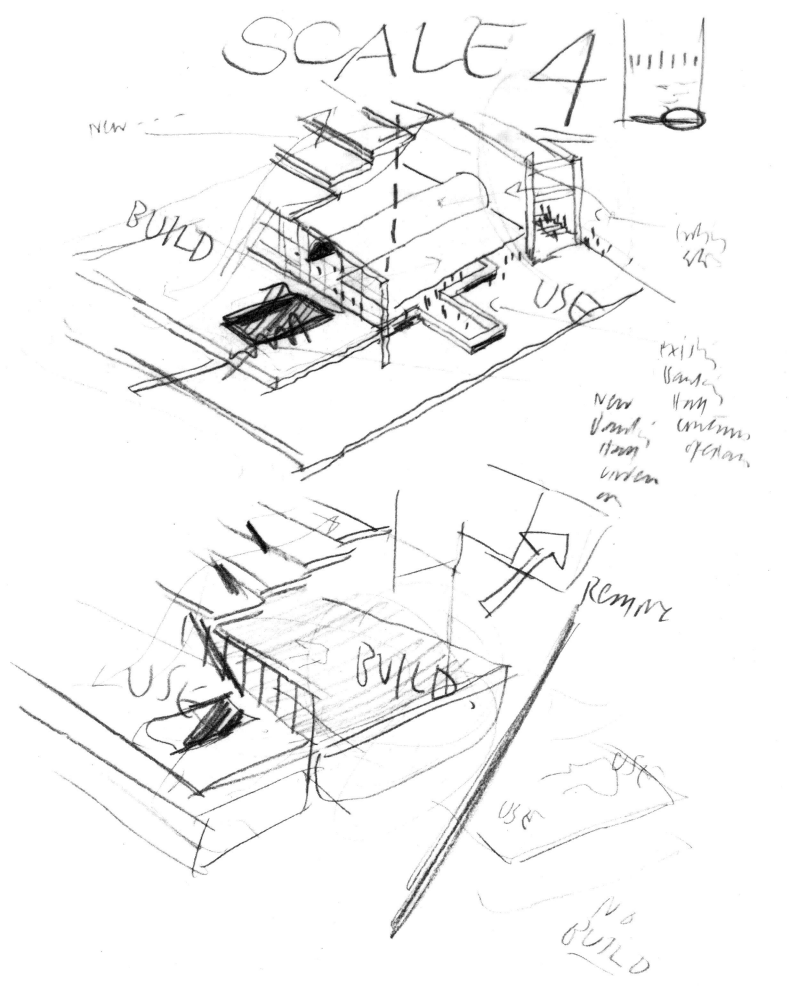

SCALE 4

NEW

BUILD

USE

NEW

Foster's first draft for the list of Design Components illustrated in the proposal: 'Concept – Systems – Hardware – Kit of Parts *also because they look good.' (from left) 'These are bridges – steel for speed and money.* Floors are suspended from these . . . shallow basement to avoid problems deeper in ground. 'Special glass was developed with Pik [Pilkingtons] for clear view and typhoon wind loads and water. Cross bracing to take wind load. There is a structural tower: it's hollow, it can take stairs, wcs, services. It is slipform concrete for speed and economy.'

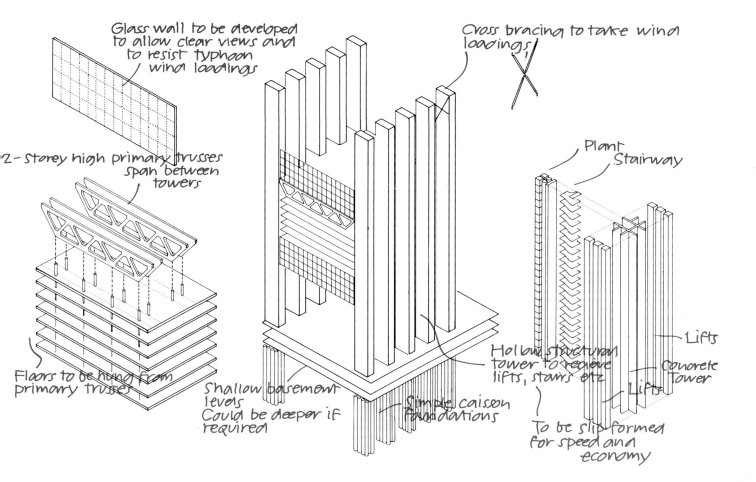

Glass wall to be developed to allow clear views and to resist typhoon wind loadings

Cross bracing to take wind loadings

2-storey high primary trusses span between towers

Plant

Stairway

Floors to be hung from primary trusses

Shallow basement levels Could be deeper if required

Simple caisson foundations

Hollow structural tower to receive lifts, stairs etc

Lifts

Concrete Tower

Lifts

To be slip-formed for speed and economy

Page 57 of Foster Associates' 'Proposals for 1 Queen's Road Hong Kong'.

The flexibility of the construction method Foster proposed extended into the interior of the new building itself. Because the floors were to be suspended, the interior could be arranged in an extraordinary diversity of ways. Portions of some floors could be left open to the air and landscaped as 'gardens in the sky'; atria could be located anywhere up the building. There could be levels where the ceilings were two storeys high, or a shallow mezzanine inserted. Escalators, staircases or lifts could be added between levels. In theory, it would be possible to expand the accommodation planned for the building in the future, by putting floors into the high-level gaps left vacant. All the main lifts and stairs, all the ancillary services and the lavatories, would be put into the structural towers on the sides of the building. With no structural columns to interrupt the vast expanses of floor, offices could be arranged in open plan, or as cells, along the windows, or in the centre of the floor. It would be possible to seal whole floors, or parts of floors, to let to outside tenants; to put in conference facilities, swimming pools or suites of apartments. The structure had all the potential to provide that essential quality Foster had so earnestly desired: the sense of moving from one kind of space to another, up the building, up through a vertical cluster of villages. For the Bank, as yet unsure of how much accommodation it wanted for its own use, the fact that this architect was prepared to think in such flexible terms was enough.

Additional flexibility for any kind of use or office arrangement was to be provided by putting all the services for the building beneath a system of fully suspended floors. The air-conditioning supply, pipework for the sprinkler system, power distribution, telephone trunking and computer wiring were all to be put into a void between the finished floor surface and structural floor slab below. The main plant for air-conditioning was to be housed in the basement, with decentralised units dispersed throughout the building. It was planned to free the roof of air-conditioning chillers by employing the same principles already used by the Bank for air-conditioning cooling, using sea water drawn through a tunnel from the harbour; and to save energy in doing so. In the same way it was hoped to do away with the fire refuge floors required in conventional tower blocks by providing terraces, that could double as gardens, on the outside of the building.

Foster's proposals for a building that could be constructed, arranged and serviced as flexibly as possible were characteristic. So were his ideas on materials. Where several of the other competitors were prepared to commit themselves to specific recommendations on materials, down to colour and finish, Foster contented himself with outlining the criteria he would use in their selection: life span, capital costs, the costs of maintenance, energy efficiency, simplicity of installation, technical feasibility and availability. Already, at this stage, Foster was conscious of the potential problems of supply and the limited number of manufacturers – anywhere in the world – who had the expertise and production capacity for a project of this size. Prophetically, the report instances steel:

The proposals for servicing the offices feature a computerised building management and energy control system linked to security and fire protection, and a deep zone under the floor for supplying fresh air, water and cabling for computers, data screens, videos, telephones and electricity.

'The supply of structural steel, a critical element to the structure, calls for an abnormally high level of planning and co-ordination throughout the production, transport, handling and erection stages. Japan seems to be the most likely source, but other offers from, say, Australia and Germany, should also be considered. Before tenders are invited, the contractor must satisfy himself that capacity is available for the high tonnage of large section steels; since the first deliveries are required in 1981, this investigation should be completed, and reservation orders placed, at the earliest possible date.'

Already it is clear that Foster would favour approaching an international list of suppliers, and that, in comparison with the other competitors, the content of his sub-contract packages was likely to be unconventional. Because of the complex interrelation between each of the engineering services, these packages, for example, might be more efficiently handled if let to one large sub-contractor than to a series of separate heating, air-conditioning and electrical specialists.

In view of the fact that the Bank set out to find an architect, not a building, the concept contained in Foster's submission in response to the request for proposals bears a remarkable resemblance to the building that stands today. The ten structural towers which Foster first envisaged in concrete have been reduced to eight, and changed to steel, while the floors of the building are suspended from a series of five, not three, horizontal trusses. The use of atria and double-height spaces remain. One moves up through the building, using the combined mechanics of lifts and escalators, through different departments, showing different aspects of the Bank's existence. The idea of landscape-gardened terraces has been incorporated and the floor of the main banking hall stands high above Des Voeux Road, with clear views north and south, over the harbour to the New Territories in front, and to the wooded slopes of the Peak behind. The building reads clearly from back to front.

In the initial concept, escalators were mentioned only as a possibility, while the lifts for the building were banked on the west side of the building, as they are in the built version; to the east, the elevation proposed in the concept is shown, as it has been built, as a series of deep recesses between the towers of the escape stairs, in order to comply with the shadow regulations. The modules designed to carry air-conditioning plant and lavatories have not yet been conceived, but are foreshadowed in the report's discussion of the need for co-ordination of the engineering services. As in the concept, the building's air-conditioning system is cooled by using water from the sea. Uncannily, the timescale proposed in the concept predicted completion of the new building for early December 1985.

After all the complex changes and dramatic events that were to follow this early proposal, final completion was in fact achieved more than two weeks earlier than that. Even more remarkably (others would say

Close-up perspective by Helmut Jacoby of Statue Square and the entrance to the banking hall.

in true Hong Kong style), occupation in fact began six months before the completion date. On 1 July 1985 the banking hall was opened to the public and, stage by stage, other areas of the building were steadily brought into commission.

In the concept, no allowance was made for building more than a very shallow basement under the north tower. The building itself was to provide a mere 52,000 square metres (560,000 square feet) of floorspace, a little more than half what was ultimately to be built. The proposals were contingent on keeping the foundations for the new building clear of the existing banking hall and north tower. By the time it came to the actual construction, a deep and massive basement under most of the site was required. At the time that Foster outlined this concept the engineering technology did not exist to build such a deep basement in such unstable ground conditions so close to other buildings. Despite this it is interesting to see that when it came to the actual construction, and profound problems were encountered trying to dig the foundations, the structural concept held true. Foundations were dug first for the main structural masts, which then started to be assembled. Building began on the upper part of the structure while the earth and rubble of the basement was still being excavated.

It is doubtful if the concept Foster Associates outlined in their submission in response to the request for proposals could have been built as it was described. Here, however, are the clear roots of the design. In spite of the development of a more coherent brief, and all the countless modifications to the design which took place after the November evening back in 1979 when Foster first outlined his proposals to the Bank's board, the final building bears clear testimony to its origins. It could not have been conceived if its structure had not, in the first place, been devised to bridge over an existing building.

At 5 pm on the afternoon of 14 November 1979, the day following the board meeting at which Foster had been appointed, Michael Sandberg, Norman Foster and Roy Munden sat down in the chairman's office to discuss the kind of facilities the Bank might want in its new headquarters. Foster was accompanied by Spencer de Grey and Loren Butt, both of whom had worked on the competition. Neil Keith, from the Bank's property department, and Gordon Graham, still retained as the Bank's architectural adviser, were also there. Foster was taking his own notes:[1]

'*This meeting*
1. *Time & cost.* Any shortening of time attractive. As many *options* as possible . . . foundations . . . consider one phase approach . . .
. . .
3. Western Tower *next to Bank*. Explore.
4. Looking like a Bank. Each a different picture. Not in Threadneedle Street – Hong Kong
. . .
7. *Other Architects* SOM/YF/time. 1 year shorter'

It was clear that something had to be done to shorten the timescale. Foster had based his concept on a completion date of December 1985; Skidmore, Owings & Merrill in their submission, however, had named a completion date some eighteen months sooner. Now as many ways of speeding up the project as possible were to be considered, including the demolition of the entire headquarters and construction in a single phase. In broad terms, the brief was that the site was to be used to the full, and the building, which it was clearly understood had to be outstanding, had to look like a 'bank'.

Then talk turned to the kind of facilities the building might contain: canteens, restaurants, a sports club with gymnasia for basket ball, table tennis, volleyball. A competition-sized swimming pool? A helicopter landing pad? Only now did the officers from the Bank allow themselves the luxury of considering all the possibilities that building a new headquarters might offer. Besides the banking hall – a large, dignified and impressive space – they might have multi-purpose auditoria for entertainment, conferences and civic events. They could have apartments, perhaps as many as 100, depending on the plot ratio

Perspective by Helmut Jacoby showing the final form of the building proposed by Foster.

implications. There was to be a medical centre, and space for the Bank archives. They thought it would be a good idea to design built-in features for attaching the Bank's traditionally lavish decorations for Christmas and Chinese New Year to the outside of the building, so that the new building would not have to be sheathed in bamboo scaffolding before each festive occasion. Foster suggested investigating laser displays, which might mean they could run screens of public information, like typhoon warnings, and the Hang Seng financial index, down the side or around the top of the building.

The meeting went well. Over the preceding few days Munden had teased Foster for drinking Campari and soda, ('not a drink for a man in the Far East'). Now:

'DELIGHTED ADVISE YOU NORMAN IMBIBED WHISKY SODA WITH CHAIRMAN PRIOR DEPARTURE STOP THIS EARLY BREAKTHROUGH IN ONE OBJECTIVE AUGURS WELL FOR FUTURE OF OTHERS'

Munden telexed Butt and de Grey afterwards.[2]

The next day Munden wrote formally to commission Foster Associates as architects for the redevelopment of 1 Queen's Road Central. Both Ove Arup and Levett & Bailey, who had already worked on the feasibility studies for the project, were to be formally appointed. But the question of who might be the mechanical and electrical engineering consultants was debated. Foster wanted a London-based firm. The Bank wanted Hong Kong expertise. Two months later Munden and a team from Fosters would interview several contenders in Hong Kong. The process eliminated all but two firms. Munden went into his office to deliberate. He came out to appoint the London office, rather than the Hong Kong branch, of J Roger Preston, who had worked for the Bank on the feasibility study.

Under the terms of their agreements, the consultants were employed directly by the Bank. As the architects, however, Foster Associates would be responsible for their direction, management and co-ordination. Ove Arup & Partners already had a substantial office in Hong Kong. So, obviously did J Roger Preston. Levett & Bailey, quantity surveyors, were a Hong Kong firm; they would share the consultancy with the London firm of Northcroft, Neighbour & Nicholson, where Levett had worked early in his career. It was a concidence that Northcrofts had already worked with Foster on his projects for IBM, and had helped to advise him on the competition. Now, Northcrofts would handle the pre-contract phases of the job and, because of expertise in the area, the mechanical and electrical servicing contracts; while Levett & Bailey would inject specific Hong Kong cost advice, and handle the post-contract period, in Hong Kong. With his appointment, those of the structural engineers and the quantity surveyors confirmed, Foster flew back to London. The next round of meetings with the Bank was scheduled in Hong Kong for late January.

In London they cracked a couple of bottles of champagne. But they had not quite absorbed the news which Foster had relayed over the telephone. The commission was more than a coup; it was a fabulous opportunity, and the biggest, most prestigious job ever to come their way. In those days, Foster Associates consisted of twenty architects and designers. It was a small, tight-knit office done up in acid green and yellow behind a slick black glass wall in Fitzroy Street. The team was young, talented and ambitious: people like Peter Busby, the Canadian who had taken the model to Hong Kong for the competition submission and watched it fall apart when he opened the crate to check it over in his hotel room; and Jan Kaplicky, trained in Prague, an inspired draughtsman whose view of the world was as one lived in the rarefied high-tech atmosphere of a space capsule. Architects with more experience and different specialist skills like Richard Horden, David Morley, Birkin Haward and engineer Chubby Chhabra were to move on and off the project.

Later others, equally talented, ambitious and young, would be recruited. Foster favoured young, obviously talented, initiates straight out of college, whose tastes in design were similar to his, but as yet unrefined. Successful candidates tended to be more interested in technology, or flying, or sailing or racing cars than in architecture. Of those who began work on the project at the beginning, only four would stay with it, following it in Hong Kong to the very end of construction: Roy Fleetwood, tall, auburn-haired, with a languid arrogance and seven years' experience at Fosters, would be responsible for co-ordinating design with industry; Graham Phillips, 'the backroom boy' who had worked extensively on IBM, would look after contract administration and site supervision; David Nelson, young, enthusiastic, a product of Hornsey and the Royal College of Art, was a specialist in furniture and would take charge of the internal systems of the building; and, lastly, Ken Shuttleworth, who had worked for Fosters for a year on Willis Faber before joining them permanently in 1977. Like Nelson, he too was young and tireless, candid and completely reliable. It would be Shuttleworth who would work up the details of the structural design with Ove Arup, and who ultimately, more than anyone, would be the man who would pull the whole project together and make the construction work in the final stages.

The London headquarters of Ove Arup & Partners was next door in Fitzroy Street. With offices in twenty-two countries, and 3,000 staff, Ove Arup & Partners were the largest firm of consulting engineers in the UK. Their expertise was highly sophisticated, varied and covered the entire range of engineering from building roads and bridges to radio masts and oil platforms, from microwave systems to transport flasks for nuclear fuels; they specialised in computer modelling. In the realm of structural engineering, the firm was rare in basing its approach on a genuine belief that structure is only the means to an end. The firm's founder, Ove Arup, had spent much time propounding that end as architectural excellence. Work they had done in the past included the

Foster Associates, 1981. The Hongkong Bank team: top row from second left: Tony Hackett, Keith Griffiths, David Nelson, Ken Shuttleworth, Ian Lambot; Chubby Chhabra (ninth from left), Jan Kaplicky (partially obscured, seventh from right), Roy Fleetwood (third from

right). Centre row: Arthur Branthwaite
(second from right). Front row: Birkin
Haward (second from left), Loren Butt
(fourth from left), Norman Foster
(centre), Spencer de Grey (sixth from
left), Wendy Foster (eighth from left).

structures for the Centre Pompidou and the Sydney Opera House. They sought to work with like-minded firms.

Arups established a small room in a nearby basement for their Bank project team. It was dark, hot and badly ventilated, and soon to be smoke-filled. For the project Jack Zunz had selected a team unlike any other that Ove Arup had previously put together. He purposely chose a team of high-fliers and kept it small, so that it could react to changes fast. At Ove Arup they had already grasped that this job would be unlike others they had been involved in, where large industrial clients proceed along an organised path, according to programme. Mike Glover, young and cheery, was the partner in charge. Under him: Tony Fitzpatrick, fast-talking, analytical, of mixed Irish, Italian and Jewish extraction from London's East End; and Ken Anthony, a highly creative engineer with a talent for excellent draughtsmanship and a special interest in wind-engineering. More than the others, Anthony spoke a language the architects at Fosters could understand. Two years later, as the wind-tunnel testing which he had initiated was well under way, he would be killed tragically in a car crash. Others were to look at how to put up the building: Tony Broomehead on the basements and substructure; and David Thomlinson, who was told to get on top of aluminium and other alloys, to look ahead, and to investigate all the available systems of fire protection. Others, like Mike Wilford, owlish and frail-looking, were to work on testing the structure and its components.

At both Arups, and Fosters, it soon became impossible to identify one person or another's contribution to the project. Ideas were a product of brainstorming, criticism and relentless questioning. Everyone was part of a team. Foster was the catalyst, the one who always made them go back to the starting point of the problem they were trying to solve; and who had the ability, with the stroke of a pencil, to turn a banal or strained conception into something which approached architecture. In those early months on the project, humour was high. At Fosters there was a tremendous *esprit*. Lunch every Thursday was an office event. It was a jokey, immensely hardworking and prolific period, when any possibility was worth consideration. It was also tense and emotional – especially for the consultants. No one was too sure of where everything was going. Foster invited Northcrofts to put their men in the office specifically to watch the drawing boards and to keep track of the cost implications. For Arups the pressure to keep experimenting with what was and was not structurally possible was intense. But even at this stage a sense was developing that this building was not going to be like anything else anyone had built before. People were becoming dedicated.

Early in the New Year, Foster Associates set up their Hong Kong office, headed jointly by Spencer de Grey, who was to work with the Bank to develop the brief, and Graham Phillips, who was to oversee the contractual side of the project and the site organisation. In March they were joined by Chris Seddon, a humorous, bearded Australian, who had worked for Yuncken Freeman on their competition design. Seddon was not only a talented designer who got on well with people, he also provided the Foster office with an essential qualification: he was registered as an 'authorised person' and would be the only member of the team qualified under the Hong Kong building ordinances to practise as an architect in Hong Kong.

Shortage of office accommodation was as acute as ever, and at first Fosters worked out of a section of Ove Arup's office. But soon they managed to find other offices in the same building. While Foster had no plans for expansion on a wider scale in the Far East, he regarded the project as the firm's most important running commission of the early 1980s, and one he would head personally. At first he was commuting to Hong Kong every six weeks. The early phases of design work, however, would take place in London. Later, the intention was to move the whole team out to Hong Kong.

Now the immediate object was the series of meetings to be held with the Bank in January. On the design side, Fosters and a special project planning group from Arups had studied a number of ways of cutting down construction time. At the same time many of the implications of incorporating apartments and auditoria, swimming pools and other sporting facilities into what was essentially an office block, had begun to be assessed. What would these facilities mean in terms of exerting extra loads on the structure? How much stronger would it have to be? What were the implications for the building's appearance, or the building regulations? How close, for example, must an auditorium be to a safe escape route in case of fire? What was the impact on the timescale? Or on maximising the plot ratio, getting as much floorspace as they could on the site? On the administrative side lay the question of how best to manage the project. What kind of people did the Bank need to run the job and to brief the architect from within their own organisation? What was the best way to supervise the construction of the project? With the help of an in-house project management team, an outside specialist project manager, or a managing contractor? This area especially was a minefield, where even experts disagreed. The responsibilities for supervision were the same. But there were marked differences in the degree of power, in their contractual position *vis-à-vis* the sub-contractors, and in their relationships with the client and the architect.

Fosters proposed that there should be 'a strong, single line of communication' between themselves and the Bank. They wanted the Bank to provide one person on whose sole instructions the architects would act. The role they envisaged was powerful, and similar to that played by the project co-ordinator on the Lloyd's building. At Lloyd's property matters are the responsibility of the Committee of Lloyd's, a part-time body. The chairman and deputy chairmen change every three years. When the Committee of Lloyd's prepared to develop in the City they set up a special committee devoted to the redevelopment, chaired by the deputy head of the secretariat and attended by the then chairman and four other members of the Council, who stayed in charge until the work was completed. Lloyd's considered that an outside project manager would inevitably intrude between themselves and their design team; instead they appointed their own project co-ordinator, as a pivot around whom and through whom all the parties worked. The project co-ordinator was responsible for ensuring that the design team had all the information it required, by the time it needed it, and that potential difficulties in the development of the design were recognised and resolved. The architects were instructed to take formal instructions from no one else. The co-ordinator was also responsible for seeing that the design and construction teams kept to the client's timetable and cost plan. Once the final design had been crystallised, it was he who had responsibility for avoiding departures from the plan, and those fatal second thoughts that could cause costs to escalate.

Fosters recommended that the Bank should employ someone similar, someone with a background in building engineering, who had experience in construction management, and knew how to control costs. They also wanted a team of people, under the command of the project co-ordinator, to work with them in detail to develop the brief. As for the physical construction of the project, Fosters recommended that a management contractor should be employed, and that the design team should be strengthened by a specialist in project planning and programming, 'for those aspects of the total project planning which would not at any point be addressed by the managing contractor'.[3]

In Hong Kong that January, the issue of how best to manage the project became the subject of fierce discussion. Six weeks earlier, Munden had written to Foster suggesting that a man called Ron Mead, then project director of the Hong Kong Mass Transit Railway, who was planning to set up his own business in project co-ordination and management, might be suitable for managing the job. He enclosed an eight-page outline of how Mead proposed to approach the project. Mead was in large part responsible for the fact that the Mass Transit Railway had come in on budget and ahead of time. With wide experience on civil engineering jobs, refineries and nuclear reactors, he came highly recommended by his boss, Norman Thompson. Thompson was the one man on the Bank's board who believed profoundly that the Bank ought to have its own man co-ordinating the project.[4] Mead called himself a 'construction co-ordinator'. The emphasis of his notes suggests a role that fell half way between the co-ordinator whom Fosters believed it essential for the Bank to employ to run the project, and a fully-fledged project manager, whose organisation would act as a clearing station between the client and architect, giving instructions, running the sub-contracts, overseeing construction, in charge of the whole project.

This brand of project management, which is usually derived from

TRADITIONAL CONTRACT
PROGRAMME TO SITE START   2

COMPETITIVE MANAGEMENT CONTRACT
PROGRAMME TO SITE START   3

NEGOTIATED MANAGEMENT CONTRACT

The differences in time taken to get on site between a traditional contract, a competitive management contract and a negotiated management contract.

experience in managing commercial property, was inimical to Foster. As architect to the Bank, Foster wanted complete authority for the project and direct access to his client. Project management was alien not only to his methods but to the whole of English building practice, where the architect is considered the leader of the building team. As has been seen, however, what Foster wanted was an experienced management contractor, one whose experience lay in the construction industry, to join the rest of the team of consultants and be in charge of holding and managing the sub-contracts and overseeing the construction. What he did not want was another tier inserted in his direct line of authority from the Bank. Mead had no sympathy with Foster's approach. The Bank, after all, would be paying the bills. He believed that, if the Bank was to retain control of the project, it must hold the sub-contracts directly and retain its own project manager with the clout to enforce them. The debate on how the project was best to be managed was to rage on for nearly six months. On one side were Fosters supported by Arups' project planning unit; on the other Roy Munden and Ron Mead, whom Munden, playing devil's advocate, had invited to help advise him. It inevitably influenced what happened next.

Unlike Lloyd's, and despite Munden's urging that a small, senior working group should be formed to take charge of the briefing of the architects, the board had decided that there was no need to appoint a special committee to oversee the project. The Bank did not work like that. Sandberg told Munden that whatever decisions he felt unable to make could be referred to him. A briefing team could be provided from within the Bank's existing resources. But there was no question that some sort of 'technical adviser' was required to bolster the experience available in the Bank's property department.

Two months later Ray Guy assumed the role of 'technical manager' for the project within the Bank's property department. In January 1981, this department was to be hived off to form a separate company, HS Property Management. Guy's immediate boss was Doug Brown. Bluff and practical, Brown was a man who had spent his working life serving the Bank in the Far East. His experience, and that of his staff, lay more in the field of property management than in construction. As far as this project was concerned, Guy was to answer to Roy Munden as project director. But it was clear from his brief that he was to possess none of the power of the Lloyd's co-ordinator, as Fosters and Arups had recommended. Guy's job was to liaise between Munden and the architects, and keep track of the day-to-day progress and costing of the project. It was Munden who was to be responsible for reporting to the Bank's board on the project as a whole. Although he was to become a director the following year (in May 1981), he was not as yet a member of the board. He continued to fulfil his other duties as a general manager of the Bank, and the board was busy with other business.

In fact, at this stage, the Bank had failed to recognise the importance of a powerful briefing team. After all, Foster had told them he liked to work with the client to draw up his own brief. He described how his team had analysed the work of the staff at Willis Faber in preparation for their designs for that building; on his visit to their headquarters, Munden had confirmed Foster's immensely detailed work on their brief. All that seemed necessary was to give the architect complete access to everyone at the Bank and await the results. If, Foster had told them, the building was to be designed to be flexible, any changes, the Bank assumed, could be taken care of later.

It was all this talk of a flexible building which in fact provided the breeding ground for a fundamental misunderstanding between architect and client, and one that would continue to plague the development of a fixed brief for the building. From Fosters, it was Spencer de Grey who had been given the task of drawing up the brief. His task was to collect information on the number of the Bank's departments, the people in them, and the relationship between one department and another. The aim was to make an accurate record of the Bank, a sort of snapshot of the organisation at a particular point in time. This record would provide a point of comparison with whatever changes in the Bank might take place in the course of designing the building, and make sure that, ultimately, the design of the new building would 'fit' the Bank. It would also give the design team a starting point to set out significant requirements like the boardroom, the kitchens, auditoria, swimming pools or computer centres and any other special requirements the Bank might have. The question of the best places to locate these kinds of facilities in the new building not only involved aesthetics, but, more significantly, because these items usually required special services, fire protection and floor loadings, decisions on their nature and location were needed before the design of the structure was finalised.

Munden had issued written instructions to all staff to co-operate with the architect in providing the information he needed. In addition to Munden, who had frequent recourse to other executives in charge, de Grey's main points of contact within the Bank were three or four people within its property department. The briefing process should have been straightforward, but somehow it wasn't. A series of meetings was held with staff of different departments to try to formulate an outline brief of major requirements but these often dissolved in frustration. The Bank had never operated according to particular strategies; given the volatile politics and economics of the region its managers had exceptional independence. Talk of making detailed plans for the future seemed to them like bureaucratic nonsense at the best of times and here they were, with the Bank growing far faster than their most optimistic predictions, being asked to say what kind of facilities they would need in five years' time. Banking itself was on the brink of a revolution brought about by the advance of electronic communication. In Hong Kong, the property market was in ferment, generating massive new lending programmes. In China, for the first time since the war, the possibilities for renewed Western business were reviving. Soon de Grey was to find that, all too frequently, those executives who had provided one set of information and some informed guesses for the brief were drafted elsewhere, and the process had to start again.

But the Bank took comfort from the knowledge that the building it had commissioned was to be as flexible as possible; if so, it would be able to accommodate the Bank in all its permutations. What the Bank failed to grasp was that this flexibility could have limitations. Despite repeated appeals by Fosters for decisions on major requirements, it was to be another three years before there would be a group within the Bank which the design team felt was providing it with consistent briefing information, and more importantly, to whom it could refer for final, binding authority.

With Ray Guy's appointment by the Bank, the argument about how the construction of the project should best be managed continued. By March, Munden had accepted 'in principle' the idea of appointing a management contractor, but he still had many reservations. In spite of Mead's preferences, Munden's assessment of project management in the past ('either a disaster or a waste of time or both')[5] made him wary of using a project manager. What he had heard about management contracting on his tour round the world had impressed him. He knew the concept had been used with success on a number of large projects in Britain. Furthermore, without a management contractor, Foster could not get the direct access he would need to the sub-contractors with whom he intended to develop the modules and other fundamental components for the building. Without a management contractor he could not fast-track; development of the site could not begin until the design of the building was finished. But the clinching factor was the advice of the Bank's legal department. In no circumstances, it advised Munden, should the myriad sub-contracts be held directly by the Bank.

There were, however, two real drawbacks to using management contracting in Hong Kong. The first was that 'sub-contractors' in the Western sense with whom formal contracts could be made were rare. Specialist labour on a Hong Kong building site was generally hired on a casual basis. It was usually negotiated and agreed between men in a teashop, who concluded an agreement by shaking hands: and then went out to find the men to do the work. The second was that Hong Kong's building regulations inhibited the fast-track construction associated with management contracting. A start on site could not be made until the final design had been approved. It was one of the reasons why so little attention was often paid to the details of buildings in Hong Kong. Given the manner of organising Chinese labour for a project, the idea of importing a foreign management contractor and telling him to get on with the job seemed mad.

By late spring 1980, time was becoming extremely tight. With the way the design was developing, Fosters wanted a management contractor

Ray Guy

on board by the end of August. They had agreed with the Building Ordinance Office that major aspects of the design like the plot ratio and shadow factor could be negotiated early to give them a good start on the overall design, while other more detailed aspects, such as fire safety, could wait until later. Early appointment of a management contractor to help evaluate methods of construction, materials and plant would save time. Despite its newness in the Hong Kong context, Fosters, Arup and the quantity surveyors remained adamant that management contracting was the best way to run the project. But they also agreed that Munden was right to insist that a contractor with substantial Hong Kong experience should be involved on the project. A joint venture seemed the obvious solution.

In the end, a detailed tender request demanding extensive management contracting experience – which they could not provide – was issued to six leading Hong Kong contractors. Graham Phillips had been to see them all beforehand. As the team had hoped, each formed a joint venture with a leading UK firm. On 8 September, the contractors were given an all-day briefing on the project. They had a month in which to submit written tenders describing how they would approach the job. Each was returned in several volumes. Three more days were taken up in hearing presentations from each of the contract teams, followed by intensive interviews. Finally, late in October, a joint venture company composed of Hong Kong contractors John Lok & Partners, whose chairman was president of the Federation of Contractors in Hong Kong, and George Wimpey International, the largest construction firm in Europe, was appointed as the management contractor. Initially John Lok/Wimpey were to organise the preliminary planning and mobilisation for the project, and to oversee the conversion of a section of the Bank's headquarters so that it could continue to operate while construction took place. Agreement of the main management contract would have to wait until final designs were formulated and costed by June of the following year.[6] It was now November 1980, one year into the project.

Back in January of that year, ten different ways of cutting down the project time had been presented to the Bank. The fastest and least expensive option was one that demolished the whole of the Bank, leaving a green field site. With a clean slate to start on, it was reckoned that design and construction would take just under five years to complete. But a less obvious option that could be completed in the same time, and cost roughly 10 per cent more, was to prove more attractive. This involved clearing the whole site except for the 1966 annexe to the Bank, and converting the annexe into a small, temporary banking hall until the new building could be completed.

In fact, the Bank had only just succeeded in finding space near by that could serve as a head office while it rebuilt its headquarters. The need for a banking hall on the site continued to be felt, however. At the series of meetings with Foster in January, the Bank gave its general agreement to the idea that clearing the site and retaining the annexe was the way forward. Gone was any economic rationale for keeping the famous north tower, or indeed much reason to save the 1935 banking hall, although investigations would later be mounted to see if the barrel-vaulted ceiling could be saved. Within a few days Fosters started looking at the ways of converting the annexe to fulfil the needs of the Bank during construction work. Conversion would start on 1 December.

At these January meetings, Foster and his team were showing the Bank flip-books of drawings which showed how facilities like a competition-sized swimming pool, a multi-purpose auditorium, or a gymnasium big enough to take ten table tennis tables, or play basketball in, would affect a building on the site. How many apartments, and how they might be arranged had still to be decided. There was no precedent in the building ordinances for determining the plot ratio for a building where floors were randomly divided between business and domestic use.[7] They showed half a dozen ways of treating the banking hall, with different arrangements of atria, mezzanines, and ways of gaining access from Statue Square and Queen's Road. The concept for servicing the office floors showed people at work, supplied from the floor with locally controlled systems for air-conditioning, lighting and all manner of telecommunications.

The Bank wholeheartedly embraced this idea. It told the architects that the objective was to create a building designed for banking in the twenty-first century. 'It is of paramount importance to ensure the building does have the most flexible design throughout to support wiring for terminals, telephones, computers, power, etc.,' the Bank's manager of communications told Munden.[8] It should be possible to supply air-conditioning to different parts of the building twenty-four hours a day. Processors, terminals and other electrical equipment might require special connections or power from stand-by generators; these should be available at any location within the building, with the least structural alteration.

They discussed colour; Foster talked about the use of red and green, colours traditionally used in Chinese buildings, to see how the Bank reacted. Arup had sketched out eleven different ways of treating the structure to show the variety of frames which could provide the . widespread flexibility to be gained by bridging the site, so that the Bank could see what they might look like. Foster showed them other well-known structures with clearly expressed structural systems, like the Eiffel Tower and the Golden Gate Bridge. The object of the exercise was to test the Bank's reactions, try out ideas, to see which of them were greeted with derision, which with grudging satisfaction, which excited interest. Once the broad strategy for the design of the building could be agreed, Foster told the Bank, there would still be time to be flexible on many fronts. The meetings went well; everyone was pleased with the prospect of finally getting to grips with the project. A major

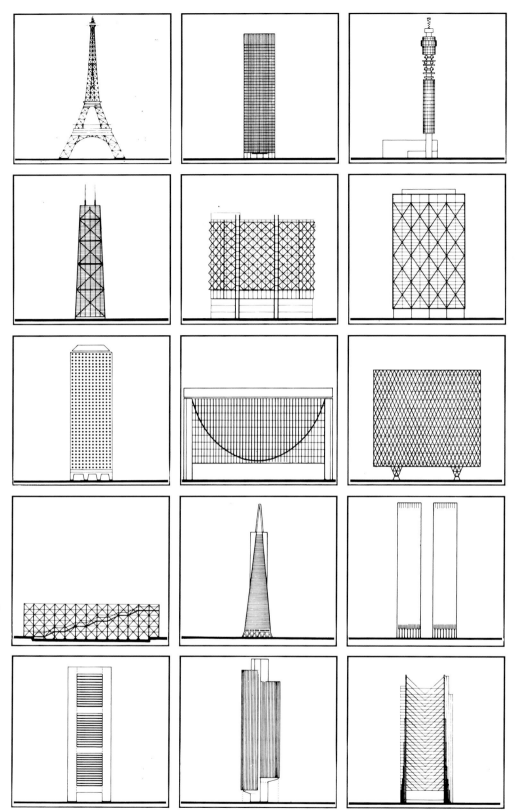

Extracts from the flip-books, January 1980: examples of buildings with externally expressed structural systems. Left to right from the top row: Eiffel Tower, Paris; Seagram Building, New York; Post Office Tower, London; John Hancock Building, Chicago; office building in Cannon Street, London; Aluminium Co. of America, San Francisco; Connaught Centre, Hong Kong; Federal Reserve Bank, Minneapolis; Group Practice Clinic, Salt Lake City; IBM Building, Pittsburgh, Centre Pompidou, Paris; William Pereira Building, San Francisco; World Trade Center, New York; OCBC, Singapore; National Westminster Tower, London; Hongkong and Shanghai Banking Corporation, May 1980 presentation.

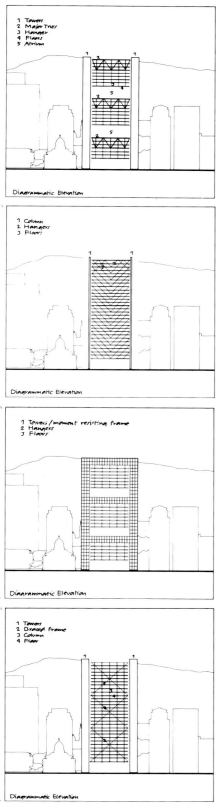

Some early options considered by Ove Arup and Fosters for the main structural system for the building.

board presentation was planned for May; the final building concept was to be ready by late November. Foster flew back to London to tell the design team the good news.

One of the structural options conceived by Jan Kaplicky with Ove Arup for the January meetings with the Bank showed a series of powerful downward-thrusting diagonals across the main façade of the building. At the side of the building were large bundles of tubes. The Bank had reacted blandly to each of the structural options, but this one showed the germ of an idea that Foster liked very much. The system consisted of tapering steel masts, connected by strong diagonal structural members, to support the floors. During the next few months, the design team was to work on preparing what they called the Chevron scheme for presentation to the Bank board in May.

The work was hard and intense. As soon as Fosters had learned in November 1979 that they had been selected as the architects to the Bank, they and Arups had 'brainstormed' the concept proposals. They wanted to get rid of the large bridge-like trusses in the building. They had also become increasingly concerned about the complexity of the proposals they had put forward. More study had shown that it would take much more time than they had first envisaged to carry out their programme of 'phased regeneration' of the old bank. In addition, their first idea of using concrete for the main structural supports would have meant that the structural columns would take up a significant part of the office areas in the building. To use steel masts, rather than concrete cores, to support the building would reduce the 'footprint' of each column on the ground by fifteen times; for Fosters, too, the use of steel throughout the building held aesthetic appeal. In the competition scheme, the double-height spaces in the building could only be located at the points where the giant trusses spanned the structure. But Foster wanted more flexibility inside; he wanted a whole variety of spaces, galleries, mezzanines and atria located apparently at random up the tower. When, in January, the team was given the go-ahead to clear most of the site, the possibility of developing the Chevron scheme, in steel, and so that it could be cantilevered over the annexe on just one side of the site, was irresistible.

The office was mobilised. Roy Fleetwood, and Mike Glover from Arup were despatched to Japan to start investigations into who, around the world, might have the capacity and facilities to make the steel. Loren Butt, and Chubby Chhabra went to work with J Roger Preston on detailed concepts for servicing the building. David Nelson, who was working on a project with Hille the furniture makers on ideas for the office of the future, began to apply this research to the internal outlines of the building. Shuttleworth and Fitzpatrick began to consider the integration of the structure with the rest of the building. The disciplines of the two, the architect and the structural engineer, had to be in harmony. They wanted the steel to be on view for all to see; its proportions had to be satisfying, and structurally it had to stand up.

103

Elsewhere, the team was looking at lift systems, and transport access to the building. The bank had also commissioned them to make a complete study for the development and renovation of Statue Square, in front of the building. In Hong Kong, Chris Seddon was opening negotiations with the Building Ordinance Office; Graham Phillips was arguing the management contracting issue and de Grey was working to further the Bank's brief. Foster himself always carried a drawing pad on which he sketched out ideas as they came to him. The rest of the team – and this was a habit also at Ove Arup – kept diaries in black notebooks, recording meetings and ideas, notes and sketches. No one worked on any idea for very long, unless it passed muster. In the next stage of development, models were built, or photomontages designed, to get a clearer idea of what one proposal or another might look like.

The most striking aspect of the Chevron design, as it was finally conceived, was its dramatic emphasis of a steel structural frame across the front of the building. Powerful red diagonals were suspended downwards from strong red vertical masts, dominating the north façade of the building. On closer inspection the masts consisted of bundles of tubes, very thin and strong. The diagonals on which the floors were supported formed part of the vertical truss system supplying stability to the building. It was a tension structure, designed to make economic use of steel. Double-height spaces could be located randomly up the building. Furthermore, now that there was no longer any need to maintain the old banking hall beneath the building, Foster proposed to try to maximise the use of the site to the limit of the building ordinance. If he maintained the concept of raising the whole building above ground level, and left the ground space beneath it free, this area could be dedicated as public open space. It would mean that people would be able to walk through from Star Ferry to the base of the Peak. If this reading of the building regulations could be used to persuade the authorities to raise the Bank's plot ratio from 15:1 to 18:1, this could give it 20 per cent more floorspace.

On the western edge, the building was to be cantilevered over the annexe, the temporary Bank branch on the site, until the end of the construction, when it would be demolished. The concept for placing the services on the sides of the building had been developed to show, for the first time, a system that put the central plant for the building in the basement, and located self-contained modules on one side of each floor. These were to contain lavatories, storage and the plant to distribute air-conditioning to each floor, as well as serving as the point from which all the underfloor services would be distributed. Each workplace in the building was to have its own light, power, air-conditioning and telecommunications supply, and the entire building was to be equipped with a sophisticated computerised building management system to control the humidity, temperature, security, sprinkler, lifts and sign systems.

Other elements of the Chevron scheme were similar to the competition

Close-up of the structural model of the Chevron scheme.

March 1980. Mock-up of a typical diagonal cross brace for the Chevron scheme erected in the Foster office to see what it would be like to live with.

The Chevron scheme from Queen's Road.

submission. There was the potential for atria, and a three-tiered banking hall at the base of the building. The building could incorporate gyms, squash courts, an Olympic-sized pool, apartments and roof-top terraces. There was to be external sun-shading and high-efficiency lighting. In front of the building, Fosters showed how the whole of Statue Square, from the Bank to the Star Ferry, could be freed of traffic to create a vast, open plaza. From early in 1979 informal plans to prohibit cars in parts of Central District had been in existence; this was the beginning of a plan that, at the Bank's request, Fosters would refine later in the year. The new headquarters itself could be finished in July 1985. Demolition of the annexe, and construction of that corner of the new building, would take until April 1986.

At the presentation to the board in May 1980 it was not immediately obvious that the scheme required a powerful system of diagonal bracing running north-south within the building itself. Even as the scheme was being presented, a vast red polystyrene diagonal beam was standing in Foster's own office to see how often people bumped into it. The design of the Chevron scheme was not going to work easily. At the end of Foster's presentation, Chinese members of the Bank's board conferred in a corner of the boardroom; their hands moved to form a series of V-shapes. They did not like the red, downward-moving diagonals of the structure. They were worried about the *fung-shui*. Red, diagonal bracing was not going to be acceptable.

It was a profound blow. Three weeks before the presentation Foster had flown out to Hong Kong to take the chairman through the scheme. He had been delighted with it. The board's rejection came as a complete surprise. Nor was it the only problem. It had been a fraught period in the Building Ordinance Office. On his first trip to Hong Kong Foster had heard that it was important to deal at the most senior levels if there was to be any hope of obtaining interpretation according to anything other than the strict letter of the regulations. When Foster made the first formal approach to the Building Ordinance Office on behalf of the team, he found himself dealing with Edward Kennard, the principal government building surveyor, to whom he had been introduced at a previous briefing. Kennard had told him that he was prepared to negotiate some aspects of the scheme in the spirit rather than the letter of the building ordinance. Foster was delighted that the team would be dealing with someone so senior, so apparently open-minded and willing to co-operate, and took great pleasure in telling the Bank.

Ten weeks before the Chevron scheme was to be presented to the board Kennard was arrested on a charge of accepting bribes. 'Norman really picks 'em, doesn't he,' quipped Munden when he heard the news. Investigations by the Hong Kong Independent Commission Against Corruption of alleged offences within the Building Ordinance Office, threw the government building authorities into disarray. Even if the board had not rejected the Chevron scheme, Foster would have had to

**Norman Foster's sketches for the
Chevron scheme.**

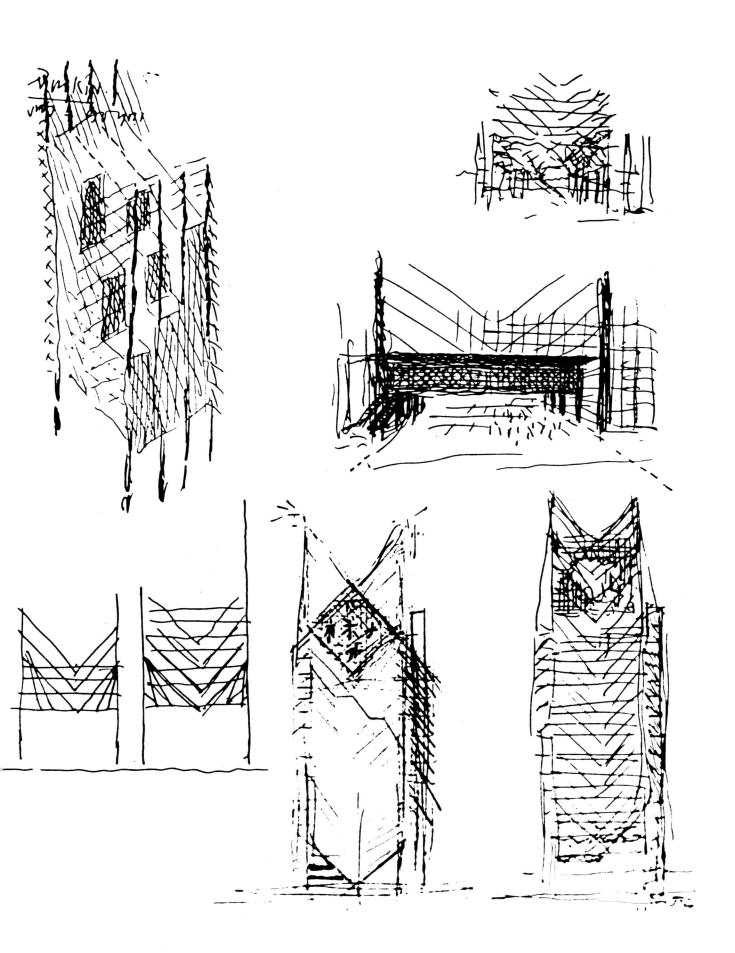

Norman Foster's sketches for the Organ Pipe scheme.

Norman Foster's sketches for the Coat Hanger scheme.

visit the authorities afresh. Kennard's arrest had made everyone in the Building Ordinance Office suspicious of any project with which he had been connected. Foster went back to the authorities and made it clear that whatever reassurances Kennard might have given him were being disregarded. His team would start again from scratch on the plans. In London, they were already back at the drawing board.

After the débâcle of the Chevron scheme, it seemed to several at Fosters as if inspiration had dried up. Having agreed that the old headquarters was to be demolished, it was now no longer necessary to bridge the site. There had been too much red in the Chevron scheme. It was time for a radical alternative, based on a different structural system. The Organ Pipe scheme, as it became known in the office, was an exercise by Foster and David Morley in massing the building so that it complied with the strict letter of the shadow regulations. It was a massive building, cut back and stepped down on an angle of 45 degrees to Statue Square. In the context of the two earlier proposals, however, its appearance looked like an aberration; Munden told Foster not to pursue it: he was going too far in the wrong direction.

But, without having experimented with the Organ Pipe scheme, it would have been difficult to proceed with conviction to the next stage. For in the meantime Ken Shuttleworth and Fitzpatrick had continued to pursue the idea of the suspended building. By the end of August they had developed a new structural concept which brought the structural masts in from the edge of the site, and suspended the floors out from the sides of the building, as if from a series of coat hangers. Now the building's structure appeared less dominant, but the internal cross bracing it would have required would have made planning the inside of the building awkward. Nevertheless it looked promising. On 31 August, Foster showed this scheme to Michael Sandberg and Roy Munden at his office in London; the chairman expressed broad approval.

The so-called Coat Hanger scheme was the breakthrough in determining the final structural concept for the new building. It was soon realised that the huge cross-braces that were needed inside the building to give the structure stability from east to west could be dispensed with if two coat hangers were joined together on the north and south sides of the building. Now the trick was to cut back the building on the east side to make it comply with the shadow regulations, without destroying the symmetry to Statue Square, which was not only required aesthetically, but could also be used as a bargaining point with the building authorities to allow a little more shadow on Bank Street. The solution was to reduce the floors at the top of the building, and to adjust the height of the building, until the amount of shadow cast on the surrounding streets fell near enough to the limits of the building regulations for negotiations to open. By late September they were ready to put a preliminary submission of the new scheme to the building authorities.

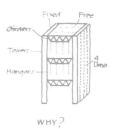

NOVEMBER 1979

Fixed   Free

Girders

Towers

Hangars

4 Days

WHY?

WHY?
BECAUSE –

1. Bridge over banking hall
2. Create mix of spaces here
3. Create clear spaces
4. Flexibility for choice change + growth
5. Image
6. Buildability

ALL ADVANTAGES –
WHAT ARE THE DISADVANTAGES?

DISADVANTAGES –

Structure compromises 6 storeys out of 32 storeys

Good buildability – but note relative size of structural concentration at these parts

– LEADS TO MAY 1980

– Chevrons solve over-concentrated structure

– all 32 floors equally flexible

– eliminates 'girders' (taste!?)

3 days now possible due to

Annexe

OK – BUT

THE 'BUTS'

– Some reaction against roof structure (1967 overtones)

– Chinese express reservations to appearance of 'chevrons'

– Questions about inclined structures internally

– Colour?

STAGE ONE – AUG 1980
STRUCTURAL DEVELOPMENT

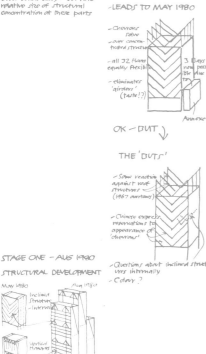

May 1980   Aug 1980

Inclined structure internal

Vertical towers

Nov 1979   Colour!
Advantages – Continuous inclined structure removed. No congestion.

Sketches by Birkin Haward to illustrate the story of the developing design, November 1979 – August 1980.

Five major issues had to be clarified before the team could go any further. In the office, the team rehearsed them. An illustrated paper was prepared to make their arguments clear. Would the authorities in fact allow the space under the building to be dedicated to public passage and, in return, grant the Bank an increased plot ratio? This regulation had been conceived to encourage developers to spare precious space for pedestrians at ground level, in return for more floorspace higher up in a new building. Normally architects would cut a corner off their site, or leave more groundspace around the base of the building, in order to gain more plot ratio. No one had tried it with space *under* a building before. The issue was worth an extra 20 per cent – an 18,600-square metre (200,000-square foot) bonus to the Bank. The answer returned was a qualified yes.

The second issue to be cleared was how much of the site they would actually be permitted to cover. The building regulations were intended to encourage the development of towers with fat podiums at the base to prevent the creation of canyon-like streets. Not only did the question of public dedication affect the amount of the site they could cover, but this building did not have a podium.

Third, there was the two-pronged question of fire protection. The first concerned refuge. The Fire Service Department strongly recommended that every fifteenth floor of a tower should be declared a 'sacrificial floor' and specially compartmented to afford protection from smoke and flames. Normally such floors are filled with plant and other equipment, and are identified from the outside of a building by the absence of windows. Fosters wanted to omit these floors, and put the plant – which in the case of fire they felt was dangerous – in the basement. Instead of sacrificial floors they wanted to build refuge terraces, that could be planted as gardens, on the outside edges of the building. These would be protected from fire within by roller shutters. The second issue was compartmentalisation. Under the fire regulations every 30,000-cubic metre (1 million-cubic foot) section of a building must be capable of being sealed for two hours against the spread of smoke and fire. The problem here was that the banking hall was four times larger than the maximum permitted volume of a 'compartment'. Fosters planned to try to persuade the authorities to allow an exception to compartmentalisation requirements by equipping the building with numerous other fire protection features. There were to be systems for sprinklers, mechanical smoke exhaust and automatic smoke alarms throughout the building, and all escape routes would be on the outside edge of the building, instead of inside a central service core. Eventually, components throughout the building – the steel, the glass curtain walls, the partitions and the doors – would also be manufactured to provide a two-hour fire rating.

Finally, there were the critical shadow constraints. They had tried following the shadow regulations precisely in the Organ Pipe scheme. The result had not been a satisfactory building. Fortunately the shadow

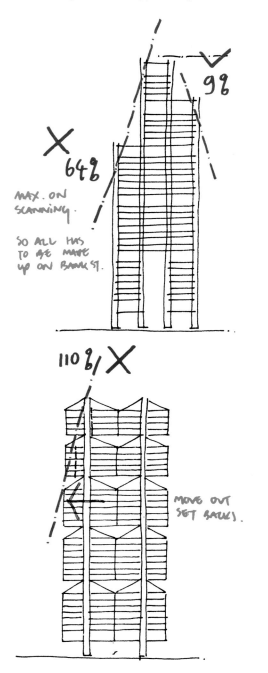

Ken Shuttleworth's illustration of the setting back of the building to meet the shadow regulations, November 1980.

regulations permitted discretion to be applied; everyone agreed that the new building looked better because it appeared symmetrical from Statue Square. In the event, after protracted negotiations and successive exercises in cutting back the Bank Street façade of the building, using models and computer formulations, they arrived not only at a formula acceptable to the building authorities but at a solution that, in architectural terms, made a virtue out of the problems. But back in the autumn of 1980, dealings with the Building Ordinance Office were only just beginning. Ultimately, clearance of the building would require over 100 separate submissions to the authorities.

By the autumn of 1980, the Bank had yet to give Foster any indication of how much money it was prepared to spend on its headquarters. The feelings of the board had been mixed, but generally relaxed: perhaps the building might cost double the price of a very good Hong Kong office block? Say HK$1,200 per square foot? In the first months of the project there was a strong feeling that no one should inhibit the architect by mentioning cost. 'In view of the prestigious and special nature of the building and of having employed one of the world's leading architects,' the meeting noted, 'it [is] not appropriate to place any particular ceiling on the price to be paid for the building.' At a board meeting in August this view was reiterated. What the Bank had been after was the right design, a building that would carry it into the twenty-first century, and rival anything else in Hong Kong at the time. As it had yet to be designed, no one knew what it might cost. No budget had been imposed.[9]

At the same time, Fosters had been extremely reluctant to name any figures on the project. While the design was still developing, too many aspects with dramatic cost implications, like the special facilities the Bank was calling for, and the phasing of the construction programme, still had to be decided. Other features, on the thresholds of building technology, could not be costed using historical cost yardsticks. Later, the quantity surveyors would devise a system of allowances based on budgets prepared by industry and the known elements like the weight of the steel, the square metres of cladding and the plant and equipment to be supplied, to estimate the costs of the modules. In the spring of 1980 Munden had insisted, however, that at the board presentation planned for May – the meeting at which the Chevron scheme was presented – the subject of costs should be addressed.

The figure for the Chevron scheme, $HK2,167 million at May 1980 prices, was greeted by the Bank's officers with an audible intake of breath. It was a fabulous sum – over seven times the average cost of a forty-storey speculative block and more than three times what Hong Kong's most expensive building so far had cost. At the board presentation, however, concern was focused on the building's appearance, those striking red diagonals, and their impact on the Bank's image. The design was rejected. Reaction to what it might have cost was almost indifferent.

110

FLEXIBILITY	20, 25, 15, 10 ▢	(15)	15/16
COMMUNICATION	10, 7, 8, 15, 14, 12, 5	(10)	10/11
SPACE EFFICIENCY	15, 25, ▨, ▨ 20 ▢	(17)	18/17
SECURITY + CONTROL	5 (M = for banking)	(5)	5
ENERGY/RUNNING COST	5, 10, 15	(9)	10/9
EXTERNAL IMAGE incl. Banking Hall	I	(20)	20
CUSTOMER BENEFITS	5, 7, 6	(5)	6
EMPLOYEE BENEFITS	12, 9, 10, 7, 5	(7)	8, 7
URBAN BENEFITS	3, 5	(4)	5

'Please vote.' Criteria used by the Quickborner Team to ascertain the Bank's priorities in the design of its new building.

After that meeting, Munden commissioned Levett & Bailey to do a cost comparison between the Chevron scheme and a typical Hong Kong tower block. Because so many items normally supplied by a Hong Kong tenant, like the servicing, were to be integrated with the structure in the Foster building, it was judged nearly impossible to isolate a 'bare building' cost in the Foster proposals. These normal 'extras', together with the auditoria, swimming pool, banking hall, sports facilities and other 'optimal extras' proposed in the Chevron scheme, were to be added on to the cost of a typical, good-quality Hong Kong block. Everyone knew the comparison was specious. Other Hong Kong office blocks were built to rent and not intended as owner-occupied headquarters. They were constructed of concrete, not of steel; and to nothing like the high standard that was envisaged here. They did not include special security equipment and vaults; they were not required to be highly flexible and to countenance frequent rearrangements of accommodation; nor, as Fosters told the Bank, did they contain atria and double-height spaces which might, at some future date, be filled with more floors. Nevertheless, adding-on the more conventional extras, by July Levett & Bailey had found that the Foster proposals were not quite double those of the typical Hong Kong tower block.

By the autumn, however, it was clear that if the scheme was to cost more than HK$2,000 million, it was unlikely to be supported by the executive directors and would therefore be thrown out by the board. Munden told Foster that he was prepared to believe that a cost-in-use analysis (based on maintenance costs, running charges and depreciation) might quell his doubts, and show that the performance of the new building would justify the high figure; but any analysis would have to be done by an independent organisation. They agreed that Foster should approach the Quickborner Team, a group of planning and management consultants based in Hamburg. Foster had first encountered the Quickborner Team earlier in the year when both of them had been commissioned by Hille, the furniture manufacturers, to help them develop ideas for the office of the future. A week later Munden telexed Foster that he would like to see 'an assumption made that our new Bank headquarters could be built and fully fitted out to good Hong Kong standards for a cost of HK$1,600 million at May 1980 figures.'[10] This figure would be used as a basis of comparison in the cost analysis. By the end of October, the Quickborner Team was established in the offices of the Bank for the duration of its study. The final scheme, its costs and a cost analysis were scheduled for the final design presentation to the board on 5 December, a little more than a month away.

Whatever Munden might have told Foster, HK$1,600 million was not low enough. On Sunday, 23 November, a meeting was held in the chairman's house, high on the Peak overlooking the harbour. The chairman decided they could not recommend that the board proceed with the scheme. A call was put through to Foster in London to tell him that they had decided to impose a budget, excluding furniture and

111

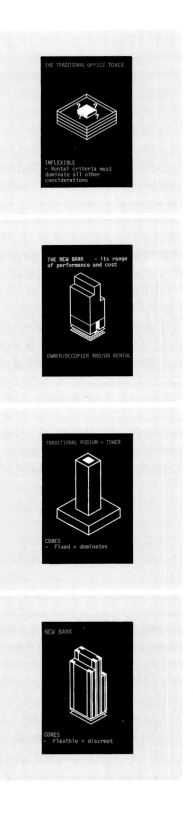

interior decoration, of HK$1,300 million on the building cost. Foster had already warned Munden that if a strict budget was imposed, they would have to start work on the design afresh, using costs, not a brief for the best building, as their starting point. On Tuesday the board was informed that the presentation of Foster's plans for the building, scheduled for 5 December, was cancelled.

Two weeks later the board met again. In the meantime Foster and the rest of the consultants had flown out from London as they had originally planned. The Quickborner Team had finished its study. Foster gave senior management a slide presentation that compared his concept for the new Bank with a traditional office tower. Unlike a typical office tower, the new Bank had the potential to expand, by up to 30 per cent, by plugging extra floors into the areas left void in the building. Its wide-span floors created the potential for extraordinary flexibility in office arrangements, and, because of the system of underfloor servicing, office moves could be easily accommodated. Changes in technology were much more likely to be able to be incorporated easily. Different floors, or sections of floors, could house quite different functions, a flexibility which was reinforced by the use of escalators for internal transportation. Because they could be linked by escalator, large departments could be accommodated on more than one floor with hardly any loss in communication.

Foster's statements were backed up by the findings of the Quickborner Team. These showed that the wide-span, column-free space for both the banking hall and the upper floor levels yielded a significantly higher gross rentable area than other buildings. At the same time, Quickborner reckoned that the average nett to gross space percentage (that is, the ratio of actual floorspace a tenant can call his own, as opposed to space like reception areas, lift lobbies, lavatories and passageways, which would be shared with others) was 73.5 per cent: ie 8.5 per cent more than a traditional tower. During 1980, the Bank had spent nearly HK$15 million in moving staff and departments. Quickborner calculated that the ease of adapting space in the new building to accommodate changes in workspaces would reduce this figure by ten times.[11] It appeared that the present concept *was* going to give the Bank high value for money – but it could not be built for HK$1,300 million.[12]

These were potent arguments, and, as Munden explained to the board, the Bank's executive had once more become reluctant to abandon Foster's concept. There was another factor, powerfully persuasive. The property market was booming. Allowing for authority to erect a standard commercial podium and tower block with a 15:1 plot ratio allowance, the current market value of the site of the Bank was reckoned to be HK$2,250 million.[13] It was crazy for the Bank to be so underdeveloped.

Munden now instructed the quantity surveyors to draw up new cost

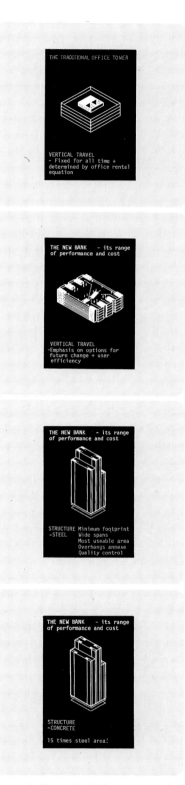

estimates. These were to be broken down into the basic cost of the shell of the building plus special features for the Bank. Fosters were to take these costs and try and reduce them significantly without compromising the concept. Foster, Spencer de Grey, Doug Brown, Ray Guy, and Gordon Graham sat down to the task. Three days later, Fosters delivered a schedule of exclusions from the complete cost plan to the Bank. By eliminating the 'fit-out' costs of the headquarters – the utilities (such as the telephone installation, satellite link, clock systems, and the wiring for computer terminals) and furnishings and other fittings (like landscaping, water dispensers) – the figure for the 'basic building' was eventually reduced to HK$1,380 million at November 1980 costs, not including fees (HK$207 million) and contingencies (HK$76 million).[14]

It was to prove a fatal beginning. The decision to divide out the costs of the shell of the building ('all those extraneous items which we do not normally present to the board when seeking authority for a building cost')[15] from the total cost of the headquarters was taken in accordance with the Bank's normal methods of dealing with new buildings. The board exercised control over capital expenditure on buildings, but the chief executive usually had a delegated authority to dispense funds, capital or not, on items relating to normal banking operations. Whenever comparisons between the concept and a 'typical' Hong Kong tower block had been mooted during the year, the architects had warned Munden that trying to separate shell costs and special Bank requirements from the fitting out of the building was impossible. The quantity surveyors, Levett & Bailey, who had already been thrown into a considerable professional dilemma by being instructed to prepare estimates by the client over the head of the architect, deplored this method of accounting. Very soon the Bank's executives, too, would come to regret it. Each time the tender for a sub-contract was to be prepared, its cost would have to be put forward on the basis of two budgets, the 'shell' and the 'fit-out'. The architects found themselves having to seek authority to transfer amounts from one budget to another on a highly arbitrary basis. Potential for confusion was to be even greater because, while the shell cost represented a firm fixed sum, authorised by the board, the 'fit-out' budget was never fixed. Each item under the 'fit-out' was considered individually on its merits. These included an estimate of its costs-in-use. In frequent cases it was applied to items like the building management system, the sunscoop and the system of flexible servicing for which much research had to be funded, and for which there were no precedents in building. Nevertheless, the immediate problem of reducing the costs to some sort of apparently realistic level was solved. It looked as if the Bank was going to get that building. On Christmas Eve Munden telexed Foster to tell him that the day before the board had agreed to receive a presentation of the final concept – as modified to reduce the cost – on 23 January.[16]

That day Norman Foster presented his final outline scheme to the board. It was the critical board presentation. Foster was in his element,

wearing a suit, outwardly relaxed, urbane and fluent. The presentation was marked by superb photomontages of how the new building would look in its surroundings. Foster was followed by Dieter Jaeger of the Quickborner Team, who went through the costs-in-use analysis. Not everyone was convinced. But on 27 January, the Bank's board ratified the decision to proceed with the project on the basis of the design Foster had presented, for an estimated cost for the shell of HK$1,380 million – at November 1980 prices – plus fees and contingencies. There was as yet – and this was important – no allowance for inflation. At a press conference two weeks later, the plans were unveiled to the public for the first time.

To those who had followed Foster's career in England, and believed in what he was doing, the Perspex and silver model of the proposed new Bank was a revelation. It was a fulfilment of hopes, it fired the imagination. Here was no cosmetic treatment of a normal tower block, no superficial coating of timeworn floorplans with an elegant new cladding system. There were no gimmicky additions or lavish decorations to a tower that was basically banal. The plans for the Bank represented a total reworking of the skyscraper in the late twentieth century, and a heroic exercise to address its problems.

Now the design had come full circle to reapproach the original competition-winning submission. The basic ideas of a structure which bridged the site, from which floors were to be hung like a series of suspension bridges, remained. But, now, eight huge steel masts replaced the massive concrete core towers of the original conception. The walls were of glass, clear and translucent, and framed by long silvery sunscreens. Inside, were the great, wide, clear, spanned spaces of Foster's initial concept, now sharpened and refined. A huge ten-storey-high atrium (it was on a scale with the interior of Amiens Cathedral, the team had discovered), hung with plants, was to be the centrepiece of the building: the banking hall. It was to be lit with daylight scooped by a series of mirrors on the outside of the building. More light would filter down the building through translucent strips in the floors running between the masts.

Movement vertically up the building was to be by lift, for fast commuter traffic, up to double-height reception spaces. From there, local transport through the building would be by escalator. Fire refuge terraces located on the outside of the building were to double as gardens in the sky. Plant and lavatories for the building were located in steel-encased modules on either side of the lift shafts on the western side of the building. Services, water, clean-air ducts, and cabling were distributed up the building in a series of 'risers' pinned to the outside of the building, from where they would be further distributed in a void between the structural floor and a system of lightweight floor panels. On the east, the Bank Street elevation, where the shadow regulations had dictated a structured setting-back of the façade, was a richly expressive frontage formed by ranks of glass-encased escape stair

The new Bank viewed from the harbour front: photomontage presented to the Board, January 1981.

towers. The base of the building was to be an open public plaza, with a vertical wall of water at one end, and a floor of translucent glass, which was intended to allow light to filter into the Bank's archives and vaults in the basement below. Around the world, architectural critics greeted the plans with applause. This new tower was to be a triumph, and a masterpiece of the genre.

Perspective drawing by Birkin Haward of the entrance from the plaza to the banking hall presented to the Board, January 1981.

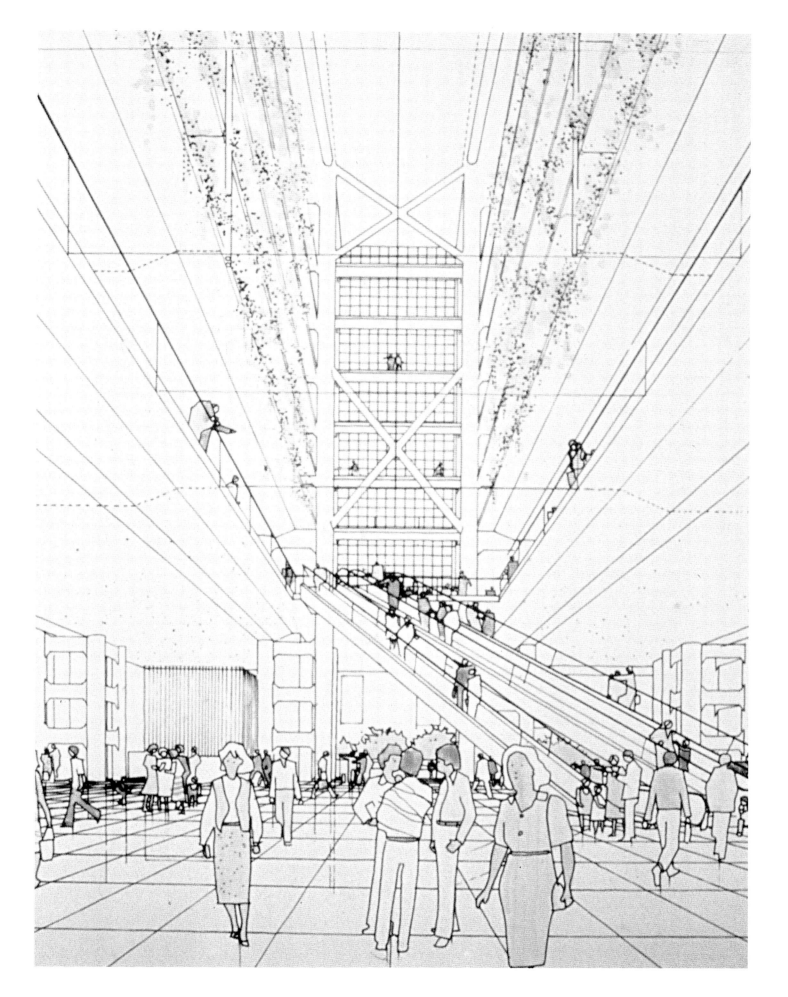

With outline plans approved, more prosaic, practical aspects of getting the headquarters built now commanded attention. Fosters faced five main challenges as they considered the construction. The programme was extremely short, the site was highly restricted and the ground underneath it consisted of decomposed granite, muds and sands. Hong Kong produced few building products locally. Furthermore, their client, who would tolerate no noise, dirt or grime from the works, planned to carry on business right next door.

When Foster unveiled his outline scheme to the board in January 1981, he told the Bank that he aimed to hand over its new headquarters, finished, in November 1986. As we have seen, however, occupation of most of the building was to take place nearly eighteen months earlier, in the summer of 1985. The final months of the construction programme were to allow for the demolition of the annexe, and the filling-in of the lower floors of the western portion of the building. To all intents and purposes, Foster aimed to have the Bank ready in four and a half years. But the pressure to complete the building even sooner was relentless. During the year Fosters had spent designing the Bank, steel frame construction had arrived in Hong Kong. New towers were visibly rising, at the rate of a floor a week. The opinion of the Bank's board at that January presentation was unanimous. The programme was 'very long' compared with the erection of other steel framed buildings now going up in Hong Kong. They demanded to know why.[1]

To erect the structure – steel or reinforced concrete – and fit-out a basic floor for one level of a Hong Kong high-rise building takes between 10 and 16 days. Forty-two floors take between 18 months and 2 years to erect. Another 6 months is needed to finish those floors, leading to a total of 24–30 months to put up a building. Arup's project planning group, whom Foster had first commissioned to help the team prepare alternatives to speed up the programme at the beginning of 1980, reckoned that the steel frame for the new Bank could go up at a rate equivalent to $1\frac{1}{4}$ weeks per floor, to take 15 months in all. The rest of the cladding, servicing and finishing would be done at the rate of $1\frac{1}{2}$ weeks per floor, or 15 months all together. At the time of the Chevron scheme, the construction programme had been planned to take 39 months; the 9 months over and above a traditional Hong Kong building programme was the time it would take to dig a basement 10

A typical Hong Kong excavation.

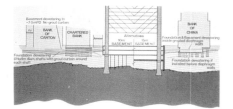

Close neighbours, unstable ground conditions: the implications of digging deeper basements.

metres (33 feet) deep. In addition, it would also take 6 months to demolish the existing building and clear the site.

The real problem in the programme were the basements. In terms of losing time, costing money, and potential damage to surrounding buildings, going underground is the most dangerous part of any contract. The deeper the excavation, the higher the risks become. The ground under the Bank provided a classic example of the kind of unstable conditions that are notorious for serious movements during excavation. During the digging of the Mass Transit Railway, the near-by Legislative Council building had settled 150 millimetres (6 inches), with devastating effect to its structure. Digging the foundations of another near-by tower brought about the collapse of nearly a block of Queen's Road, which brought weeks of traffic chaos to the city centre. After the rejection of the Chevron scheme the previous June, the Bank had asked the architects to increase space in the building. The only way they could do so was to sink the basements a further 5 metres (16 feet), to 15 metres (50 feet) below ground – deeper than any basement in the neighbourhood, and increasing the risk of exposing the foundations of the buildings next door. Now, a diaphragm wall, to box-in the site and keep the sides stable, would have to be inserted all around the site down to the level of the bedrock. Working 17 hours a day, it would take at least a year to excavate the 60,000 cubic metres (over 2 million cubic feet) of earth, rubble, and rock down to 15 metres below ground level and, then, to build giant caissons down to the bedrock, another 17 metres. If the Bank was to have these basements, the programme Foster outlined was the fastest one possible.[2]

Shortage of time was not the only pressure on the project. Like any other in Hong Kong's Central District, the Bank site was extremely constricted. Being just under half a hectare (an acre) in size, it was larger than most. The logistics were those of stacking up a building some eighteen times greater than the ground area it stood on, in a coherent manner. There would be no room to store building materials. The site had to be kept clean and safe; it had to have catering facilities and lavatories, and storage for tools and offices for the contractor and sub-contractors. The organisation of the site was John Lok/Wimpey's responsibility: they had to consider how to demolish, transport and dispose of the old building; remove the earth and rocks from excavating the basement; bring in the steel, the concrete and all the other new materials to the site, as well as determining how many people it was feasible to have working on site at any one time.

Access was severely limited. To the south of the site was Queen's Road, Central District's main traffic thoroughfare; on the harbour side was Des Voeux Road, the main tram route. The only daytime access to the site was from Bank Street, 6 metres (15 feet) wide, between the Bank and its neighbour the Bank of China. Beneath the two main roads ran the city's sewers, power lines and other main services. A fracture to the district's old water main, which in particular was in poor condition, would cause a major land slip. Furthermore, during 1980 plans had been mooted to run an extension of the MTR line, only one metre away from the proposed diaphragm wall of the new Bank's basement. Investigations were now under way to work out how to protect the Bank's new premises from noise and vibration. Meanwhile, if either of the main road surfaces were blocked or damaged by settlement the repercussions on the surrounding business community would cause widespread indignation. And just next door were two highly sensitive neighbours: in the east the Bank of China, to the west the wall of the Chartered Bank, separated by a mere few feet from the annexe.

Within a month of Foster's appointment, both the Bank of China and the Chartered Bank had written to the Bank to express their concern over the redevelopment and the possibility of vibrations disturbing their computers. Munden wrote to reassure them: 'We will always have a fully operating branch on site,' he told them. There would be the minimum of noise, dust and vibration.[3] The message was passed to the architects. No one was to be given any opportunity to criticise either the noise or safety standards adopted for the project.[4] There could be no disruption, and there was to be no noise and no mess. Arup Acoustics, a special unit from Ove Arup, was taken on to measure noise and vibration throughout the construction. If for any reason the strict control levels required by the Bank were exceeded (at first, these were so stringent they were scarcely louder than the threshold of human perceptibility), the Bank would want to know why, and penalties would be extracted.

There was another dimension to the Hong Kong reality. The place was like a village, it fed on rumour. Hong Kong had its own conventions, its own ways of doing things. Outwardly open and helpful to newcomers, people tended to distrust strangers. Within the Hong Kong property world there was deep suspicion – more, resentment – of this high-powered design team with its new ideas fresh out from London. Long before any plans by Fosters were published elements of them were common knowledge. 'You know, they're keeping the banking hall. They're going to keep that ceiling,' companies in the building industry whispered to one another. 'You don't stand a chance of getting that contract unless you have an office set up in London first.' True or false, the team was well advised to bear in mind that construction was a well-hated nuisance in Hong Kong, and that any opportunity for malicious gossip would be fully exploited. The Bank had to be seen to be above reproach. The pounding of pile-drivers, traffic hold-ups and dirt were bound to provoke a torrent of public abuse which the Bank simply would not tolerate. It was prudent public relations for Foster to announce that the caissons for the building would be dug by hand, and therefore silently, and that no sheet piles would be driven to secure the perimeter wall.

To the problems of a tight schedule and a restricted site were added the fact that, except for indigenous supplies of granite and concrete, everything for the building would have to be imported. With 100,000 square metres of building to be planned, the sheer scale of the project, let alone its radical character, meant that no manufacturer would have sufficient stocks of any of the required components for the building to enable them to be purchased from stock. Time had to be calculated for their design, manufacture and shipment, and for clearing customs. Once materials had arrived on the site, Foster was determined to forestall a further, and very real problem. Hong Kong's normal standard of hand finishing was all too often slipshod: grout oozing between ceramic tiles in bathrooms, chunks of cement render left heaped in corners, sleazy handrails fixed badly to the walls were commonplace.

Foster's reaction to these limitations was characteristic. To match the deadlines of an ordinary Hong Kong timetable for construction – that is, about two-thirds, even half, the time it might take to build a comparable building in Europe – and still provide a headquarters of exceptional quality, he aimed to fast-track the design process for the project in a fiercely ambitious and sophisticated manner. He christened the process 'strategic designing': separate primary design decisions from secondary design decisions and deal with these first; then identify the pieces of the building that will take the longest to manufacture, or are needed first in the construction programme. Design them, get them into production, move on to the next stage. In order to meet the exigencies of the tight site during construction, the pieces of the building would be programmed to arrive in order: first the steel for the structure, to be lifted from a lorry into its appropriate slot in the structure, then the modules, next the cladding, then the lifts and escalators, and so on. While the structure was being erected and the modules were being secured, the design work on the details of partitions and doors for the interior, their handles and hinges would be finalized, ready for production lines that would deliver them to 1 Queen's Road, finished and ready to be locked into place in the building. Trade the time it would take to finish a building with care by hand on site for time to design the parts of the building in detail with the manufacturers. Then deliver them, ready finished, to slot into place on the site.

As he had done in the past, with the glass on Willis Faber and the aluminium cladding panels on Sainsbury, Foster planned to develop the components of the building in conjunction with manufacturers in appropriate fields. In this way the architects could learn from the experience of the fabricators and together they could produce the components which would best suit the needs of the Bank and the new building. The economies of scale alone justified a certain degree of custom design even if, in fact, there was no other way that the building could be constructed. The structure was comparable to that of a bridge or a North Sea oil rig; it could hardly be made up from beams off the peg. No one had ever used containerised modules to service a building before; they would have to be designed, prototyped, tested and manufactured. The complex external shape of the building, with its glass walls set back behind the steel frame, was far too complicated to allow for filling the cladding contract from catalogues. Many manufacturers might be able to provide service systems to be placed under raised floors; but no one before had aimed to put *all* the services – the air-conditioning, smoke detection, a sprinkler system, the public address and security systems, as well as the more common cables for power, telephones and data systems – beneath an office floor. So it went on. Once one important part of the building had been designed, it would have to fit with the next; and every component after that would have to fit with them.

Furthermore, if finishing could be done as part of the manufacturing process, it reduced the risk of failing to achieve excellent quality. In factories effort could be concentrated on the details at hand, in clean, well-organised conditions subject to quality control. Fit the lavatories, plumb the basins, spray-paint the partitions, cut the carpets, apply the door handles far away from the site. Then bring in the modules, the doors, or whatever, in order, and fit them into place in the building. Here was to be the realisation of Foster's earliest vision of the building as a kit of parts, a Meccano set of pieces, to be designed, manufactured and then assembled on site. At least this was the theory. If Foster had always worked with industry before, he had never before done so on this scale. In reality, the complex problems of co-ordinating the details of designs that were being developed under a dozen major sub-contracts with manufacturers located in widely different parts of the globe were later nearly to prove the project's undoing.

The construction was to be managed conventionally, through a number of large sub-contracts. As the design had developed during 1980, the content of each of the sub-contract packages – the structural steel, the modules, the lifts and escalators, the cladding to cover the steel frame and glazing for the curtain wall, the sub-floor services, the raised floors and ceilings – began to be established. In parallel with efforts on the design, a mass of research was going on. The team needed to know about the latest methods of servicing buildings, and the best kinds of materials and components to consider for use in the new building. It didn't take them long to realise that if they were to have the building's components when they wanted them, they would have to reserve factory production time very soon – as well as that of the engineers who would help them develop their design. But before Fosters could implement their strategy they had to find the companies across the globe with the capacity and willingness to do what they wanted. Did they have the facilities to make prototypes and test them? Were they in the business of innovation themselves? The answer to this was important. Chemistry counted. Were their minds open? Were they willing to explore? The first important sub-contract was that for the supply, fabrication and erection of the steel structure.

The question of who might make the steel was considered when Fosters and Arups first set to work on the concept for the competition. At the end of the first detailed talks with the Bank in the January of 1980, Roy Fleetwood, who was to be responsible at Fosters for setting up the sub-contracts, and Mike Glover, the engineer from Arup in charge of the project, left Hong Kong for Tokyo. They wanted to see for themselves what the steel industry in Japan could offer. By then, Fosters were familiar with many of the products and capacities of the European building industry. Arup had brought their knowledge of heavy industry to the project. The Krupp steelworks in Germany, for example, had supplied the steel for the Centre Pompidou in Paris, while Arup had done the structural engineering for it.

Fleetwood and Glover left for Tokyo as the first germs of the Chevron scheme were being nurtured. Here the vertical structure was to be made up of bundles of huge steel tubes, rather than the masts that were subsequently developed. They were therefore particularly interested to see how the Japanese handled thick plate steel, how they rolled tubes and fabricated large pieces. The Nippon Steel Corporation are the biggest steel makers in the world. At one of their strip mills in Yokohama, Fleetwood and Glover stood on a high-level walkway in a factory nearly half a mile long, watching red hot metal pass through presses at more than 60 mph. Bang! In a wave of heat, the steel was wound in an instant into a drum. This was thin steel for refrigerators and car bodies rather than buildings; none the less, the whole process was totally automated and highly impressive. At Osaka is Kubota, the world's largest manufacturer of cast tubes. Here they saw very thick, spun-cast tubes, called G-columns. Each one ended in a thick lip. Stacked up, one on top of another, they would look like giant sticks of bamboo; a nice idea to incorporate in the Chevron scheme?

It was fundamental to the design that the steel structure should be clearly visible throughout the building. Foster wanted people to be able to understand logically how the building worked, to get a sense of inside/outside. As visitors drew closer and closer to the building, he wanted them to experience a breakdown in scale, to move from a general view of the building from the distance, to take in more and more details of the structure as they came closer.

The dilemma was how to expose the steel structure to view and yet protect it against fire and the corrosive pollutants and humidity in the air. There were a number of ways of solving this problem, but none seemed satisfactory. To protect the steel from fire, it could be painted with intumescent coatings, which bubble up at the touch of flame; but these would give only one hour's worth of fire protection. They would also need constant maintenance, an unacceptable prospect for the Bank, who wanted a building that would have a life of fifty years. They could coat it with enamel, but the joints would show. The conventional approach was to smother the structure in 50 millimetres (2 inches) of concrete. With all the rain that Hong Kong endured this solution was highly disagreeable from the aesthetic point of view; it would be messy and difficult to achieve. At the Centre Pompidou, and another building, Bush Lane House in London's Cannon Street, Arup had filled the steel structures with water, to keep them cool in case of fire. This was what they planned to do for the Chevron scheme. If the steel on the outside of the masts of the Bank could be stainless it also would not corrode.

Shin Nippon Kokan did bimetal casting, lining pipes with stainless steel. Yes, they could reverse the process to put stainless steel on the outside of the Kubota tubes; this would solve the corrosion problem, but the surface would look pickled. In south-west Japan where Nippon Steel fabricates oil platforms to float out to Alaska and the Gulf, Fleetwood was interested to see the thick corrosion protection – a kind of coal-tar epoxy full of big lumps – which is sprayed on to rigs to provide abrasion resistance in what they call the severe splash zone, above the water line. In Muroran in southern Hokkaido they visited the centre for 95 per cent of the world's production of clad steel.

Oil rig production, Japan, January 1980.

Clad steel – mild steel lined with a molecularly bonded layer of stainless steel – was used to make pipelines. Maybe it could be turned inside out and used for the masts for the building? But Fleetwood and Glover found that clad steel production was geared exclusively to the needs of the petrochemical industry, focused on pipes made to withstand pressures forcing outwards, and resisting highly corrosive acids, not for building vertically. Because it was made of two different steels, it would also be difficult, if not impossible, to weld clad steel to be strong enough to form an upright structure.

Fleetwood and Glover's trip to Japan lasted nearly three weeks. It was an exhausting trip, up every morning for meetings at 7 am with guides and officials. The trip confirmed Foster's early view that the steel for the project might well be manufactured there; and in Japan they had also been able to see examples of the use of risers – prefabricated packages containing all the pipework for a building – similar to those being conceived for the building. They were able to look at conventional Japanese cladding systems and examine the two known examples of modules in high-rise building construction: Kurakawa's Sony building in Osaka and a student hostel in Tokyo where small-scale modules for bathrooms, made on site rather than in a factory, had been used. Otherwise, not much else was achieved. The tantalising problem of how to protect the steel against corrosion remained.

Meanwhile, in Hong Kong Munden and Graham Phillips from Fosters were sorting out the management of the project and Spencer de Grey was exploring the Bank's detailed requirements. Now that the Bank had decided to demolish its building, except for the annexe, in its entirety, there was a major task in sorting out the logistics of moving all its departments out of the building and redistributing them elsewhere, as well as putting in train the conversion of the annexe. At the same time, in London research in a host of areas was beginning to gather

Derek Tuddenham of J Roger Preston
(with back to camera), David Nelson
and Ken Shuttleworth at work on the
servicing.

pace. Who made the best lifts? What about escalators? What was the
latest on fibre optic wiring, on natural and artificial lighting systems, on
furniture? Who produced localised air-conditioning systems, raised
floors and document conveyor systems? Who produced the best
equipment for bank tellers? The brief from the Bank was to select the
best from world markets, although in terms of electronic equipment
Hong Kong's experience showed that it was usually easier to adapt
American products. Mail shots were despatched, technical literature
culled.

Fosters had first conceived the idea of using raised floors throughout a
building in their work on the transport interchange for the
Hammersmith Centre. Now, on the Bank, they wanted to incorporate
all the services – including the air-conditioning and a pop-up sprinkler
system – under the floors. The problem was that maintaining the fan-
coil units which supplied water to individual air-conditioning units
from below the floor would be difficult, to say nothing of the problems
of such a sprinkler system. While both ideas had been tried and seen to
work before, it was not only their client whom Fosters had to persuade
of the desirability of certain features that they wanted to bring into the
building. Early in 1980, the architects had refused to consider concrete
for the floors in the Bank. Their fellow consultants told them they were
mad. The problems of fire and acoustics would be overcome somehow,
Fosters said; now what they wanted to do was to make the floors as
lightweight and flexible as possible. They had their eyes on aluminium
honeycomb panels, like those used in the aircraft industry. In the
spring, Ken Shuttleworth and Jan Kaplicky from Fosters took Ken
Anthony, David Thomlinson and Tony Fitzpatrick from Arups and
Derek Tuddenham from J Roger Preston on what they called a mind-
expanding exercise. First stop a visit to the chief structural engineer of
Concorde at Bristol. With them they had taken the plans of the
Chevron building.

Priorities at Concorde were altogether different from those in the
building industry; here the engineers were obsessed with making
components as light as possible. There ensued a fascinating exchange
of views on materials and underfloor air-conditioning, and a surprise
discovery: should there be a fire, sprinklers popped up from the floor of
the hanger underneath the plane.

The next stop was Christchurch in Hampshire and the Ministry of
Defence. In the murk of deep fog (too thick for Foster, who had flown
down, but was unable to land in his helicopter), the assembled team
watched experimental vehicles throw bridges made of pins of maraging
steel across a 12-metre-wide ravine in 30 minutes. Fosters and Arup
were interested in the strength of the specially developed high-tensile
steel; the army wanted to get the erection time down to 10 minutes.

Wanton? Indulgent? Perhaps. But a suggestion here, a door closed
there, one step on these trips led to another, and eventually to the

answer that they wanted. Working with the Quickborner Team on the project on the office of the future for Hille, David Nelson had learned of a German company, Schmidt Reuter, who had developed a system of underfloor air-conditioning for a building in the early 1970s. In October 1980, Nelson, Shuttleworth and Derek Tuddenham flew to Düsseldorf for a whirlwind day with Schmidt Reuter seeing systems they had installed in buildings. Schmidt Reuter maintained that, to use underfloor air-conditioning, at least 10 per cent of the air had to be pushed up through a desk top. Fosters were not interested in that kind of limitation. But seeing a system of underfloor air-conditioning in action helped convince all of them it could be done. It would take until mid-1983, by which time Fosters and J Roger Preston had gone back to the first principles of air-conditioning, before they could develop a suitable system of floor outlets that gave them the levels of air-conditioning they required on the Bank.

By October of 1980, it was ten months since Fleetwood and Glover had visited Japan. The Chevron scheme was dead. It was not going to be possible to fill the newly designed structure, with its long horizontal spans, with water to protect it in case of fire. A concrete coating was impracticable. Reluctantly the team had concluded that the only way to protect the structure from fire would be to wrap it with some kind of fibre blanket; in the meantime some way of protecting the steel against corrosion also had to be found. These decisions made it clear, however, that such layers of protection to the structure would also have to be covered and protected. Aluminium was the only metal that was sufficiently lightweight, strong and resistant to corrosion to be worth considering.

By now, the team had nearly completed a list of a dozen potential steel suppliers from the Common Market and Japan from whom tenders could be invited. They had also investigated nearly forty companies in the UK, Europe and Japan, to find one organisation capable of making the aluminium with which to clad the structure and the glass curtain wall for the building. One company in Germany was judged to have the capacity and expertise for the contract, but Roy Fleetwood, who was heading the investigation, was worried that it had little high-rise experience. In North America there were only two companies in the field of custom-making high-rise curtain walls who he believed could handle the project: Flour City, based in Long Island, and Cupples Products in St Louis, Missouri.[5]

Flour City had first attracted the attention of the Foster office when they had been investigating glass walls for the Hammersmith Centre. Flour City had supplied the curtain wall for Hugh Stubbins's Citicorp Tower in New York and it looked, as Roy Fleetwood said later, 'pretty slick and interesting at the time'. In the autumn of 1980, he and Ken Anthony from Arup went to see them. At their Long Island drawing offices, he found their approach tough and aggressive. They seemed unsympathetic to what Fosters were proposing to do on the Bank. He

127

felt it would not be easy for the team to work with them. In 1980, however, there was also much news in England of another building. Foster had taken Philip Johnson to visit the Sainsbury Centre while he and John Burgee were at work on the now completed, and splendid, 'Crystal Cathedral', the Garden Grove Community Church in California. With its beautiful walls of reflective glass panels, supported on an immaculate silicone structural system, it was a magnificent building. The glass walls had been made by Cupples. Cupples had also clad four of the world's tallest buildings: the Standard Oil building (1,136 feet), the John Hancock Center (1,127 feet), and the Sears Tower (1,450 feet), all in Chicago, and the twin towers of the World Trade Center in New York. After talking to Flour City, Anthony and Fleetwood flew west to Missouri, to see Charles Beason, the vice-president at Cupples in charge of engineering and a leading expert in the field, to talk about the Bank project.

Beason quickly grasped the complexity of the cladding that Fosters were proposing. Here was no ordinary box of a building that needed to be covered with a neat wall of glass. The actual 'building' was to be enclosed within a frame of steel. That frame would need to pass through the walls at a whole variety of points. The difficulty of devising a system to cope with this exercise was compounded by the complexity of the façades themselves. To the north and south the building presented a fairly regular, almost symmetrical face. The main discrepancies occurred at the five double-height levels, where the glass wall was to be recessed, and the fire refuge terraces to be built. On the east and west sides of the building, however, the façades were massively complex: on the eastern side of the building the shadow regulations had resulted in a deeply recessed façade of parallel towers containing escape stairs. On the west, especially where the double-height spaces within the building occurred, the pattern of the modules and risers and lift shafts had led to an equally diverse arrangement. By comparison with a conventional tower, for which Cupples might be presented with perhaps six drawings, in the first forty-two levels of the building above ground thirty-three different floor plans alone would later be required as a basis for producing this cladding.

Cladding the walls of the building was only one aspect of the potential contract; there was also the cladding to cover the steel masts and the rest of the structure. Cupples were specialists in aluminium panel cladding, but designing the cladding for this building would be like devising a hard surface to wrap around and seal an off-shore drilling rig. Beason told Fleetwood that the most difficult building Cupples had ever done was the Hancock Center in Chicago. It was 100 storeys high and every floor in it had been different. Cupples would never do another job with so many specials again. In any case, this whole project sounded like pie in the sky. Who were the Hongkong Bank anyway? Cupples had heard of Norman Foster all right, but when Fleetwood told Beason that the practice had never built a high-rise building before he could hardly believe it.

The Crystal Cathedral, the Garden Grove Community Church, California, by Philip Johnson and John Burgee.

'So you've never built anything over three storeys?' concluded a bemused Beason. He told Fleetwood and Anthony to go down to Houston, where the climate features hurricanes and extremes of heat and humidity similar to those that affect Hong Kong, and look at at least a dozen high-rise buildings Cupples had clad. But even more than they were going to need the experience of a company like Cupples to help develop the cladding systems for the building, Fosters were going to have to have the expertise of a manufacturer to help them develop their concept for the modules. More than any other sub-contract on the project, the production of the package for the service modules lay outside the conventions of the building industry.

What they wanted to develop was a kind of standardised prepacked container, fully equipped with plant and store rooms, lavatories and pipework, which could be plugged into the building to provide the plant required to service each floor. The concept for the modules was a logical extension of Foster's initial attempt to re-analyse high-rise construction. If you could eliminate the central service core – with its lifts, and all the pipework, heating and air-conditioning ducting – from a high-rise building, you could also eliminate floors packed with mechanical and electrical plant. Conventionally these are provided at intervals of fifteen or twenty storeys in order to supply heated or chilled air to the floors in between. Centralising boilers and air-conditioning chillers not only means that whole huge parts of a building – instead of just a single floor – must be heated and cooled at the same time, but they also cost a client valuable office space in the upper levels of his building. If the Bank were to have such floors devoted only to plant, it also meant that Foster would have to control his desire to create a free flow of spaces and movement up through the building.

Fosters believed that if plant could be dispersed throughout the building it would not only save valuable floorspace but also energy. Heated and cooled air would need to move shorter distances. It was logical to locate the lavatories, with their requirements for plumbing and fresh air, next door to the boilers and air-conditioning plant. Given Foster's priorities for the shape of the building, the lack of space on site, the potential for damage at the finishing stages, and above all the need to save time, it was but a short step to consider the possibility of getting a factory to prefabricate a series of containers equipped with plant and lavatories that could be tested, then sealed in the factory, transported to the site, and craned up – like the sections of the steel frame – to be plugged into the building.

But what kind of company could do this job? Cases of the use of prefabricated modules in building were scarce. The team only knew of the student hostel in Tokyo and Kurakawa's Sony building in Osaka, where nine – simple – modules containing lavatories had been built, one for each floor of the building. Coincidentally, Richard Rogers was also planning to use modules in his new Lloyd's building, but his team were not yet ready to look for manufacturers.

Cut-away diagram of a typical module as it was eventually built combining lavatories, heating, ventilation and air-conditioning plant.

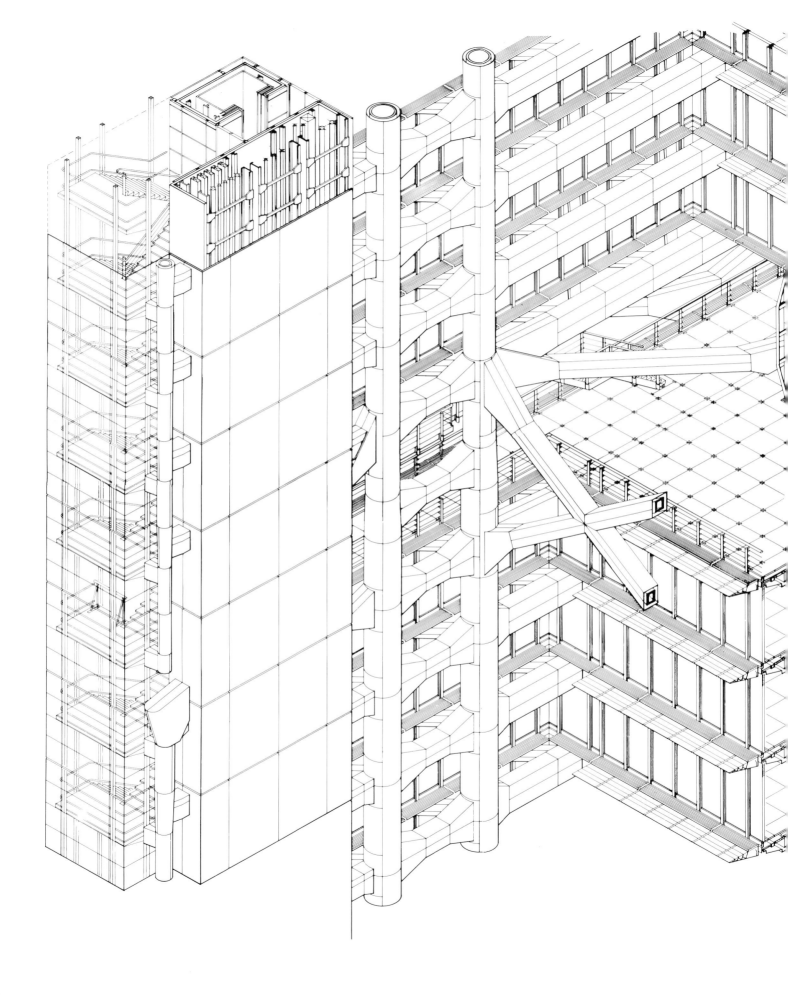

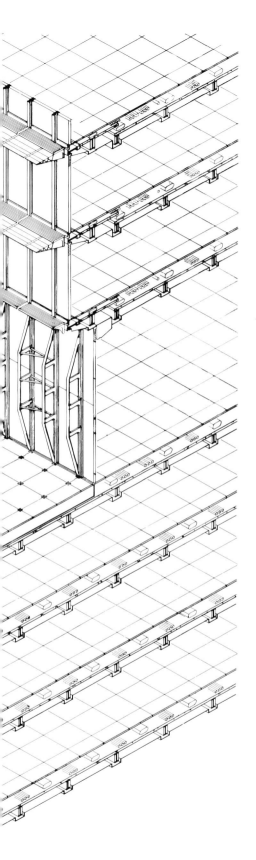

In Foster's case, the requirements for the modules were diverse and highly complex. The expertise Fosters needed might come from a heating and ventilating company, or a manufacturer of air-conditioners. It could come from a producer of ocean-going containers, or from within the offshore oil industry, where huge, raw-steel-framed containers are built to house workers and facilities on the rigs. Fosters, J Roger Preston, Ove Arup and Wimpey had already carried out intensive research into the kinds of company that might be able to handle the contract. But none was an obvious candidate. They decided they would have to rely on several stages of selection to eliminate contenders. Now, in January 1981, having gained the board's approval of the outline scheme, the team prepared to go out to tender.

East elevation showing the complexity of the cladding system for the building. From left: staircase towers, hangers, masts, cross braces, curtain walls, mullions and sunscreens.

131

On 12 January 1981, ten days before the board of the Bank in Hong Kong was convened to approve Foster's outline scheme, a meeting was held in Wimpey's headquarters in Hammersmith in west London. In the lobby outside the darkened lecture theatre a model of the building was mounted. The purpose of the meeting was to brief twelve steel-fabricating companies on the requirements to prequalify, and therefore be included on the list of those who would be invited to tender for the contract to fabricate and supply the structural steel for the Bank. This was the beginning of a long, arduous and detailed selection process for the most important sub-contract of the project. The procedure would be repeated and repeated over the next four years until, ultimately, 150 different sub-contracts, large and small, had been awarded.

Fosters and Ove Arup had begun talking informally to steel makers and fabricators the year before. Big contractors who had bid for the management contract on the project in the previous autumn had also sought advice from steel companies as to how they should handle the erection of the building, so details of the building's concept had been circulating in the industry for some time. The steel contract was the key contract on the job. The start on site of the steel structure was to be the point from which all else on the construction was to follow. Excavation of the basements was due to start in ten months' time, in December 1981. These would take a year to dig. It would then take two and a half years from the erection of the first steelwork to complete the building. Thus, if the main part of the building was to be finished in the summer of 1985, the first consignment of steel had to reach Hong Kong by January 1983 – and a steel contractor had to be appointed by the end of 1981. Such was the critical path. Once construction of the structure had begun, the modules and the cladding, the lifts and the escalators were all to follow on. The order of the work was strictly sequential: the steel had to start first, and any delay on any contract would have an important knock-on effect.

The formal procedure for appointing sub-contractors for the project was laid down by John Lok/Wimpey. Each sub-contract was to be let competitively on a fixed-price basis. But before any sub-contractor could be awarded a contract he had to go through a two-stage process. First, he had to succeed in being invited to 'prequalify': to join a list of around ten companies to be considered for inclusion in the tender list.

The Kubota tubes, Japan, January 1980.

At this stage, he was given a description of the package, the timetable and the general strategy for carrying out the works. He was asked to complete a questionnaire on how his company proposed to manage the job and on its programme, manufacturing capability and experience. This application was then followed by interviews. Prequalification was intended not only to narrow a widely international field of potential tenderers, but also to give Fosters the opportunity to gauge the kind of input that a particular manufacturer could contribute to the project, especially on packages that would need substantial design development. The qualities that they looked for in their sub-contractors went beyond considerations of cost and programme and normal contractual procedure. Fosters wanted sub-contractors who would enter into the spirit of the venture, who would come up with ideas of their own and contribute to the project. Different manufacturers might make the same kind of component in a different manner, out of different materials, with different finishes. Generally, the architects did not want to prejudice good ideas, or special processes, which manufacturers might be able to offer by tying them down to the much more hard-and-fast design specifications which would be required in the formal tendering process.

Thus the twelve companies who were now invited to be considered as potential tenderers for the steel contract – three British, one French, two German, an Italian and five Japanese – were told that the detailed architectural and structural design of the project was not yet complete. It was likely that the design would have become refined by the time tender documents were issued; but, even then, the design would not be finished. The successful sub-contractor would be expected to participate in the finalisation of the details. Then it would be up to the sub-contractor to fabricate the steel. Because of the novelty of the structure, prototype testing of several key elements was an essential part of the programme.

Replies to the prequalification exercise were to be judged by a team of representatives from each of the consultants, John Lok/Wimpey, and the Bank. Any team member could veto a contender. Four, at most five, companies would go forward to the final tender list. Documents produced by both parties for the tender would provide the basis on which the contract for the work would be agreed. Once the tenders were received, two months of evaluation, discussion with the client and negotiations would take place before the award. The company that offered the best deal – the lowest bid, with the fewest riders – would get the job.

Of the three British companies on the prequalification list, one was regarded by the consultants as a rank outsider: Dorman Long Technical Services. Dorman Long is among the most famous names in British engineering. Most of Britain's suspension bridges – the Severn, the Forth, the Humber – and many of its power stations, steel mills and oil rigs in the past 100 years have been built with steel and men from

Dorman Long. Internationally, the company made its name when it fabricated and erected Sydney Harbour Bridge in 1932, and it was Dorman Long who had supplied and built the steel structure for the 1935 Bank building. Since the war, in Hong Kong alone the company had supplied the steel for more than a dozen buildings and for the Cross-Harbour Tunnel. In 1967, the company was nationalised: its steel-making and rolling operations were merged with the rest of the British Steel Corporation's steel-producing units; its fabrication and erection sections were combined to form Redpath Dorman Long, one of BSC's forty-six constituent companies. RDL had two major subsidiaries: Redpath Engineering Ltd, with fabrication works in Glasgow, Edinburgh, Manchester, Warrington, London, Scunthorpe and Middlesbrough; and Redpath Dorman Long International in Bedford, to handle work overseas. Up in Middlesbrough, Dorman Long's expertise was channelled into the construction arm of BSC to build a massive programme of steel plants – at Scunthorpe, Ravenscraig, Redcar – as part of a new nationalised drive aimed at producing 30 million tonnes of steel in the UK by 1980. In 1978 the work stopped, as it seemed to those on the shop floor, overnight. Rising energy and production costs had dried up the demand for steel. Among those facing redundancy was a unit of forty designers and 200 draughtsmen at Redpath Engineering in Middlesbrough, men with some of the most comprehensive experience in steel fabrication and erection in the world. Their managing director was Bill Boswell.

With his staff facing redundancy, Boswell decided to set up a technical unit to capitalise on the expertise of his designers. Its role would be to act as a consultancy, advising civil and structural engineers on the best way to fabricate steel for a particular purpose. If they could provide such a service for consultants, perhaps they could get work into the Middlesbrough fabrication shop. They reverted to the old famous engineering name and called themselves Dorman Long Technical Services. By 1980, they were beginning to succeed. They had recently engineered a complete chemical plant, which had been floated out to Africa, then mounted on a 1,000-tonne barge and taken up the Zambezi River, to be craned on to its site.

When news of the Hongkong Bank contract began to circulate during 1980 Boswell and his Dorman Long Technical Services at Redpath Engineering were out in the cold. Any bid being put together under the British Steel umbrella would be done by their sister company, Redpath Dorman Long International at Bedford. Then Boswell heard that RDL International planned to team up with Nippon Kokan to supply the steel from Japan. Cleveland Bridge, the other British contender, was also going in with the Japanese, at Kawada Industries. No purely British bid was going to be put together. At a dinner at the Ritz to celebrate the fiftieth birthday of the Tyne Bridge, an MP asked Boswell why his group was not going to make a bid for the Bank. After all, Dorman Long *had* built all these bridges. Boswell was joined by someone from British Steel. Money? Perhaps they could help?

The Severn Bridge completed in 1965.

The Forth Road Bridge completed in 1964.

By eight the next morning, Boswell had met Stan Gaston, head of the group's Britannia Works at Middlesbrough, and his other senior managers. Gaston had joined Dorman Long in time to work on the final stages of the Sydney Harbour Bridge. He was one of the most experienced men in the field of steel fabrication in Britain. It would cost at least £50,000, money they did not have, just to get the bid together. But they all agreed that they should make a try for it. Boswell telephoned Arups and asked to be put on the prequalification list. For Redpath Engineering, Middlesbrough, it was all or nothing.

Two months later, when their two volumes of prequalification documents were assessed, the team judged the technical part of the Dorman Long submission to be 'well thought-out'. Commercially, however, the consortium they had put together was viewed with grave concern. Boswell had secured British Steel's agreement to bid for the project. The British Steel Corporation and Redpath Engineering would go into the job as equal partners: BSC to supply the steel, and Redpath Engineering to fabricate it. But BSC, a nationalised industry, was making heavy losses. Strikes plagued the industry. Wimpey knew that if the BSC/Dorman Long Joint Venture, as it was to be called, won the tender, the Bank would insist that the British government guarantee BSC's performance. If strike action was to affect either the supply or fabrication of the steel there was no way that delay could be avoided on the whole project. Wimpey and Fosters were adamant that to employ the BSC/Dorman Long Joint Venture would be to court disaster. The consultants recommended that four other groups – two Japanese, Krupp from Germany and the Redpath/Kokan consortium, featuring Redpath Engineering's sister company – should be invited to tender.[1]

From London Ray Guy telephoned Roy Munden to tell him the news. There was to be no purely British representation on the tender list.[2] It was early March 1981. In the Bank, plans were being laid to take over the Royal Bank of Scotland. Munden told Guy that he was sure that the Bank would be unhappy at the lack of any purely British representation. Guy relayed this news to John Lok/Wimpey. The consultants protested; but the client's view was clear. The BSC/DL British Joint Venture was put on to the list of steel tenderers.

Three months later the five competitors for the steel contract received the tender documents. They had two months in which to put together their proposals and prices. Then at 12 noon on 28 August 1981, at the offices of John Lok/Wimpey in Ice House Street, Hong Kong, the tenders from the five steel companies were opened. On the face of it, the bid by Redpath Dorman Long/Kokan was the lowest. Next was the offer from BSC/DL, some HK$24 million higher. Krupp's offer was the highest. Technically, however, the consultants agreed: BSC/DL and Krupp were in a class of their own, demonstrating a deep understanding of what the structure had to achieve. Close study of the bids also showed that RDL/Kokan had excluded several items from their tender; while Krupp had added others in.

A meeting was held with Krupp. Even though Krupp felt able to make a number of cost savings on their bid, it could not be reduced sufficiently to compete with BSC/DL and RDL/Kokan. After adjusting the tenders for currency fluctuations, and making additions for firm prices, the final approximate totals were:
British Steel/Dorman Long HK$608,000,000
Redpath/Kokan HK$617,000,000
Krupp HK$636,000,000

Not only was the BSC/DL bid the lowest, but financial benefits such as the British government's Export Credit Guarantees entitled the Bank to additional savings of up to HK$120 million (£10.5 million), around 20 per cent of the tender price. Quite apart from the high quality of the technical sections of the tender, on a commercial basis the project team could not but recommend BSC/DL. But the consultants' fundamental reservations about the consortium remained. While closer investigation had reassured them that the picture of industrial unrest was not as gloomy as they had first suspected (at Middlesbrough, where the fabrication was due to be done, only three man days due to industrial action had been lost in the preceding three years), British Steel's financial plight still added an element of risk to the project that they were reluctant to accept. The programme for the steel was exceptionally tight. There was now less than fifteen months left in which to develop the design, prototype and test sections of the structure and manufacture the steel. Erection had to begin on site in Hong Kong by January 1983. The financial fortunes of British Steel lay in the hands of the government and the government had refused to guarantee Boswell's promise to perform.

On 1 October, Ray Guy flew to London to be on hand during the final days of negotiations with BSC/DL. Sandberg and Munden were to follow on 5 October and would see presentation details on the contract then. The chairman of the British Steel Corporation, Ian MacGregor, had supplied his personal guarantee of his corporation's performance; but the Bank wanted one from the government. Sandberg's main reason for visiting Britain, however, was to review progress on the Bank's bid for the Royal Bank of Scotland, which had been referred to the Monopolies Commission. He went to see Patrick Jenkin, Secretary of State for Trade and Industry, to discuss both the bid and the question of British Steel's capability. The government was not prepared to guarantee BSC's performance.

By now Krupp and RDL/Kokan were making reductions in their tenders. The process was threatening to turn into a Dutch auction. Wimpey warned Munden that if they were to reconsider the Krupp and Redpath/Kokan offers they would have to give the same chance to BSC/DL. The whole procedure would take at least three weeks. The project team wanted nothing to do with it. Munden and Sandberg talked the situation over. They agreed to recommend that the contract go to BSC/DL. On 14 October, the decision was announced.[3]

Meanwhile, early in the new year, Roy Fleetwood had approached the American cladding company Cupples for a second time. By late February, Cupples had agreed to negotiate – but would not bid for – the contract to supply the cladding. With nearly 186,000 square metres (2 million square feet) of cladding required on the inside and outside of the building, the contract would eventually be one and a half times greater than that for the World Trade Center, and the biggest one Cupples had ever had. They knew that the commission for the Bank would stretch their expertise to its limits. But, for reasons of professionalism and the sheer audacity of it, this was a venture that they wanted to be part of. Cupples also knew they were in a commanding bargaining position and they were prepared to be tough. They would not go forward except on the basis of a negotiated contract – a procedure that was completely at odds with the agreed policy that all the sub-contracts for the project were to be let competitively on a fixed-price basis.

On 24 March, the board of the Bank was given the list of the companies who would be preparing tenders for the structural steel contract. At the same meeting, they agreed to allow John Lok/Wimpey to negotiate with Cupples for the contract for the manufacture, supply and erection of the complete external fabric and cladding for the steel frame as long as the contract was within the approved cost plan.[4] On behalf of the Bank, Ray Guy and a team from John Lok/Wimpey, the quantity surveyors, Arups and Fosters flew to St Louis for talks with Cupples. John Lok/Wimpey reported them 'tough but responsive'. The company was sound (not only John Lok/Wimpey, but the Bank as well carried out credit investigations on each sub-contractor), and was willing to install new plant if necessary. Its budget figure, HK$360,258,040 (November 1980 costs), was HK$35,000,000 more than the quantity surveyors had estimated, but judged to be realistic.[5] An interim agreement with Cupples was signed. Negotiation would continue as the details of the cladding system were developed. The firm contract would be drawn up for signature in late summer.

By September 1981 negotiations on the agreement with Cupples for the cladding contract were nearing completion. As the contract was negotiated, there were no bills of quantities. During these months while tendering for the steel and modules proceeded, Cupples had been working on a time/cost basis on the design with Fosters. Before the contract could be costed, they needed to look at the principles of the cladding system, and rough it out with Fosters in detail. During the five months since the interim agreement had been signed, Cupples and Northcrofts, the quantity surveyors, had established the guidelines for what the cladding was to cost, based on the design as it developed. By September, the design of the façade up to level 42 was complete. Cupples and the consultant team had agreed the thickness, the wind and heat loading and the configuration of the glass for the curtain wall. They had agreed the sunshades, the glazed grid wall, the module panel wall, the structural cladding for the masts and cross-bracing and the costs of mock-ups and testing. Any changes in these components, which were now defined in two volumes of 300 detailed drawings and specifications, would incur more costs. Nor, under the contract, were Cupples obliged to carry out any variations before the costs had been agreed (but they were not allowed to stop work, either).

In reality, a dangerous situation was developing. The design of the steelwork was still due for modification once the steel contractor was appointed, and the most basic concepts for the modules were far from finalised, yet the details of the skin that would cover these elements, and make up the walls between them, were now being finalised with Cupples. Cupples planned to start manufacturing shortly after the contracts for the manufacture of the steel and the modules had been let, long before the design for either had been finalised. Everyone recognised that there were many areas of the building yet to be developed that would require further negotiation later on. But it was not conceived that these might embrace the exterior form of the steel frame or the outside of the modules. These paths had now been closed. After days of final negotiation, in mid-September a fixed price of US$139,788,000 (HK$645,821,000) (including inflation and erection) was agreed.[6]

Meanwhile, twenty-seven companies from Britain and Scandinavia, Germany, the USA, Japan and Hong Kong had been invited to take part in the first stage of the prequalification submission for the modules. The range of experience covered by the companies was exceptionally diverse and extensive. There were those who manufactured modules for North Sea oil platforms, steel companies who made the rigs themselves, representatives from ocean-going containers, and all types of air-handling and mechanical and electrical engineering. The all-day briefing session at Wimpey's London headquarters was packed. Fosters had drafted rough performance specifications for the modules early in February. Technically, the ideas were no more than preliminaries. They had deliberately decided to present their concepts for the modules to potential sub-contractors in rudimentary form. The architects did not want to inhibit manufacturers from proposing solutions that might improve their own ideas. The, companies were told that the architects envisaged the manufacture of perhaps 530 modules, 150 to contain staircases; the remainder to contain lavatories and plant. Each module was to be 3.9 metres (13.2 feet) high, and 3.6 metres (11.75 feet) wide; the longest was 9.6 metres (31.5 feet) long. The structure was to be steel, with finishes in steel or aluminium or, on the inside, glass-reinforced plastic. All the modules were to be sealed on arrival at the site. On the basis of this two-page outline, and a further dozen pages of notes on the technical plant specifications, the prequalification documents were issued.

The companies were to propose their strategy for handling the contract. The team wanted to know how and where they would manufacture the modules, transport them to the site and erect them. Their comments on the content of the sub-contract and its commercial viability – especially in view of the 'exceptional standards of material quality, workmanship, finish and precision' which were expected – were welcomed.[7] The whole exercise was loose, exploratory. The consultants wanted to arrive at a sensible number of contenders for a place on the tender list, and also to cull ideas. At the end of this initial stage, seven consortia presented themselves for consideration as candidates for the tender list. Nearly all the contending companies on the prequalification list had joined forces with one another, or engaged other companies, to provide the expertise that they lacked. Only two companies had withdrawn altogether.[8]

Now a second stage of prequalification commenced, to whittle the seven consortia down to three or four. Each of the seven consortia gave a one-hour presentation. This was followed by four hours of intensive interviewing to determine technical and commercial capabilities, conducted by Fleetwood and Shuttleworth from Fosters and a team of representatives from Ove Arup, J Roger Preston, Northcrofts and John Lok/Wimpey. Early in June, four groups were recommended to the Bank to go forward to the tender stage.

It was the unexpected combinations of expertise that the prequalification process called forth which intrigued the design team. From Sweden: the Consafe/Flakt consortium. The main contractor was Consafe AB. The company had more than ten years' experience in the North Sea, supplying modules of higher quality than most to the oil rigs. In order to transfer their experience in manufacturing modules for oil platforms to a land-based building, they proposed to link up with Sweco, a large firm of consultant engineers. SV Flakt, the largest air-treatment manufacturer in Europe, would provide all the air-handling equipment. Flakt had the test and research facilities to test the modules, which they proposed to ship complete from Sweden to Hong Kong.

A similarly experienced consortium had been formed between the Hong Kong-based Jardine Engineering Corporation and the Bedford-based branch of the steelwork company Redpath Dorman Long, who by now were also preparing tenders for the steel contract. Redpath Dorman Long planned to capitalise on their North Sea oil rig experience. The modules would be made in England, and shipped to Hong Kong by Jardines.

From Japan: HMT Consort represented the combined forces of Hitachi, Mitsubishi and Toshiba. The group had been formed in 1975 to bid for the construction of the Hong Kong Mass Transit Railway, and remained as a standing consortium ready to compete internationally for contracts for urban transport systems and other complete turnkey contracts. Now it was the Mitsubishi Electric Corporation (MELCO) arm of the consortium who wanted the module contract. With its potential for high quality mass production, and for shortening the construction period, MELCO foresaw a fine future in Foster's concept for the modules, especially in industrial building. MELCO would manufacture the modules at its heavy steel transformer factory at Ako, Japan, where they would be tested and commissioned. The modules would be shipped complete to Hong Kong, and be installed by HMT personnel. But the expertise MELCO was offering lay in the field of heavy electric transformers, not construction. HMT Consort looked like the weakest contender.

The consortium which intrigued the design team most was one proposed by Haden International, a major British heating, ventilating and air-conditioning services company. Haden planned to team up with a firm of structural engineers and Metro-Cammell, coach builders and manufacturers of underground trains. It had been Metro-Cammell who had been successfully awarded the tender to supply carriages for the Mass Transit Railway. The vision of an elegant monocoque construction for the modules – using a single stressed skin for strength, as a fire barrier, and acoustic control – rose seductively before the eyes of the architects.

Tender documents had gone out for the modules a week before the tenders for the steel contract were received at the end of August. For the design team, the royal wedding day had been spent in Foster's new Great Portland Street offices. Spencer de Grey brought in a television set. Ray Guy had flown in from Hong Kong to spend the day in a crunch meeting with the design team and J Roger Preston on the preparation of the module tender. By now complete drawings and detailed specifications for the modules had been prepared and a wooden model of a typical module had been built. Guy and Prestons wanted the tenders for the modules to be issued at the very least on the basis of schematic drawings of the modules. But Fosters, who had been heavily influenced by the attractiveness of Haden's monocoque proposals, were against the idea. Once again, they were reluctant to be too dogmatic in their own presentation lest they should risk prejudicing the ideas and proposals which the manufacturers might put forward. The deadline for issuing the tenders was the middle of August. A decision had to be reached. Fosters' arguments prevailed.

By now, the design team's ideas had undergone a number of changes. Roy Fleetwood and Ray Guy had been to Tokyo to talk to Mitsubishi, and Fleetwood had been to the Ekofisk oilfield in the North Sea with Frank Archer, the man who would be in charge of the construction for John Lok/Wimpey, to look at modules built by Consafe. In the process they had picked up more ideas. It was clear, for example, that several of the functions which the design team had initially allocated to separate modules could more economically be combined. The idea that the steel staircases for the building might be constructed as modules had been abandoned. A new concept however had entered the module package: all the risers, the ducting and pipework, running from top to bottom of the building, were now to be prefabricated in sections.

Ideas for prefabricating the risers developed from the same philosophy that produced the concept for the modules. Fosters' desire to isolate plant and equipment in the modules in one area of each floor of the building found a parallel in a wish to box-in, organise and prefabricate the underfloor services. During 1980, David Nelson had examined how far it would be possible to prefabricate the underfloor services. It was going to be too difficult. But the vertical ducting and pipework in the building? Fleetwood had already seen that prefabricated risers were in fairly common use in Japan. There could be positive advantages in laying all the pipework out flat, and preparing all the joints in factory conditions. The specifications for risers written into the module tender were for three-storey lengths, to be anchored to the outside of the building, and plugged into the plant in the basement of the building, the boilers and stand-by generators at the top of the building, and the modules in between.

Because the design team's ideas presented in the tender were deliberately sketchy, each of the companies invited to tender for the module and riser contract was asked to prepare its own bills of quantities, and a formula for flexible pricing for the changes that would invariably come along, on the basis of its own design solutions. The team supplied performance specifications. Late in October, the tenders were assessed. It was clear that three out of the four contenders required more consideration.

The three lowest bids were extremely comprehensive. To the disappointment of the architects, Metro-Cammell, authors of the elegant monocoque module, had withdrawn from the Haden joint venture; but, technically, Haden's submission was excellent and it was strongly favoured by the mechanical and electrical consultants J Roger Preston. It was the highest of the three bids, but until detailed assessment and comparison between the tenders had been finalised it was difficult to say by how much. The next lowest bid came from Jardine/Redpath Dorman Long. This bid was within a mere few hundred thousand Hong Kong dollars of the price quoted by HMT, the Japanese consortium, and it was judged to be of similar merit technically. But, to Fosters, HMT's submission represented the best understanding of what they were attempting to achieve. In ten volumes, it was certainly the longest. Over the summer the consortium had secured the assistance of Takenaka, a leading Japanese building contractor, which had its own large architectural department; the company, in fact, that had built the modules for the Sony building in Osaka. A few days after the receipt of tenders on 23 October, Consafe was dropped from consideration, and negotiations opened with the remaining three contenders.

The negotiations took the form of intensive question and answer sessions with representatives from the entire design team. There had been a mere six weeks to prepare the tender; for all the potential suppliers there were many aspects of the structure of the modules

142

which remained to be developed. Even as they talked with the design team, more of the ideas for how the structure of the modules might be designed changed. Where could they be stored on arrival in Hong Kong? How would they be transported to the site? The size of the cranes it was planned to use to erect the building meant that no module could weigh more than twenty-five tonnes. In HMT's case, there was not only the language barrier to be overcome, but the fact that the standards of details and certain specifications in Japan were lower than those required in Britain and Hong Kong. How would each consortium handle quality control? Did the export credit guarantees they each proposed make commercial sense? Each of the three tenders was subjected to rigorous financial and technical analysis.

In the end, the battle for the award of the modules contract came down to the peripheral issues. Whose modules would weigh the least? Who required the least time to mount them? Whose plans for transporting them through central Hong Kong made most sense? One company test-drove a lorry through the streets of Hong Kong with an outsize container on its back, to gauge the formidable logistic problems. As the time drew near to award the contract the lobbying grew more and more intense. In the end, HMT offered to clad the outside of the module in stainless steel for no extra cost. It proved the clinching detail. On Christmas Eve, the board of the Bank confirmed the award of the contract to HMT Consort Ltd.[9] The three main contracts for the job had been awarded.

The long, hard, detailed slog of the tender process: the briefing of companies, the preparation of drawings and documents, the checking of details, the interviewing, the evaluating and negotiating, was really only the beginning. Besides the steel, module and cladding contracts, those for the lifts and escalators had also been processed during the year, and preparations were now being made to continue the process for contracts for the raised floors, etc. Meanwhile, during 1981, development work at all levels gathered pace. Fosters worked on their own and with the consultants to consolidate their ideas for items like the modules, raised floors, the lighting, the air-conditioning system and the sunscoop. At this stage of the project two areas were particularly revealing in demonstrating the lengths to which the project team would need to go before they could even begin to commission the manufacture of most of the components of the building: first, was the analysis and testing of the steel structure of the building and the early design development with British Steel/Dorman Long; second, was the process of development which took place in the early stages of design with Cupples, before the negotiated contract was signed in September 1981.

Fosters and Ove Arup had no sooner agreed upon a satisfactory structural concept for the building in the late autumn of 1980, than Arup began conducting a thorough analysis of the whole structure. By that time the superstructure of the building had become very different from that of the early Chevron scheme. The 'kit of parts' for the Chevron had looked simple: three main structural elements; tubes, hangers and floors. Now there were five main elements to the structure:

first, eight *masts*, arranged in two parallel rows of four. Each mast ran from the lowest basement to the top of the building. The section of each mast for each floor was to be made up of four tubular steel columns, connected by haunched rectangular beams, which became known on the project as *vierendeels*;[1]
second, seventeen pairs of suspension *trusses*, located at each of the five double-height spaces up the building;
third, 102 *hangers*, from which the floors of the building would be suspended from the trusses;
fourth, twenty-four *cross braces*, each two storeys high, designed to connect the masts inside the building at the double-height spaces; and two great three-storey-high cross braces at either end of the atrium, to

The complexity of the underfloor services as they will later go down in the building.

145

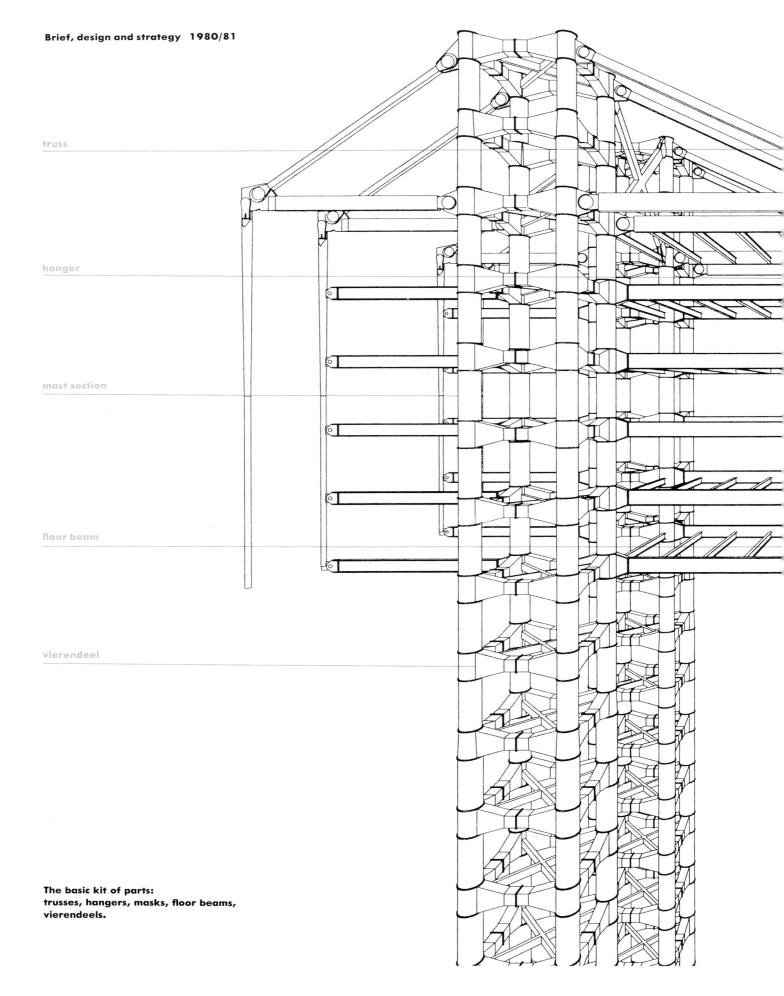

truss

hanger

mast section

floor beam

vierendeel

The basic kit of parts:
trusses, hangers, masks, floor beams,
vierendeels.

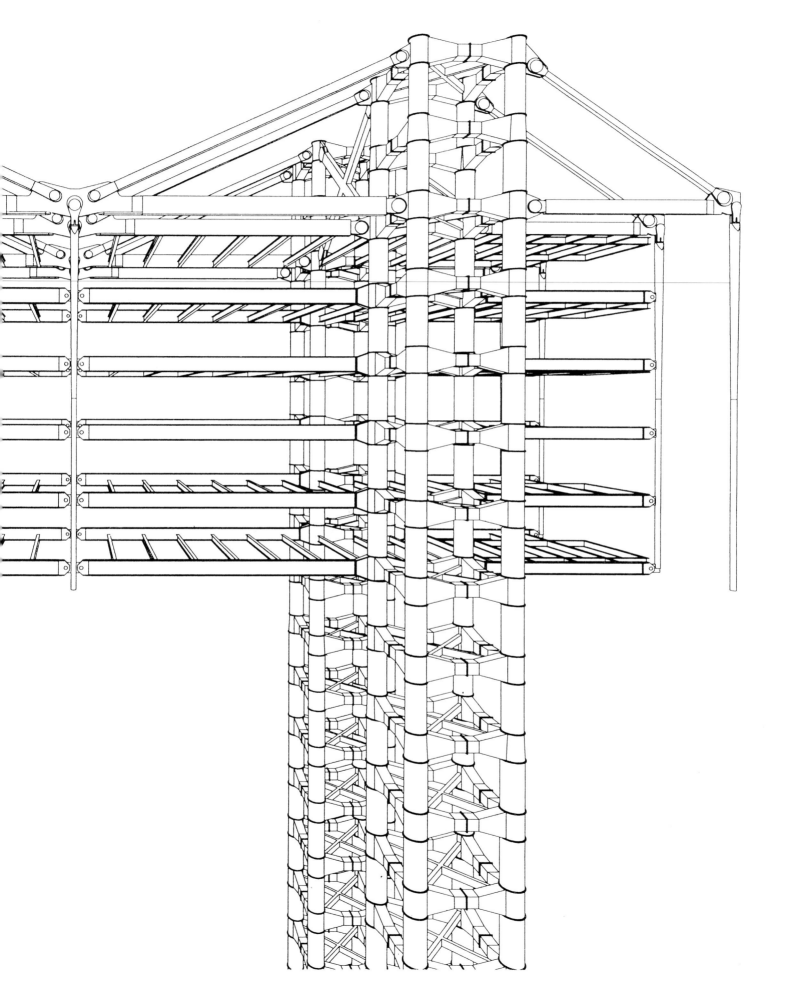

provide north-south stability;

fifth, forty-three *floors*, framed by a series of primary and secondary beams, decked with steel and topped with a 100 millimetre (4 inch)-thick reinforced-concrete slab.

Not only was the configuration of the masts unique, the whole assembly really represented five buildings stacked up one on top of the other. As such a structure had not been built before, the entire frame and its elements would have to be subjected to first-principle analysis. Arups needed to find out how strong the structure was and whether it complied with the Hong Kong building ordinances. They needed to know how the building would behave under different wind loads, and how much the steel frame would move during construction. Later, the strength and stiffness of particular key elements in the structure would be tested to destruction at Middlesbrough.

Arups used their own computer analysis programme to predict the way in which the structure would move. Steel expands and contracts as the weather gets hotter or colder, and shortens and extends as loads on it increase or decrease. Because of the building's unusual shape – with its vigorous set-backs on the eastern façade, and fully extended floors and lifts on the west – the distribution of the loads in the building would not be symmetrical, but weighted on its western side. Predictions of the loads it would take – people, furniture, computer equipment, the modules – had to be extremely precise if accurate predictions of the final geometry of the frame were to be obtained. This was crucial. Because of the desire for precise architectural expression of the steel structure, the cladding was designed to fit the steel structure like a glove. Each module would have to fit into a precise space, at a precise location, and be connected to the structure with predetermined fixing points. At the same time an accurate allowance for movement between each element of the structure would have to be predicted. Later, during construction, tolerances of astoundingly minute dimensions, less than two millimetres (less than a twelfth of an inch) between any elements of the steel structure, some of them weighing as much as forty-six tonnes, would be required. A single inaccuracy in the erection of the steel frame would increase by orders of magnitude as it was transferred on through the other elements of the building.

Arups also wanted to make sure that the structure would be capable of supporting an 'expansion' of the building in the future. If the Hong Kong building regulations changed to permit more floor area on the site, the set-backs on the east could be filled in. The building designed for completion in 1985 had to be capable of being filled in, and its loads adjusted to become symmetrical, sometime in the future. The computer model was also subjected to the impact of earthquakes and tsunamis, and, at the request of the board, explosives wielded in a terrorist attack. Efforts projected by the SAS to blow up elements of the building failed to bring about even partial collapse. The configuration of four columns on each mast, connected at each floor level, turned out to be

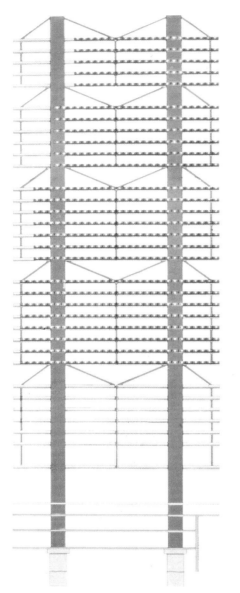

How the building was to work. Blocks of floors were to be suspended from hangers dropped from trusses supported by the masts.

particularly robust when subjected to explosion. The likelihood of a tsunami – the event postulated by the Bank's insurance company was a wave 30 metres (almost 100 feet) high travelling at 30 knots – in the shelter of Hong Kong harbour was remote in the extreme. And, although Hong Kong is in a region of low to moderate seismic activity, designing the structure and the building to withstand the strongest typhoons, which constituted a much more real threat to the building, would give it the capacity to survive an earthquake.

At the same time as these tests were going on, chemists in Arups' research and development department were dealing with the problems of the corrosion protection for the steel. It had been envisaged that the tubes and hangers of the Chevron scheme of the year before would be made of stainless steel and filled with water. The rest of the structure would be protected conventionally, corrosion protection being supplied either by coatings or, possibly, by making the steel thicker, building-in a 'corrosion allowance'. But as soon as the design began to approach its final appearance, its long, horizontal spans meant that protecting the structure from fire by filling it with water (which must always be kept moving) was no longer feasible.

The steel was therefore to be wrapped with a thin fibre blanket to protect it from fire; which in turn would be disguised by the smooth finish of the Cupples aluminium cladding. But as the Cupples cladding could not be made airtight, and fibre blanket absorbs water from the air, this decision made it impossible to guarantee that the steel could be kept dry. Conventional corrosion-protection paints were ruled out as they would have to be maintained. Cement, with its alkaline properties, which, if anything, means that it protects even better when it is wet, remained the only material that could withstand a soaking during construction or the effects of moisture trapped inside a fibre blanket of fire protection and still protect the steel against corrosion for fifty years. In the spring of 1981, it was decided to develop a barrier coating, say 12 millimetres (0.5 inch) thick, based on using cement, fibres of glass or steel to make it tough, and a polymer to help adhesion, that could be sprayed on to the steel to provide corrosion protection. Trials began first at Wimpey's laboratories, and then continued under British Steel's aegis at Teesside the following year.

It was the threat of typhoons which made an accurate prediction of wind loading obviously important to the design of the building frame, the glazing and the cladding. But the strongest winds of typhoons, which dictated the standards of strength and safety for Hong Kong's buildings, only occurred on average three times a year. If anything, Arups were more concerned that the building should be comfortable to work in, in everyday conditions. Hong Kong's wind records were comprehensive, but the complex topography of the colony's islands and mountains meant that there were substantial local variations in wind conditions. Arups needed precise and accurate knowledge of wind speeds around the Bank. No comprehensive wind study had yet

149

Ken Anthony of Ove Arup and Partners and Professor Alan Davenport at the University of Western Ontario.

Setting out the 1:2500 topographical model of Hong Kong in the wind tunnel.

The 1:500 proximity model inside the wind tunnel at the Bounday Layer Wind Tunnel Laboratory, University of Western Ontario, January 1982.

been done in Hong Kong. The Bank agreed that one should be commissioned.

On their trip to North America to see Cupples for the first time in October 1980, Roy Fleetwood and Ken Anthony had also investigated three wind-tunnel test centres. At the Boundary Layer Wind Tunnel Laboratory at the University of Western Ontario in Canada they met Professor Alan Davenport. Unlike the other wind specialists they had met in the USA, Davenport was a structural engineer. His team understood climatology and had been involved in the design of most of the tallest buildings built in North America in the preceding twenty years; their expertise and resources for wind-tunnel testing were unparalleled in the world. The wind engineering study they were to undertake for the Bank would take nearly two years, to become possibly the most exhaustive ever undertaken for a building project.

They began by making a complete reassessment of the wind climate of Hong Kong to establish a mean set of wind speeds. To do so they built a 1:2,500 topographical model, the size of a tennis court, of the island of Hong Kong and most of Kowloon. The model provided a basis for correlating wind records between different sites in the colony. Then behaviour of the winds around the Bank site alone was tested. Not surprisingly they found – as men sailing the South China Seas had discovered long before – that the site, on the edge of the harbour, was particularly sheltered by the height of Victoria Peak.

To test the behaviour of the winds immediately around the building itself a larger-scale 1:500 'proximity' model, containing a detailed model of the new Bank and all the buildings and other features within a 600-metre (2,000-foot) radius of the Bank, was built. Finally, a second 1:500 model of the Bank, all shimmering Perspex, and designed to follow the complex geometry of the full-scale building exactly, was made to measure the peak pressures and suctions on the surface of the building; 520 pressure taps, connected by tubes to a computer, were applied to the model to measure changes in suction and pressure as a variety of winds, generated by huge fans, were blown at it from different directions.

What this testing revealed was that Hong Kong's statutory regulations for wind-loading were more than adequate, even conservative, for the structure and cladding on the Bank, lying in the shelter of the Peak. It was also interesting to find that, except for the two or three times a year that severe tropical storms threatened Hong Kong, and wind-loading increased dramatically, the average wind climate of Hong Kong appeared to be somewhat less severe than in temperate regions: normally, the winds had roughly 75 per cent of the strength of those in a city like London.[2] As a result of the wind engineering tests it ought to have been possible to make some savings in the steel used in the frame; unfortunately, the tightness of the programme and the need to release information for construction did not allow time to negotiate a

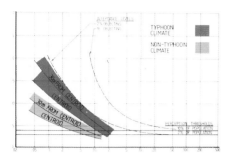

How much do people feel a building move? Peak accelerations at the top of the building during typhoons and ordinary wind conditions measured against perception thresholds.

Overleaf:

From the Board presentation, January 1981: the first proposals for the plaza under the building. The slope of the site, and the plaza, is not clear.

reduction in the design wind load for the building with the Building Ordinance Office.[3] But the most amazing fact to emerge at the end of the tests was that, being designed to resist the strongest typhoons, the structural frame was judged to have a life of 10,000 years.

October 1981: the final negotiations on the structural steel contract are under way. The programme for the steel was not only extremely tight, it was very risky. Because there was no room for error once materials had arrived in Hong Kong for erection, the whole of the manufacture and fabrication of the steel was to be subjected to the kind of stringent quality control reserved for the defence and nuclear industries. It was the way in which BSC/DL had suggested handling the fabrication and erection of the steelwork that had impressed the design team. Now that the contract was secure, the BSC/DL Joint Venture was formally established as a separate entity jointly controlled and staffed by British Steel and Redpath Dorman Long. It was Bill Boswell's intention that Dorman Long Technical Services would lead on the design; fabrication would be sub-contracted to other RDL machine shops, according to their specialisation in making different forms of steel.

Erection of the structure was due to start on site in just over a year, on 3 January 1983, but the design was still being worked up. Besides the 'design development' which needed to be done with BSC/DL, additional provisional costs had been allowed in the contract to cover staircases, internal access bridges, cladding connections, as well as the system of corrosion protection which was still being developed and the 'top of the building', which had yet to be designed. Building Ordinance Office permission for the design of the structure had yet to be sought; even the general plans for the building had not been accepted. At this point it looked as though the structure would not be approved by the authorities before the end of April. Then, shortly before the steel contract was awarded, Fosters realised they had an architectural problem with the design of the structure, where it hit the ground.

The reason why Foster had proposed that the whole structure of the building should be suspended above the site even after the need to retain the old banking hall had disappeared was purely commercial. He saw the opportunity to increase dramatically the Bank's plot ratio, and therefore its floorspace, but only if he could persuade the building authorities that a plaza under the building constituted open space for public use. It was an unprecedented interpretation of the building ordinances.

It had been Foster's intention to create a plaza underneath the building that would be like the kind of space to be found inside some of the great Italian *gallerie*, such as those in Naples or Milan. People would be able to walk freely across it, and underneath the masts of the structure, which would form an arched passageway. There was, however, a substantial slope across the Bank site. The architects had realised that

151

anyone trying to walk up the slope, under the arches of the masts, would be unable to do so without banging their heads, bumping their chests, or, finally, knocking their knees on the first level of vierendeels in the masts. If the public could not walk freely under the whole building, Foster feared the authorities would argue that this part of the plaza did not constitute public open space and would then refuse the 18:1 plot ratio. Debate over how best to solve this problem took several weeks. Finally, Foster decided that the vierendeels must come out.

With Arup, Fosters examined the structural implications of removing the vierendeels at such a low level in the structure. Jack Zunz was confident that if they thickened up the walls of the masts at the bottom of the building, they could safely remove the vierendeels at first level. They could make up the extra tonnages of steel required at the base of the masts by reducing the amount needed at the top of the building. When Munden and Ray Guy arrived in London for the final negotiations with BSC/DL, the problem was put to them. At this time BSC/DL told Arups there would be no increase in costs as a result of this change; but they would require design information sooner so that the special thick steel they would need would be available in good time. Vierendeels at level one came out of the building. It was a simple decision – one of hundreds of similar changes that would be made on the design and one that Foster and Zunz have always maintained was one of the best they made on the project. Its consequences were to grow out of all proportion to its significance.

For the six weeks after the contract was awarded, Ken Shuttleworth and Tony Hackett from Fosters and a team under Mike Glover from Arups worked intensively with the three members of Dorman Long Technical Services, who had put the tender together. All three were structural engineers: Stan Gaston, the works manager, would oversee the fabrication of the steel; Dick Stainsby, whose father and grandfather before him had worked for Dorman Long, would handle the working design; Ron Plews – his father had erected the steel on the 1935 building – was Dorman Long's chief steelwork erector, with nearly forty years' experience on big bridges and power stations: he would plan and oversee the construction of the frame. All three were approaching retirement; as they said afterwards, this was the job they'd trained for all their lives.

It was the joints of the steelwork which were concerning this team. The problem was to devise ways to bolt the main suspension trusses to the masts, and to bolt the main diagonals of the truss to the horizontal floor beams. For the tender, Arup had devised a scheme using dozens of high-friction grip bolts at each joint. It was a cumbersome solution. The bolts would be difficult to make, and when clad the whole joint would bulge. It would be much neater to be able to use a single large pin to fasten the pieces, but unless a way could be devised to fit the pin *exactly* into the bearing, whenever the structure moved in high winds the pins would be wrenched against the sides of the bearings. Clunk,

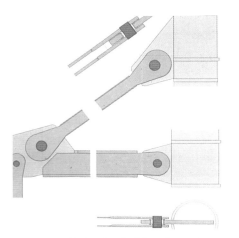

The final solution for bolting the main suspension trusses to the masts.

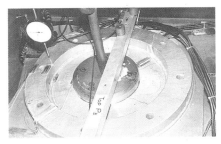

Testing of the British Steel Corporation prototype for the spherical bearing truss connection.

Prototype of the steel mast erected at Middlesbrough.

click. It would not be long before the bearings would fracture. The problem lay in the size of the pins. They would need to be up to 350 millimetres (14 inches) in diameter, and pass through 3 plates of steel, each up to 175 millimetres (7 inches) thick. Short of totally impracticable solutions, like treating the pins to baths of liquid hydrogen on site to make them shrink temporarily, neither Fosters nor Arups could think of a way to make such a large pin fit perfectly. Indeed, no one in the building industry had attempted to work steel of that size to these extremely high tolerances.

Then Gaston said: 'We can do it like this.' They would put the edges of the plates exactly together, and mill them through in one go. The holes would be cut to the same size and orientation. Then they found a German company who could make spherical bearings to vary in size from 150 to 600 millimetres in diameter (6 inches to 2 feet), to an accuracy of within one thirtieth of a millimetre (a thousandth of an inch). These would get rid of the clunk, click problem. The bearings would only be required to move during construction. Once in place, the joint between the plates could be sealed with a double protective layer: a sophisticated neoprene gasket, covered with a silicone sealant.

The spherical bearings also provided the answer to a problem they could foresee in the erection. The diagonal booms of the suspension trusses were 20 metres (65 feet) long. They had to fit on site, within a tolerance of a quarter of a millimetre, the thickness of a razor blade. How could this possibly be achieved? Hang the boom down. Pin it into place in the centre of the truss. Then drop it into place on to the mast. The spherical bearings turn to allow the diagonal booms to be correctly aligned. It fits like a glove.

Together, they arrived at further refinements to the structure to make it simpler, and more accurate to construct: they reviewed the arrangement of diaphragms which would strengthen the inside of the tubes of each mast section; they examined the way the hangers would be bolted to the floors. Now, the key elements of the mast structure had to be tested. The team needed to know how strong the elements were, and whether the designs of the details would work in production as they hoped. They needed to know how each piece would perform when it was erected. The engineers commissioned prototypes of the main building blocks of the structure: a section of the main vierendeel beam and column of the mast and the new pin and spherical bearing connection for the giant trusses. They also tested a complex thirteen-piece connection, typical of the kind of joint that would be used to connect the north/south cross braces to the masts, on the inside of the atrium. Finally, prototypes were made to test the huge screw couplers which would be used to drop the hangers from which the floors of the building would be suspended.

Around 250 millimetres (10 inches) in diameter, the hangers were to be erected in three pieces, and connected together using screwed couplers, a method that had scarcely been used in building before. They had to test which of two different kinds of threading to use, and how best to align the hangers for connection. Although by now the Britannia Works, where Gaston and his team were based, had been closed, the testing house remained open. Its 1,270-tonne test machine, built in the 1920s to test prototypes for the Sydney Harbour Bridge, was Britain's largest. All the prototypes were manufactured as they would be in production, and then tested, first to the actual loads required, and then to destruction, to see how they performed.

By the close of 1981, the contract for the modules had been let. Cupples were about to begin production of a series of prototypes for different areas of the cladding which would be subjected to tests for wind and water penetration, air infiltration and structural stability – as well as static tests. By now, Stan Gaston had set out the basic method for fabricating the masts. Each tubular section of the masts would be connected to two vierendeels. They were to become known on the job as the 'Christmas trees'. Four of these Christmas trees would make up a double floor section on each mast. The basic kit of structural parts – the masts, the trusses, the hangers and the floors – looked simple; but each of the joints in the structure required many more pieces. Furthermore, at each level up the building everything changed size. As the masts rose up the building, their diameters reduced; the hangers tapered as they went down. Every piece of the masts and all of the steel for the floors had to be fabricated to within 2 millimetres (0.08 inch) of true. All the other elements changed in proportion. In the end, more than 3,400 drawings would be required for the fabrication of the structure and more than 700 for its construction.

At the same time as the theoretical testing of the structure continued, Fosters began work in earnest with Cupples on the development of the cladding system. The first sketches for the details of the structural cladding date from the last week of March 1981. After the negotiation of the interim contract in St Louis that month, Roy Fleetwood had stayed on for some days to start work with Cupples. In order to estimate the price of the cladding contract, Cupples and Fosters had had to be sure they were speaking the same language; in order to do so the main components of the cladding systems had to be agreed and designed.

Three weeks later, in early May, Phil Bonzon, vice-president in charge of design at Cupples, flew to London with Russ La Plante, the engineer from the company who would oversee the production, and with an estimator, a structural engineer and Al Long, the vice-president in charge of construction. Bonzon had already discovered a rapport with Fleetwood. The team from Cupples had walked into Foster's green and yellow open-plan office in Fitzroy Street. It was not large. 'Is this the reception?' they asked. With Fleetwood, and Tony Hackett, who would be assigned to help with the design of the steel at the end of the year, the team from Cupples was to spend the next three weeks working in the cavernous and still empty offices Foster had found in Great Portland Street.

Bonzon, who had a gift for understated humour, was to have an enormous influence on the Foster team. A former art student, he had joined Cupples in 1955, and then trained as a structural engineer. Bonzon is one of the great unsung heroes of the modern movement, and a brilliant designer. During all those years that Cupples had manufactured curtain walls for the skyscrapers of America, it was Bonzon who had worked with the architects – people like Mies van der Rohe, Skidmore, Owings & Merrill, IM Pei, and Philip Johnson (he had even worked with Frank Lloyd Wright, but Cupples had never supplied any cladding to him) – to design the clean and shiny walling systems for countless towers all over the United States. At Fosters, he would sit down at the beginning of the day and begin to draw, Russ La Plante beside him, discussing the production realities. These two worked rapidly and highly creatively, taking up ideas, roughing them out and exploring the practicalities of details for the cladding from the drawing board right through to erection. Bonzon drew on yellow tracing paper with black felt-tip. Soon others at Fosters were using the same materials. The rapport between Fleetwood and Hackett, Bonzon, La Plante and the rest of the Cupples team was immediate and long lasting.

Cupples and Fosters had begun by looking at the masts to see how water would run down and off the outside, and at the directions in which the masts would move. The skin had to move when the steel did. Where should they place the joints between the pieces? How big ought they to be? The proportions of each of the major steel components – the masts, the vierendeels, the hangers for the floors, the giant trusses – were designed to reflect their different loads. The steel masts were 1,400 millimetres (55 inches) in diameter at the bottom of the building. As they rose up the building they reduced in size: from 1,400 millimetres in diameter to 1,200 millimetres (48 inches) and, finally, down to 800 millimetres (31.5 inches) at the top of the building. Similarly, the hangers decreased in diameter as they tapered down. The cladding had to follow the size of the structure absolutely, or the building would look bizarre. They started to list some of the sizes that might be needed: 1,700 millimetres (67 inches) at the bottom of the masts, reducing in stages to 1 metre (39.37 inches) in diameter at the top. In order to lend a monolithic appearance to the structure, and at the same time make the building look as if it had been precisely engineered, each of the joints had to be as tight as possible. The designers wanted it to appear as delicately tuned as a fine Swiss watch.

With Arups' advice, Cupples and Fosters established a hierarchy for the joints on the structural cladding. A gap of 150 millimetres (6 inches) was to be left between the steel frame and the cladding, to accommodate the welding and anchor points, the layers of corrosion protection and the fire proofing. The tolerances for each piece of the

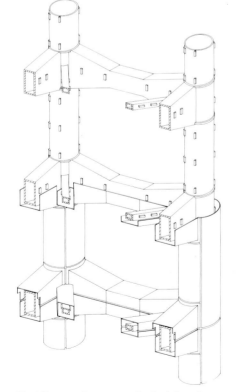

Cladding each mast to the height of a single floor would eventually require 34 shop assemblies, erected in a sequence of 18 steps.

cladding were set at $\pm$ 3 millimetres (0.125 inch). A fixed joint on non-moving sections of the cladding, like the vierendeels, would be 6 millimetres (0.2 inch) wide. The joints that took all the movement, like the floor-to-floor vertical joints, were permitted to be as wide as 18 millimetres, roughly three-quarters of an inch. Joints at points with less degrees of movement were allowed to be 9 millimetres (0.33 inch); and so on.

The line of these joints was critical. It had to be logical and consistent over many hundreds of square metres of the building: where it was drawn could alter the whole appearance and proportion of the structure, making it look clumsy or elegant. Defining the line of those joints would prove to be a nightmare not only because of aesthetic considerations, but because it was the one weak point, where weather could penetrate. The cladding had to be watertight. The line of the joints also established the order in which each piece of the cladding was to be mounted. On the masts alone, the joinery of the cladding was to become massively complex. Eventually onsite, cladding each mast to the height of a single floor would take 34 shop assemblies, erected on the building in a sequence of 18 steps. Each of these assemblies was made up of between 20 and 30 pieces, put together in the factory. At this point, the team from Cupples was looking at which piece should go in first. When the time came to put up the cladding, they did not want, as it were, to paint themselves into a corner.

Although Cupples had established that there should be a tolerance of 50 millimetres (2 inches) in every direction, when it came to fixing the cladding on to the building Bonzon and La Plante could see that the extremely minute tolerances, $\pm$ 3 millimetres (0.125 inch) on each piece of cladding, was going to require a degree of accuracy in production that was impossible to achieve using their current methods. All the cladding for the steel structure was to be made of aluminium and then painted with a fluoropolymer finish – intended to resist the moss-building effects of Hong Kong's heat and humidity for at least fifty years. To achieve this durability, Cupples treated pieces of cladding to nine stages of cleaning, coating, rinsing and painting, finally baked on at 260 degrees centigrade (500 degrees fahrenheit). The problem here was to form the shapes. Traditionally, Cupples made large columnar pieces of aluminium by roll-forming – passing sheets of aluminium through a series of rollers to get it the right shape. Slow and expensive, the process would be too ponderous here; and not nearly accurate enough. Could large curved pieces of cladding be formed by die-stamping? Back in St Louis, investigations began on other forms of production.

But production difficulties for Cupples were really among the least of the problems raised by the minute tolerances required on the structural cladding. These tolerances set the standard for the whole building, where, as yet, a tremendous amount of design work remained to be done. Because there was no room to give on the cladding there would be no room to give on the components of the steel frame, the joints, the floors, the partition walls or any other part of the building. Steel is not like concrete. It expands and contracts with heat and cold and moves as loads on it increase and decrease. The frame would move throughout construction. Even when the manufacturers were able to achieve the perfect dimensions specified by the design team, matching the pieces and making the building fit was to become a nightmare.

Having worked out the principles for the steel cladding, Cupples considered the requirements for the rest of the cladding. They had already agreed that modules and the risers were to be clad to match the covering of the steel structure. The solid sections of the walls of the Bank were to be made of aluminium honeycomb panelling, which could be sprayed with the same silver-grey polymer being used to finish the cladding for the steel and the modules. Lightweight, immensely strong – similar panelling, for example, is used to clad the outside of the space shuttle and to form the blades of the Bell helicopter – the special adhesives used to laminate the panels were developed by Cupples for buildings in conjunction with Boeing aircraft. Precise and machine finished, the panels could be made very large, and would fit flush.

Next, Bonzon and Fleetwood began to look at the principles of the curtain wall system. First, the 'main' curtain wall on the north and south façades. Each floor was to be framed by sunshades to help reduce solar gain. Further reductions in heat gain were to be achieved using 12 millimetre (0.47 inch)-thick silver-tinted reflective glass for the walls. The sunshades, they decided, should be on a level with the surface of the raised floors; therefore the floor slab would need to be set lower than the sunshades. How should the covering of the floor slab meet the mullion connection? How much building movement would there be between floors? They started to work using a tolerance of ± 20 millimetres (0.75 inch). Later this would increase to ± 37 millimetres (1.5 inches). They began to look at the pieces they would need to make the wall work: the sills, the anchors to lock the sunscreens and mullions to the structure, the mullions themselves. On the five double-height spaces, with their fire refuge terraces on the outside of the building, the glass for the curtain wall would need to be twice as high as the standard 3.9 metres (12.7 feet) for each of the other floors. They would need to design a second kind of mullion to support this glass. Bonzon showed Fleetwood a mullion he had designed for Riyadh airport. Entirely coincidentally, it was similar to one which Foster had developed for Willis Faber. They decided to work on it further.

They worked up the aluminium sunscreen that was to frame the long walls of glass. The sunscreen was to double as a catwalk for maintenance, but they also wanted people inside the building to be able to see through it down to the street below. It would obviously be dangerous to exert a heavy load on the edge furthest from the building. Bonzon proposed designing blades along the outer edge of the sunscreen that were so open that no one would dare to walk on them. Close to the building they designed a compact grille, so that it looked safe to walk on. Then they found out Michael Sandberg's height, and investigated how far back people normally stop from a wall when they come to look out of a window. They found that people were uncomfortable less than an arm's length from a wall. They plotted the angles of each blade of the sunscreen to accord with the angle of a man's view down and out of an office. Finally, in a classic demonstration of the kind of maniacal quest for precision that would characterise the project, the angle of the bottom slope of the sunscreen was designed to be the same as the angle of the ceiling line and the flared edges of the vierendeels: no more, no less than 15.524 degrees.

At the end of the three weeks in London that the Cupples team spent in May 1981, they had arrived at the system for the curtain wall of the building. It showed a full-height glass wall that looked as if it disappeared into the floor. Each of the joints was designed to be fail-safe and provided two lines of defence against water penetration. From the outside of the building, each floor level on the south façade was framed by a line of sunscreens. Inside the building, the wall was supported on round mullions of extruded aluminium, successors to Bonzon's Riyadh airport and Foster's Willis Faber exercises. In the double-height spaces appeared a striking trussed mullion, to support the greater height of glass. Foster liked the look of this mullion more than a thinner, solid mullion; it made more efficient use of metal and it looked much lighter.

The Cupples team was planning to leave London for St Louis on a Wednesday. Bonzon wanted to get the aluminium dies made for the mullions and the sunscreens, and to start the preparation of the production drawings. Cupples wanted to schedule production so that the Hongkong Bank project never took up more than a third of their capacity at a time. Once the prototypes had been tested and the Building Ordinance Office had agreed the plans, production was scheduled to start in December. A meeting was organised with Foster for the Monday. At about four o'clock he arrived with Fleetwood. 'Hello, Phil,' Fleetwood said sheepishly. 'Norman just wants to talk to you about turning the wall around. I'm off to Paris. Cheerio!'

Foster told Bonzon that the mullions were so handsome that they shouldn't be hidden behind the wall. They should be on the outside of the building for all the world to see. The mullions also conflicted with the junctions of the grid for the space planning of the interior. Throughout the building was planned on the basis of a modular grid of 1,200 millimetres (48 inches). If the curtain wall was built on the same grid, each vierendeel of the steel structure would crash into a mullion as it passed through the curtain wall. Could they turn the wall around? For a moment Bonzon was speechless. Then he told Foster that if they couldn't do it by lunchtime the next day, they weren't going to do it. The team from Cupples retired to a pub near by. Sipping a large

Russ LaPlante, Engineering Supervisor from Cupples working in Fosters' new offices, May 1981.

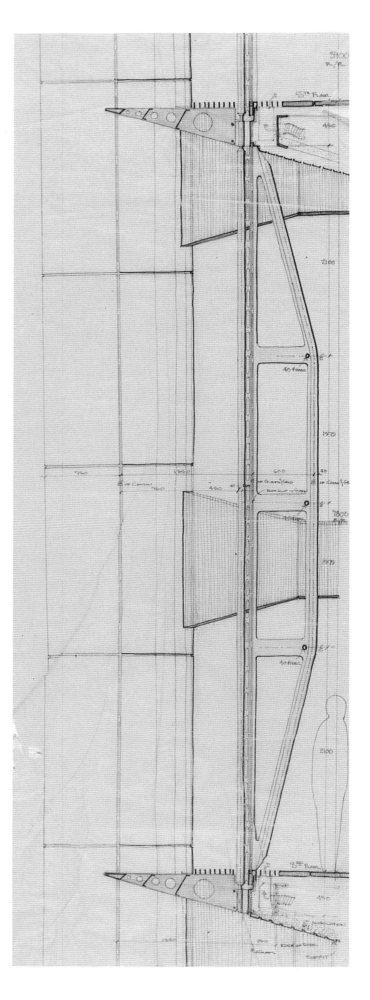

Double height truss mullion, shown on the interior of the building, May 1981.

Right:

The relations between floors, ceilings, sunscreens, mullions and masts. Cupples sketch, May 1981.

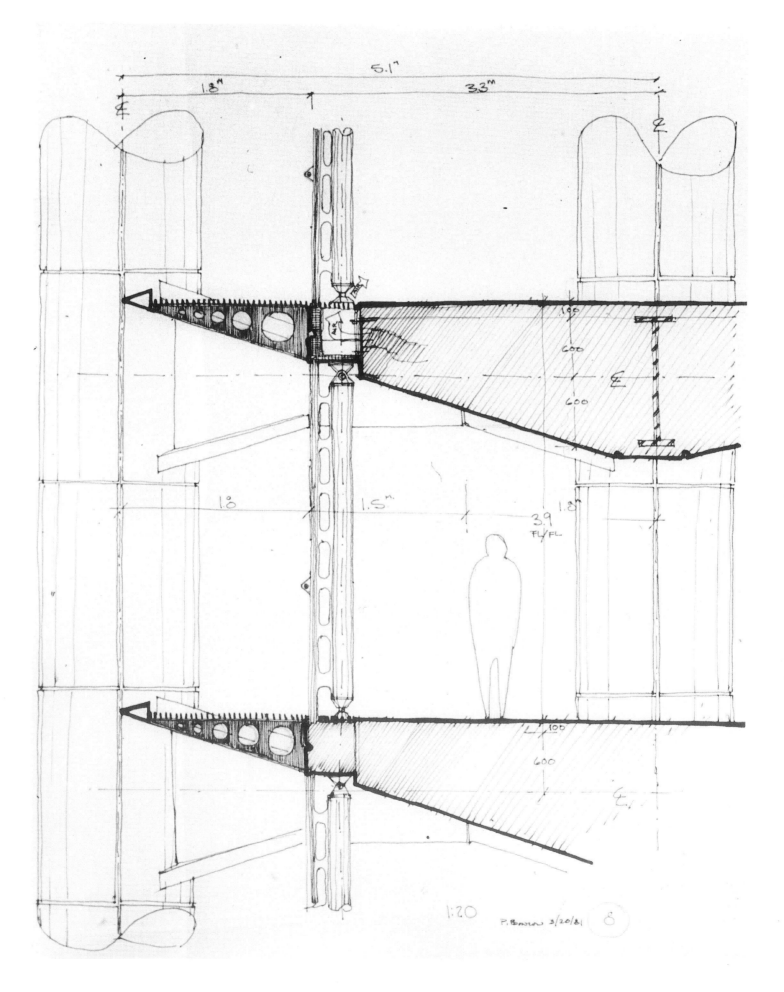

5.1ᵐ

1.8ᵐ   3.3ᵐ

100

600

€

600

1°

1.5ᵐ

1.8ᵐ

3.9
FL/FL

100

600

€

1:20   P. Benton 3/20/81   8

'The design is a moving target.' Foster secures the final solution for the curtain wall, May 1981.

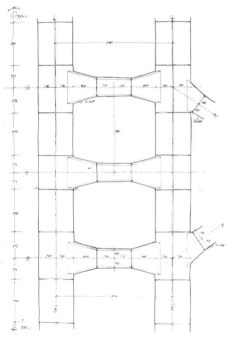

The final solution for the mast cladding, June 1981.

whisky, preparing to put in a night of it, Bonzon roughed out the first stage of the new wall on the back of a business card. By the next morning, they had the solution. They shifted the grid for the curtain wall 600 millimetres (23.62 inches) to the side of centre. Now the vierendeels would always pass through glass. And the mullions stood on the outside of the building.

For the meeting with Foster, Bonzon bought a dartboard. He put it up on the wall. 'For weeks I've been told "the design is a moving target",' he told Foster. He pinned up the drawing of the typical curtain wall on the dartboard.

'Now the design has stopped. There will be no more changes in these elements.'

Foster called Shuttleworth and Hackett over to look at the drawing. 'This is it, isn't it?' he said.

In London, the main horizontal lines of the building – the all-important points where the joints would be made – were agreed. The main weathering expansion joint, 150 millimetres (6 inches) down in the floor slab, was selected as the obvious starting point for the horizontal lines in the cladding. From there all the rest followed: the grid arrangements of the glass in the walls of the staircase towers on the east and west façades, the panel walls around the lift shafts, the grid for the partitions inside the building. On the structural cladding, it was decided that the joints should line up with the centre lines of the structure, with divisions at equal spaces up the masts. In this way the lines of the cladding ended up in the middle of each floor. They traced the joints all the way through the building. A model showing what it would look like was built.

On the plane back to St Louis that May Bonzon realised that the joints on the structural cladding were in the wrong place. The system they had devised might work well on some parts of the building; in others, such as the double-height spaces and the refuge floors, it didn't. They were forcing a solution. Landing at St Louis, he telephoned Roy Fleetwood to tell him they had a problem. Then he caught the plane back to London. Bonzon wanted to rotate all the lines on the structural cladding by 45 degrees all the way up the building. About a week later, they had traced the new lines all the way through the structure. Now, some of the steel members were expressed to their full height; the columns looked longer, and they saved some aluminium.

By late summer the designers were discovering that the decisions they were taking were going to raise many issues on other contracts. When work began on designing the cladding systems the modules were little more than a concept and the design of the structure was still being refined. The top of the building had not even been designed. They found dozens of areas that required individual treatment. Inside, glass-enclosed bridges to run across the sides of the atrium, glass-walled lift shafts and handrails needed to be designed. These related to details on other contracts such as the structural steel, the raised floors, the lifts. Everything would have to fit together exactly, in the end. The discipline was no longer one of solving problems, of asking 'What do we do next?' Cupples planned to start manufacturing shortly after the contracts for the manufacture of the steel and the modules had been let, long before the design for either of these areas had been finalised. Now it was a question of trying to predict how current decisions would affect sub-contracts on other parts of the construction, and to write those into other specifications. The design of the cladding was leading the design of the whole project. What if they forgot something?

Summer 1981. At the same time as Cupples and Fosters were beginning to become aware of the implications of their work on the design of the cladding, in Hong Kong the fundamental and practical work of developing the brief with the Bank, clearing the site for the start of construction and negotiating permissions with the authorities was under way. With the exception of the demolition, nothing was proving straightforward.

That July, the management contract formally appointing John Lok/Wimpey had been due to be signed on the 20th. By 3 July there was little indication in Hong Kong that the details would be finalised in time. By its nature, fast-tracking the design and construction programmes meant that a number of elements could not yet be 'fixed', as Fosters informed Ray Guy. At the same time, the Estimated Prime Cost, the figure on which the management contract was based, had to reflect the final cost of the construction accurately. It was a chicken and egg problem and was handled with last-minute brinkmanship. In the end, a compromise had to be reached. Some items in the EPC could be agreed and others were accepted as intelligent estimates; on other items, however, where there was still not enough information to go on, John Lok/Wimpey qualified their agreement to the figures. On 20 July, the EPC was settled at HK$2,217,171 million at November 1980 prices, excluding contingencies and fees.[1] John Lok/Wimpey's formal appointment as management contractors to the project was ratified.

Work on the details of the brief was continuing, but with more frustration than real progress. Early in the New Year, Spencer de Grey's first attempt to produce a written brief of the Bank's detailed accommodation requirements was not wholly acceptable to the Bank. The forecasts on which it was based were disputed; and for the time being it was laid aside. In the attempt to define accommodation, however, some arcane aspects of the Bank's operations had been revealed. The entrance to the banking hall had to be spacious enough to accommodate a forty-foot Christmas tree and a grand piano, the architects were told. 'We have now established that there will be no need for wastepaper-bin rubbish to be kept for three days and this practice has been stopped,' was another of these communications. Instead, the architects could expect to make provision for the disposal of a cubic foot of uncompressed waste-bin rubbish per day from each

22 July 1981. The old Bank shrouded and scaffolded for demolition.

165

The newly converted Annexe, a 1966 extension to the old Bank originally built to house computer equipment, viewed from Des Voeux Road.

Preparing to move the lions to the front of the Annexe. Wooden models were made in order to ensure the most propitious and accurate alignment.

of a maximum of about 6,000 staff.[2] The new building could expect 1,275 messengers from outside organisations delivering mail every day.[3] On busy days – considerably more before and after the Chinese New Year – some 752 people, at the rate of 120 per hour, needed access to safe-deposit boxes.[4]

Within the Bank they now debated whether the building's new telephone system ought not to be unique. Ray Guy told the architects that the Bank needed personnel location systems, a vertical document transport system, and telex cable would have to be run into every square foot of space. The building was to be capable of having its own direct satellite link. The Bank's computer centre would require a network system throughout the building, using double the present quantity of data lines, power supplies and air-conditioning. But, as yet, no decision had been taken as to whether the building would have to incorporate computers or not. As fast as some decisions were taken, others were rescinded. It was clear, for example, that if all these services might need to be expanded in future, the new Bank would have to be equipped with the raised floors that Foster had prescribed. Now, however, the Bank appeared to be voicing serious second thoughts about them. What if pipes underneath the raised floors leaked, they asked? What were the hazards to the 'electrics'? How durable could any raised floor be? What kind of finishes were needed to protect it? Particularly in areas like the banking hall, they told the architects, only marble would do.

There was no agreement as to how space in the new building should be allocated or what special facilities were needed, nor even how much of the building the Bank would occupy. For the Bank, it was simply proving too early to make these decisions. Fosters, however, were growing increasingly anxious about the lack of a coherent brief. They were very much in need of detailed and consistent input from a single source. As the date for demolition approached, the separate departments of the Bank which had lived together in one building were being dispersed throughout Hong Kong. Many of them remained in Central District; but others, like Group Methods Research, with whom Fosters were working on particular details of the planning of the new building, were removed to Quarry Bay, a long slow drive through thick traffic towards the eastern end of the island. They were going to have to make much more effort to meet face-to-face.

Demolition of the 1935 headquarters began on 6 July. They salvaged many items: the bronze gates at the Queen's Road entrance, and other screens and panels from the interior. The vast mosaic ceiling of the banking hall, however, had proved beyond safe-keeping. Elaborate discussions had taken place with *fung-shui* advisers to agree on the most propitious dates to move the lions to a new position in front of the annexe, which would serve as a token headquarters until redevelopment was complete. Any error in the casting of the most auspicious date for moving the lions into their new positions could lead

The entrance to the Annexe.

Looking through the tellers' screens down the length of the Annexe.

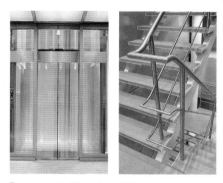

Entrance to the glass lifts.
Staircase and balustrade details.

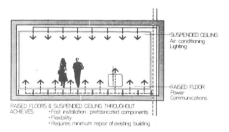

RAISED FLOORS & SUSPENDED CEILING THROUGHOUT
ACHIEVES
• Fast installation: prefabricated components
• Flexibility
• Requires minimum repair of existing building

SUSPENDED CEILING
Air conditioning
Lighting

RAISED FLOOR
Power
Communications

The principles of servicing the Annexe were on similar lines to those for the new Bank: raised floors to cover power and communications and suspended ceilings to house air-conditioning and lighting throughout.

to the direct opposite of a prosperous future; and even to 'a state of belligerence in the elements', as one newspaper had reported.[5]

With the lions carefully placed at its Des Voeux Road entrance, the annexe had opened for business a few days before demolition began. Here, for the first time, the Bank had had the opportunity to see for itself the sort of ideas Fosters were proposing for the new building. The client was not entranced. For the architects, the conversion of the annexe had provided some intransigent problems. Previously it had provided a private gangway into the bank's vaults, and, on top of this, room for computers on five floors. The building was only 7 metres (22.75 feet) wide and a city block deep. The entrance from Queen's Road was totally anonymous, up a flight of steps, through darkened sliding doors to a space with disturbingly low ceilings that could not be raised. To convert the building for public banking Fosters had had to gut the interior, but the basic structure of the building and the exterior they did not change. Inside, however, they had inserted a package that showed several ideas for details in the new building.

The walls were lined with a metallic, pressed-steel panelling, which hid the servicing. There was studded rubber and carpeting on the floor, both in an elegant dove grey. The lighting was a subdued combination of spotlights for emphasis and task lighting at each counter. The acidic green of the neon signs, used to direct customers, was repeated in a green layered view through a series of thick, bullet-proof glass screens supporting the tellers' counters along one side of the building. The screens were as simple as possible: sheets of glass bolted together with square steel patches at each corner. Interview offices were glass boxes, lined with white venetian blinds. The lifts at one end of the building were its most fascinating feature. Of clear glass, all the cables (black), the workings (painted white, with red and navy details), and passengers were exposed to view.

The annexe had been conceived to allow the Bank to maintain at least a symbolic presence on the 1 Queen's Road site until the new headquarters was erected. It was planned that it should stand for some two years, until June 1983, by which time construction on the new building would be well advanced. But for the Bank the annexe also represented a fully operational prototype, and gave it an opportunity for the first time to see and test some of the concepts Foster was proposing for the main building. The Bank did not regard it as a success. The staff made immediate complaints about the task lighting. There was no doubt that the place had an atmosphere of 'controlled gloom', as the architects later confessed. Teething problems or not, Fosters' concept for individual worktop lighting would have to be substantially modified in the main project. The glass lifts were worrying, too: some of the Bank's female customers felt 'exposed' in them. Ray Guy passed on the instruction that plans for their use in the new Bank were to be abandoned. Very soon, too, the Bank realised that commercially the branch was not making sense. No one recognised its

February 1982: the top of the line of sheet piles.

bland exterior as the Hongkong Bank, while around the corner at the China Building, to which the main retail operation had been moved, long queues were forming. By the end of 1981 the annexe would be enjoying its last few months of life. Other factors were to make it clear that demolition of the annexe was essential if the construction was not to be impeded on the western side of the site.

For, already, they had run into major problems on site. Preparation had started in November. The first job was to install a diaphragm wall, one metre thick, around the perimeter of the site down to the level of the bedrock. Its purpose was to provide a retaining wall, to seal the site against groundwater while the basements were dug out, and to prevent the kind of ground movement that would endanger the surrounding buildings and roads. Work had scarcely begun on the diaphragm wall when it came to an abrupt halt. Geotechnical surveys had failed to show up a line of sheet piles that framed the site along its length of Des Voeux Road. The only way the piles could be removed was to dig them out by hand. The spectre of a four-and-a-half-month delay on site loomed.

The Bank's pressure on the consultant team to get on with the job as quickly as possible was all the time relentless. Now it increased. Late in November Roy Munden called a full meeting of the consultants. He wanted a comprehensive re-evaluation of the building programme with a view to accelerating it so that the building could be completed as much as one year sooner than scheduled – by June 1984. As part of the same exercise, Munden also asked whether there was still a chance to increase the size of the basements from 8,000 to 12,000 square metres (86,000 to 130,000 square feet). Six weeks later, in early January 1982, John Lok/Wimpey, Arup and Fosters reported back to Munden. They showed the possibilities they had examined; and reported back on their talks with the main sub-contractors. Even if they were to pay huge acceleration payments, the short answer to such a degree of acceleration was 'No'. The consultants pointed out that, by now, considerably more work had been included in the programme than had been envisaged when the completion date had been set back in January 1981. The building was now more than twice as large as the concept Foster had proposed when he was first commissioned. Already, work on the diaphragm wall around the basement was being done on double time. They recommended the demolition of the annexe to ease problems of congestion on the site. As for enlarging the basements, this, the consultants conceded, was just possible.

By now, it was the New Year of 1982. Chris Seddon and Graham Phillips were having trouble getting the general plans of the building, due for clearance on 22 January, approved by the Building Ordinance Office. The hold-up was technical, but serious. Fosters had always been nervous about their arguments that throwing the plaza beneath the building open to the general public would entitle the Bank to an 18:1 plot ratio. It was a precedent. In talks with the Director of Public

Works, the need for clear, unobstructed passage under the building was emphasised.[6] Now the authorities insisted that before they would sanction the increased plot ratio, and clear the plans for the building, the Bank must provide a formal deed dedicating the groundspace beneath the building to public passage, twenty-four hours a day, for as long as the building stood on the site.

The issue of the Deed of Dedication was only one of hundreds of similar, highly complex problems that the redevelopment posed. It raised, for example, a host of unforeseen legal issues for the Bank. Who would police the area? Who would clean it? How would they close it in case of a typhoon? What would happen if there was a riot? Would it flood? Who even said that space *underneath* a building could be a nice place anyway?

Munden, for one, had always been sceptical about the kind of environment that could be created in the banking hall, which at this time was left open to the air, and on the plaza below. 'When you first showed us an open space our immediate and firm reaction was to ask what the environment would be like in terms of wind, heat, cold, humidity, dust etc. etc.,' he telexed Foster that January:[7]

'We did not see how such a space could have an acceptable environment but, once again, we were happy to wait for the Foster magic to work and show us why our doubts are unfounded. We are still waiting.'

Indeed, the plaza was not proving an easy place to design. It was Foster's intention to try and link the space under the building to the open spaces near the Bank: the lush, tropical greenery of Battery Path which descended to Queen's Road to the south of the Bank, and Statue Square, between the Bank and the Star Ferry. Making the plaza attractive also meant that it had to be well-lit, and comfortable. Munden had specified that it should be no more breezy than sitting under the shade of a palm tree in Statue Square. But in the autumn wind-tunnel tests at the University of Western Ontario had shown that such an open space underneath a building was bound to act like a funnel, sucking strong winds through the area. One solution – expensive, and hardly appropriate in a building that had some pretensions to energy-consciousness – would be to insert an air curtain across the boundaries of the space. Another would be to drop some kind of shield across the zone. Foster came back to Munden to request permission to carry out further wind-tunnel tests on a 1:200 model of the bottom of the building alone.

The Galleria Vittorio Emmanuele II in Milan.

Besides reducing the winds under the building, Foster wanted the plaza, and beneath it, through a glass floor, the first level of the basements, to be lit with sunlight. The principle of the 'sunscoop' he had conceived for the Bank worked in the same way that some have suggested the Egyptians may have illuminated the inside of pyramids. Sunlight, captured on a set of mirrors on the outside of the building, was to be

VISUAL LINKS BETWEEN BANKING HALL & SPACES BENEATH

Foster sketches for the treatment of
the plaza: translucent floors, sunscoops,
and glimpses up to the banking hall.

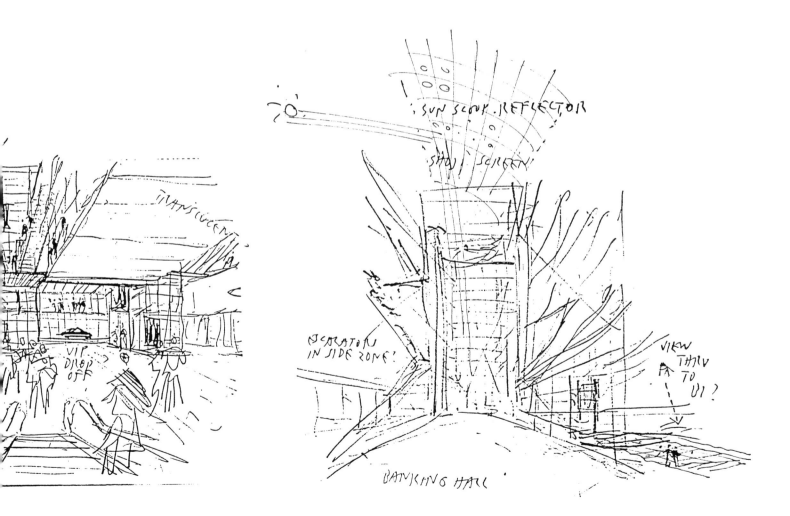

SUN SCOOP REFLECTOR

SHOJI SCREEN

ESCALATORS IN SIDE ZONE?

VIEW THRU PA TO UI?

BANKING HALL

ANSLUCENT FLOORS · SUN SCOOPS . . . .

Competition model showing water feature at Queen's Road, escalators on a north-south angle, and a walkway from Battery Path.

reflected onto a second set of mirrors at the top of the atrium, where it would shine down into the floors below, then through a glass 'underbelly' of the building on to the plaza. But at this point in the project, early in 1982, Fosters were still in the throes of trying to find a company to help make the scoop a reality.

Fosters wanted to enhance the space with a water 'feature' (it was expressed as a kind of waterfall) at the Queen's Road end of the plaza. But by the New Year Hong Kong was in the grip of one of its periodic phases of water rationing. The water feature looked as if it would now be politically unacceptable. The whole plaza area, crucial to the concept of the building, needed much more work. Meanwhile, millions of dollars were at risk until the plans were approved. The Bank would have to take Foster's word for it that the space would be attractive. The building plans had to be passed.

In the middle of January, Doug Brown and Ray Guy had flown into London from Hong Kong for their monthly series of progress meetings with Fosters. As the first meeting began, a telex arrived from the Bank. Could the number of safety-deposit boxes be doubled, from 15,000 to 30,000? It meant an increase in the size of the vaults to something in the order of 2,000 square metres (21,500 square feet). Together with Munden's request the previous November, this demand now meant that the total size of the basements was to double to over 15,000 square metres (160,000 square feet). Could Ray Guy please clarify the position?

Two weeks later, Foster and Jack Zunz flew out to Hong Kong to resolve the issue in a series of meetings with the Bank. The Bank's revised requirements for the vaults and the basement were high on the agenda. The Bank was warned of the cost – and the risks involved in digging a further 5 metres (16.5 feet) deeper into the ground. The chairman confirmed the Bank's requirements for the enlarged basement and vaults. With the diaphragm wall under way, and the sub-structure out to tender, a new design for the basement would have to be drawn up and submitted to the Building Ordinance Office.

By the end of February, Fosters and Arups had totally redesigned the basements. To reduce the possibilities for delay in Hong Kong's notorious geotechnical conditions (the ground contained sections of the nineteenth-century harbour wall as well as the sheet piles), Arups had advised that they should not plan to dig the basements any further than 15 metres (50 feet), three levels down. Now, to accommodate the new vault space, the basements would need to go down to 20 metres (65 feet). That extra 5 metres (16 feet) could add as much as four and a half months to the programme and cost in the region of a further HK$83 million at November 1980 prices.[8] While the architects wrestled with the conflicting demands of the mechanical plant and the vault requirements of the Bank, which both needed to be housed below ground, John Lok/Wimpey and the French basement sub-contractors,

Dragage et Travaux Publics, thrashed out the dilemma of how to make up the four-and-a-half-month delay on the diaphragm wall and still build hundreds of square metres of extra basement in time to get the steel on site in less than a year.

Until the discovery of the sheet piles, it had been planned to excavate the basement using a conventional form of 'top down' construction, digging out one level, inserting a floor, then another level until they reached the bottom of the shallow basements. Then caissons, into which the bottoms of the steel masts could be sunk, would be dug down to the base rock. Arups had always been aware that the concept for the structure of the building meant that it ought to be possible for the superstructure to be built at the same time that excavation of the basements proceeded. So had John Lok/Wimpey. Now, John Lok/Wimpey and Dragages worked out the practical details of putting the theory to the test.

They would dig a series of 58 caissons, 2 metres (6.5 feet) in diameter, to the bottom of the basement. Then 8 vast caissons, 11 metres (36 feet) in diameter, for each of the masts, would be sunk. Each of these would be supported by 4 more caissons sunk 15 metres (50 feet) into the bedrock below. With the giant caissons complete, steel for the base of the masts could be installed, cranes mounted and work begun on the erection of the superstructure. At the same time, excavation of the basements could start. As the ground was cleared away, the 58 smaller caissons, containing steel columns ready to support floor slabs for the basements, would be revealed. Simple, ingenious, and – because of the massive pressures of the surrounding water table – dangerous, the method was to represent an exceptional and highly impressive engineering achievement.

The designers, however, were running out of time to accommodate many more such changes. Munden had warned Foster that any alterations that could cause delay would have to be omitted.[9] This was all very well, but many aspects of the brief – let alone the design – were far from finalised. Decisions on the size of the basements should have been agreed at least a year earlier. As yet the Bank had not decided whether or not to let part of the building (which was fine), or whether it ought to have a swimming pool somewhere in its higher reaches; or house a computer centre, a requirement which could take up seven floors and require some two tonnes of extra loading on the superstructure to cover the weight of the paper alone (which had important implications for the steel contract).[10] The architects were still not receiving consistent briefing information from the Bank.

Signs that communication between architect and client were not all they might be were easily overlooked because of the good relationships on the personal level. Foster's secretary was by now familiar with Munden's favourite drink mix for the times he visited the office. The team got on well with Doug Brown, and warmed to Ray Guy's

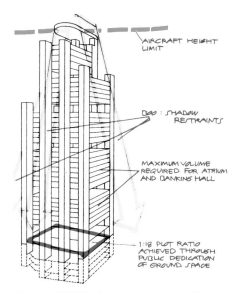

AIRCRAFT HEIGHT LIMIT

Boo : SHADOW RESTRAINTS

MAXIMUM VOLUME REQUIRED FOR ATRIUM AND BANKING HALL

1:18 PLOT RATIO ACHIEVED THROUGH PUBLIC DEDICATION OF GROUND SPACE

January 1982: the constraints on the form of the building, illustrating the significance of the plaza in plot ratio terms, prepared for the Board presentation that February.

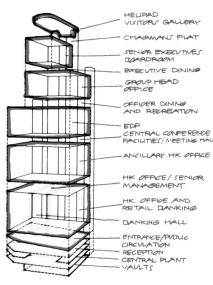

HELIPAD
VISITORS' GALLERY
CHAIRMAN'S FLAT
SENIOR EXECUTIVES BOARDROOM
EXECUTIVE DINING
GROUP HEAD OFFICE
OFFICER DINING AND RECREATION
EDP
CENTRAL CONFERENCE FACILITIES/MEETING HALL
ANCILLARY HK OFFICE
HK OFFICE/ SENIOR MANAGEMENT
HK OFFICE AND RETAIL BANKING
BANKING HALL
ENTRANCE/PUBLIC CIRCULATION
RECEPTION
CENTRAL PLANT
VAULTS

The 'stacking plan' for the building, January 1982.

enthusiasm for the project. All three men from the Bank were tough and there were frequent sharp exchanges; Munden's pen could be especially caustic. But, face-to-face, discussions were punctuated with jokes and moments of high humour.

The first major setback had come early in 1981, when the detailed brief and plan for the interior of the building prepared by Spencer de Grey had been put to one side. At that time, the outline design of the building had nearly been completed and the consultants were preparing to go out to tender on the main contracts. By now, some fifteen months later, Foster had made numerous applications to Munden to appoint someone with the skills and clout to fix the Bank's requirements for the interior of the new building so that the team could get on with the detailed planning. Although charged with keeping track of costs, and the timescale of the project, Doug Brown and Ray Guy were not authorised to take decisions or brief the design team. While Munden was next in the chain of command, many major decisions lay outside his purview, and had to be taken in consultation with others.

The fact was that, for the Bank, it was simply proving too soon to take decisions on the details of the internal planning of the building. Munden and Doug Brown were accustomed to finding new space to rent, or commissioning a new branch to be built: once they had obtained it, they would then take the decisions as to how it should be fitted-out and arranged. They could not see the urgency for the detailed level of planning Fosters desired at this point. In addition, the Bank itself was embarking on an unprecedented expansion. It was moving into America, consolidating in the Middle East, trying to expand in the UK and opening dozens of new branches in Hong Kong and throughout Asia. New personnel were being hired, new departments formed. Senior executives were constantly on the move. No one could tell exactly what the Bank's needs would be in three or four years' time.

However, partly to answer Foster's persistent requests, the previous October Munden had formalised the administration of the project by establishing a monthly steering committee whose 'interest is [to be] confined to a high level report on the major project milestones'[11] to keep him abreast of events. Unfortunately this was a reactive rather than an initiating body; its creation introduced a committee structure and timetable into the chain of decision making. At the same time, Munden's other responsibilities were becoming increasingly heavy. In his spare time he was chairman of the Redevelopment Committee of the Hong Kong Club, which was now under construction to designs – on the surface very similar to those he had prepared for the Bank – by the Australian architect Harry Seidler. Besides his other duties in the Bank, Munden was also the chairman of Wardley, the Bank's merchant banking subsidiary. As work had begun on site in the previous November, major financial problems had been uncovered in the Carrian Group, a property and trading company functioning on huge loans, in some of which Wardley was involved. In the coming year the

Solar collectors in Sicily.

In Mexico.

First experiments with the external sunscoop at Bartenbach & Wagner January 1982.

Interior of banking hall showing light descending from the sunscoop.

task of keeping track of the affairs of Carrian was to become one of Munden's main preoccupations.

Another aspect of the problem was that much of what had been agreed between Foster and the Bank was not written down. The overall design of the building was presented to the board of the Bank by Foster in private, using slides and drawings, questions and answers. Both parties regarded this forum as the one where approval for any major items of design and policy was to be obtained. Yet many of the more detailed and practical aspects of the project were never referred to the board at all. During his visit to Hong Kong that February of 1982, Foster had made a 'final' presentation to the board. The members had not been convinced about many items in the design. Using both lifts and escalators in the building was a key element in the original Foster concept, an essential ingredient in the final design. The tenders had been let for six weeks. Now the board wanted detailed justification that a combination of lifts and escalators was a more efficient way of moving people up a building than by lifts alone. They wanted to see detailed proposals for the helipad that was being mooted for the top of the building, and for the plaza below.

The board had only a vague impression of what colours were suggested for use in the new building. Foster's earlier idea of using Chinese reds and jade greens had received a cool response. Now, all they had was an impression of greys and silvers. Was this to be all?[12] The board wanted to know more about the landscaped refuge floors, the sunscoop, and the 'gull-wing ceilings', Fosters' shorthand for a system combining curved suspended ceilings with indirect, low-energy lighting for the building. According to Foster's strategy for the project, these more detailed aspects of the design were only now beginning to receive thorough attention. It was clear that at this so-called 'final' presentation of the scheme, both the design and the client were still in a considerable state of flux.

As a result of this board presentation, reports on all these aspects of the design had to be prepared, and the case for their inclusion agreed anew. In the meantime, negotiations continued with the building authorities for planning permission. Detailed talks were going on with the Fire Services Department; as a result the team were investigating the implications of making the whole building two-hour fire rated. There were complications on arrangements for driving the seawater tunnel which was to bring water from the harbour to cool the building's air-conditioning system. At first the government had flatly turned down Fosters' proposal to replace the Bank's 1935 seawater tunnel. The Bank had protested. The government had replied suggesting the tunnel might be increased in size to meet the future requirements of one of its own buildings, and possibly those of the nearby Hilton Hotel and Bank of China. But by now, early in 1982, negotiations with the government, which included talks on sharing costs and asking leave to drive the tunnel under Crown land, had become immensely protracted. Tenders

for the tunnel *had* to be finalised: construction was due to start in June. It was becoming too late to change these plans without jeopardising the project's programme. The enlarged seawater tunnel would have to go ahead, the board decided, even if, at the end of the day, the Bank had to foot the bill.[13]

At the same time plans to extend the colony's Mass Transit Railway, with its new line just one metre from the diaphragm wall of the new building, were to go ahead. Quite apart from the effect of its construction on the Bank's redevelopment, when finished, vibrations from the trains would travel up through the new Bank, affecting security systems, computers, and other electronic equipment. No, the line could not be shifted. The only way to protect the building would be to persuade the authorities to run the trains on floating tracks next to the building. Further negotiations would have to be held with the powers-that-be. It was small wonder that Graham Phillips and Chris Seddon felt besieged at times in Foster's Hong Kong outpost. 'Please be aware,' Phillips telexed London one day, 'we have received 18 letters from HSPM [HS Property Management] today.'[14]

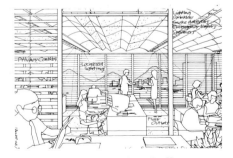

View from typical enclosed office incorporating the gullwing ceiling. Interior perspective by Birkin Haward.

Preceding page:

October 1981: 1:10 model of the gullwing ceiling, photographed with a backdrop of the view towards the harbour.

January 1982: the three major sub-contracts for the building – the cladding, the steel and the modules – have been let. Together with those for the lifts and escalators, 65 per cent of the estimated project cost has now been committed.[1] In Middlesbrough, 4,000 tons of ingot steel are due for delivery to start fabrication of the components of the structure. Mike Glover from Arups, Tony Hackett from Fosters and Stan Gaston and his team are about to achieve their breakthrough on the pins to bolt the structure together. In London, the new offices of Foster Associates in Great Portland Street are filled to capacity. Conversion work is still taking place. In the basement, there is no air-conditioning, no proper lighting and the acoustics are terrible. Work on a full-size mock-up of a section of the future interior is in full swing. Following the issue of a letter of intent to HMT Consort just before Christmas, a team of a dozen Japanese designers from Takenaka, Mitsubishi and the HMT administrative team have flown in from Tokyo to start intensive design work on the modules with Fosters, J Roger Preston and Arup. There is one year to go before the steelwork is due to start being erected on site.

Early progress with HMT was shaky. The Japanese consortium had supplied a simultaneous translator to each of the three teams working on the modules: one for the structure, one for the mechanical and electrical plant, and one on the architecture. Each team was made up of representatives from MELCO, Takenaka and Fosters, Arup and J Roger Preston. In the Japanese manner, it was development by committee. To the Westerners it was painfully slow, and apparently directionless. Each morning long discussions would be held to decide exactly what they were aiming to do; then the teams set to work. By the spring, however, excellent progress was being recorded. Ken Shuttleworth had developed an uncanny method of overcoming the language problem. He just drew all the time, extremely fast. Quite soon he and the Japanese designers communicated entirely through sketchbooks. The main challenge facing the designers of the modules was to fit all the required components into the strict confines of the space. On the risers, it would be the design of the connections that could produce fatal leaks, which would prove difficult. Now a wooden mock-up of a typical module and riser, complete with actual plant, was being built in Tokyo; its purpose was to see whether all the pieces of equipment specified could be fitted into a module and still be reached to

Drying the fluoropolymer finish on curved sections of mast cladding.

be serviced in the future. This would also provide the first opportunity to test the connections between the modules and the risers. Foster and several of the team were to fly out from London to inspect it in April.

Around the world, more and more companies and people are being drawn into the project. In Pittsburg, HH Robertson, Cupples's parent company, are about to stage a major presentation in a bid to secure the contract to build the Bank's raised floor system. In Crayford, Kent, Delta Plant Hire will soon win a sub-contract from the British Steel Corporation/Dorman Long Joint Venture for six giant hydraulic tower cranes, specially designed to climb to 182 metres (600 feet), withstand typhoons and operate in concert above the Bank's tight site. In Hong Kong, Otis Lifts, who have won the lift and escalator contract, will soon announce their plans to develop them using techology developed in association with the NASA space programme. At the same time, nine companies in the Common Market, the United States and Japan are being approached to see if they are willing to join the prequalification exercise for the gull-wing ceilings for the interior of the building.

Phil Bonzon and Norman Foster at Cupples Products, St Louis, Missouri, January 1982.

In St Louis, production on parts of the curtain wall has begun. Cupples are due to test their second prototype. In the last week of January, Foster and Roy Fleetwood fly to St Louis to witness the test on the prototype of a section of curtain wall. By now, Phil Bonzon is spending one week in every month in London furthering the design on other details of the cladding. Standing in the chill of a grey winter day, looking at that prototype was like seeing pieces of the finished building. The daylight showed up the subtle differences between the greys of the paint and the tints of the glass. They climbed up on the sunscreens to feel for themselves how reluctant a future maintenance man would be to approach the edge. They felt the finishes, and stood behind the curtain wall to watch for leaks as the propellers of a Second World War Corsair aeroplane hurled water at the rate of eight inches an hour at the front of the glass.

Behind glass walls. The dynamic water test in progress, January 1982.

Cupples were moving apace. By March, nearly 80 per cent of the basic curtain wall had been manufactured. Plans were in hand to test Prototype 4, a section of the mast cladding. Cupples cut and formed the aluminium for the mast by hand. As a result they couldn't fit the prototype together. The pieces had not been sufficiently accurately made. Next they tried half-production tooling; but they still could not put it together. To get over the problem of cutting the pieces, Cupples purchased a special numerical cutting machine made by Trumpf in Germany. Programmed by computer, with an automatic tool changer, the acquisition of the Trumpf machine meant that Cupples would be able to cut an endless stream of intricately patterned sections of aluminium for the structural cladding to within an accuracy of a fortieth of a millimetre (a thousandth of an inch). They were also working on other production problems: how to make the accurate, smooth-curved shapes for the mast columns would be overcome by the development of a series of small dies which stamped out a precise

Producing the curved sections of the mast cladding at Cupples Products.

curve; but the real challenge was to find some way to manufacture the truss mullions which provided the main support for the glass in the double-height areas, support which had to be capable of surviving the full force of a major typhoon without breaking or buckling.

More than 7.5 metres (25 feet) long, each truss was designed to be made up with 10 joints, some of them up to 400 millimetres (16 inches) long, and 16 millimetres (0.62 inch) thick. Yet the mullion had to function and appear as if it were all of a piece. Any air pockets, cracks or flaws would weaken the joints. But because it melts at comparatively low temperatures, aluminium easily overheats and distorts during welding. The dangers of shrinkage and distortion along the whole length of the truss mullion were too great to allow it to be held in horizontal position while one side of the joints were welded, then turned over and welded again. To do the job holding the mullions vertically would make these problems easier to control – but only if two welders were to perform absolutely simultaneously. The answer was robots.

It was to take Cupples more than a year to design and build the robots for the process. They set up a test rig in an empty warehouse, and made three runs of trials before they came near to a solution. There were problems with the design of the joints on the mullion, and with matching pieces accurately enough to achieve a perfect weld. But finally the system was sufficiently well developed to move into the factory in St Louis. Time after time each weld on the truss mullions was to come out perfectly.

The Unimate robotic welder at work on a truss mullion.

April 1982: Norman Foster viewing the prototype of the module at Ako, Japan.

In spite of the pressures from the Bank and the problems in Hong Kong, there was an atmosphere of exhilaration on the project during the first months of 1982. By March, most areas were reported on programme and going well. Work on the diaphragm wall was going on twenty-four hours a day, six days a week. At Munden's behest, Ray Guy paid a visit to the site several times in the small hours of one morning to confirm John Lok/Wimpey's reports that hand digging of the caissons was going on round the clock.[2] Preparation of a draft Deed of Dedication by the Bank's solicitors persuaded the Building Ordinance Office to allow the bonus plot ratio until the deed could be formally executed. The general plans for the building were passed.

Back in Foster's London office that spring, all seemed set fair. On the steel contract, Fosters reported first-rate progress with BSC/Dorman Long on the development of the design. They disputed any ground for a claim that BSC/DL was putting forward for increased costs. Early research and testing for the new type of spray-on corrosion protection treatment for the steel had been completed, and a comprehensive report analysing the vertical transportation in the building which demonstrated substantial savings in space (1,300 square metres: 14,000 square feet), travel in off-peak times and capital costs had now been prepared for the board.[3]

1982. Detailed design had reached the top of the building. Model of the helipad.

November 1982: prototype of the glass floor being fitted in the Foster warehouse at King's Cross, North London.

January 1982: photomontage of the new building prepared for the presentation to the Board that February.

Back in London major areas of the building had yet to be developed and costed: the gull-wing ceilings, the sunscoop and the helipad; the glass floor that had been proposed for the plaza beneath the building and the water feature; now back in the brief. The detailed appearance of the banking hall and many of the other special areas within the Bank was under way. It was planned that most of the team would move out to Hong Kong in a year's time to oversee the construction. In the meantime, those involved in the detailed design of the banking hall and other public areas were to spend several months in the colony.

It was in Hong Kong that rumours began to threaten the atmosphere of confidence surrounding the project. Part sour grapes, part speculation, some of what was being said had a basis in truth. As has been seen, the annexe had scarcely been a successful advertisement for the new headquarters to come. Over Christmas Ray Guy had heard that someone at Dorman Long had said that the final cost of the steel contract would have little bearing on the original tender, as the architects were constantly changing their design.[4] Such remarks moved around town fast. By the spring, rumour that trouble was afflicting the project was spreading in Hong Kong's small, but powerful, financial community. Most of it was associated with the wild speculation in the property market, which was reaching its peak. In February, the Hong Kong Land Company had paid HK$4.75 billion (US $800 million), a fabulous sum, 25 per cent above the previous record price, for a 1·3 hectare (3·3 acre) site on the Central waterfront. It was to be the last of the big property deals. In March the papers announced that Wardley, the Bank's merchant banking subsidiary, had provided at least HK$2 billion to three property companies which were now suspected of being in trouble.[5] Everyone knew someone, who knew someone in the Bank, or on the board, or otherwise involved in the project. Everyone would be fascinated if this fancy new headquarters building was somehow to come to grief.

In the Chinese popular press, some 400 newspapers, the situation was also closely watched. The new placement of the lions in front of the annexe the previous summer had been analysed in detail by independent *fung-shui* experts. In one newspaper, their alignment had been disputed. Ominously, readers were told that proof of whether their orientation was right or wrong could only be obtained by a reading of subsequent events. A few days after demolition had begun, an engineer from John Lok/Wimpey, investigating a fire on the site, fell to his death down a lift-shaft. Was this portent? And was it really true, as the superstitious whispered, that once the Bank no longer stood in the way, all the gold would run down off the Peak, and into the harbour?

Now the first sign of serious trouble appeared. The January cost report prepared by the quantity surveyors showed that the figure for the steel contract had risen by HK$68 million, nearly £7 million. What, exactly, was the meaning of this? The removal of the vierendeel at the plaza level of the building, which Foster had required the previous November, had increased the cost by HK$38 million. In November, Foster and Arups had discounted the possibility of any costs for this change; they had been comforted by confirmation from BSC/DL, who had told them that as long as no other change in weight or design was involved, costs would not increase. Fosters and Arups therefore remained confident that in the final account neither the weight of the steel nor the costs for this change would amount to very much. The rest of the HK$68 million was put down to increasing the loading of the structure to allow the building to accommodate mezzanines and floors in the atrium in future, soil loading on the refuge terraces, the swimming pool and the helipad. As far as Doug Brown and Ray Guy were concerned as they examined the cost report, this expenditure was completely unauthorised. They required a full explanation.

By early summer real trouble on the steel contract had emerged. Fosters' explanations of the HK$68 million overrun identified in the January cost report had failed to pacify the Bank. Fosters discounted the sum. The extra steel tonnages that had been required to increase the loadings on the structure were deemed to be Bank requirements, the architects told Ray Guy. Accordingly they had not applied for authority to include them as provisional items in the BSC tender. Unfortunately, it was only after Guy and Brown queried the costs for this steel that it became clear that the Bank had been unaware that these items were additional to the contract as it had been awarded.[6]

Nor – because they had been informed by the engineers that this change would have no bearing on the final total tonnage of the structural steel – had Fosters applied for formal authority to remove the vierendeels at plaza level. Similarly, they had not done so before making other refinements to the design, or incorporating such changes as extending the length of the masts when the basement had to be deepened as a result of the Bank's requirements.

Months earlier, even before signatures had been put to the steel contract, back in October and early November 1981, Ove Arup's engineers had been discussing the implications of the proposed major changes to the structure with BSC/DL. They knew that as a result of these changes, and the increases in the loadings, the thickness of the steel, particularly in the masts, was going up. Ove Arup had been assured that the only problems associated with the changes were that the materials now required needed to be ordered earlier; and, therefore, in order to meet the programme they had outlined for the steel fabrication and shipment, drawings would be needed sooner.[7] It was not until after Christmas, and after BSC/DL had processed these changes to the design of the structure and ordered the steel, that the engineers were told that in specifying the substantial thickening of the steel in the bases of the masts, and diverting the manufacture of the steel plate needed to fabricate the pieces of the masts, the steel was going to cost more.

15 July 1982: site progress.

The further evolution of the banking hall and plaza: drawing by Helmut Jacoby of the interior of the atrium in July 1982. This shows the entrance from the escalator, the glass 'underbelly' of the building and the proposals for the curved sunscoop above.

In May, BSC/DL submitted a claim in sterling for £6.158 million (some HK$64.4 million), approximately half the total sum they warned that they would be claiming for the changes to the steel specifications. There would be a five-week delay on delivery of the steel. The project team had to acknowledge that BSC/DL had a legitimate case for some extra payment due to increased tonnages. As a sign of goodwill, therefore, a token payment towards the claim was made in May.[8] The Bank had little choice but to agree to prepare to pay up in order to accelerate the contract and avoid any further delays. But they were cross. Munden's steering committee recorded their dissatisfaction 'in the strongest possible terms':

'Whatever architectural justifications are made or misunderstandings which may have occurred, the Steering Committee considered the result to be not in accordance with the professional standards they expect from the Consultants.'

Those at the drawing board, however, remained unaware of the Bank's displeasure. Ray Guy was instructed to implement a rigorous cost-saving exercise. Out went any further consideration of the swimming pool. From now on the cost implications of all items that had not yet been specified were to be examined on the basis of capital costs, rather than 'costs in use'. The steering committee noted 'with regret that this policy could not be expected to produce the best building'.[9] A new programme of steel manufacture taking account of all the changes that had occurred was proposed and agreed with BSC/DL.

By late June, however, it was clear that delay in the manufacture of the steel was getting worse. BSC/DL were stepping up their complaints. Because, they said, the architects were continually late with their instructions – some of which, especially the details of the connections and fixings and the loadings of the modules, were dependent on design development with other sub-contractors – BSC/DL were being prevented from meeting their fabrication programme and their works were under-utilised. The completion of the steelwork on site could now be expected to be almost five months late.[10] The consultants were furious. They could see no reason for this situation. The Bank was seriously alarmed. Munden was determined to get the situation under control. He was not interested in who was to blame. In order to get an objective overview he instructed Fosters and Arups to keep out of the fray. He told Frank Archer, the man at John Lok/Wimpey in Hong Kong in charge of the management contract, to go to England and launch a full-scale investigation.

Like most of the men involved in running the project, Archer had no time for fools. He had thirty years' contracting experience. For this job he had been brought out of Nigeria where he had been building roads and airstrips for Wimpey to run the management contract on the Bank. He was proud of the company he worked for. At fifty-seven Archer was fit. He was a political animal, organised and effective. His handwriting was extraordinarily meticulous, his speech precise, his dress immaculate. Archer was demanding, forthright, and fast on his feet. He was also cunning.

He and a team went up to Middlesbrough. There, they found that more than 90 per cent of the steel BSC/DL had aimed to produce under the accelerated programmes agreed in May had yet to be fabricated. Archer was satisfied that the design team had released the information for the changes that were the subject of the claim in time.[11] The steel was due to be delivered in Hong Kong within less than six months. As far as the John Lok/Wimpey team could see, the BSC/DL Joint Venture had neither the plant nor the manpower to meet the programme: a view which the Joint Venture disputed strongly.

The situation had been complicated by the introduction of a new party to the contract. At the time that the steel contract was awarded and the design team began work with BSC/DL, those at Redpath Dorman Long knew that their company was being taken over and were worried about its future. In Middlesbrough morale was low, the future confused. On 18 May the purchase of Redpath Dorman Long was completed by Trafalgar House, a huge British company with wide interests in oil and gas, construction, property, shipping and hotels. The Bank had welcomed Trafalagar House's entrance on to the scene. If a company from the private sector like Trafalgar House, with its reputation for toughness and commercialism, was to be responsible for the performance of Redpath Engineering, the steel contract would certainly be kept on track.

After the visit to Middlesbrough, however, Archer had serious doubts. Were BSC/DL using the excuse of delays in design information to disguise their own lack of performance? By mid-July there was enough muddy water about changes to the design and who was responsible for them for BSC/DL to claim as much as a twenty-week extension to their contract.[12] Archer called a meeting with Ian MacGregor, chairman of the British Steel Corporation, and senior directors from Trafalgar House.

On 3 August the meeting assembled at British Steel's headquarters on the Albert Embankment in London. Archer opened the meeting. As far as he could see, he told the meeting, the content of the steel contract had only increased by 3,000 tonnes, or 12 per cent. Both the American company Cupples and the Japanese at HMT Consort had absorbed variations of a similar scale on their contracts and had not sought extensions of time. He told MacGregor that the Bank's worst fears about the competence of British industry would be realised if their building was not delivered on time. He was not prepared to accept anything more than a five-week delay on the steel frame. 'What I want from you', Archer told MacGregor, 'is a firm commitment that BSC/DL will take whatever measures are necessary to recover the time that has already been lost on this contract.'

MacGregor's reply brought Archer up short. Was he really so unaware of the magnitude of the changes to the specifications for the steel that had occurred since the original contract? He spelled it out in tonnes under headings: plate under 50 millimetres (2 inches), plate over 50 millimetres, barrels, tubes, bars, sections. He told Archer that the most significant changes had not been in the tonnage of the steel, but in the degree of fundamental change from thin plate of under 50 millimetres to the much thicker plate, over 50 millimetres, that had been required. Not only had the amount of steel in the structure increased by 6,000 tonnes, but now over 12,000 of the tonnes of steel to be supplied on the project had changed from thin plate steel, which is made according to the conventional – and cheaper – process of continuous casting, to plate steel over 50 millimetres thick. For this, ingots were required. Ingot-making is slower, more costly, and was now performed, Archer was told, at only one mill in Britain. The ingot steel was not only going to take longer to manufacture and cost more, it was also going to require major acceleration payments to produce it in time to meet the programme. MacGregor told Archer that BSC/DL were now being asked to undertake a totally different task from that for which they had tendered, and he would make this point to Michael Sandberg. The consortium estimated that, now, far from being around £57 million, the cost in sterling of the steelwork contract would be at least £90 million. Clearly the full impact of the design changes had not been appreciated by any of the parties.

Archer was staggered. But he refused to be drawn by MacGregor. The important issue, he said, was that steel erection had to start on site on 3 January, in an orderly and coherent manner. It was clear that BSC/DL were falling ever more behind their own revised programmes, which had been made with full knowledge of the changes in design for the fabrication of the masts. Unless BSC/DL took immediate action the whole construction programme would dissolve into chaos.

Discussion was heated. But the meeting had the desired result. The commercial arguments were shelved. MacGregor undertook to honour the consortium's undertakings to give the Bank its building on time.[13] Three weeks later there were clear signs that fabrication of the steel for the base of the building was finally under way. The bulk of the steel was now in the fabrication works. In Middlesbrough they had put on extra shifts; two fabrication shops on Teesside that had been closed down were reopened. Appeals for help had gone out to sub-contractors in Cumbria and Humberside, Krupps in Germany and Mitsui in Japan. But if BSC/DL were to maintain this momentum, John Lok/Wimpey knew that they had to have a commercial incentive if they were to deliver the steel on time. On 28 August, Archer met Roy Munden and Ray Guy, Foster, Gordon Graham and a representative from the quantity surveyors at Foster's Great Portland Street office. Ove Arup had not been invited. Archer wanted a mandate from the Bank to open negotiations with BSC/DL in an attempt to resolve the programme and the cost of the steel contract. He got his authority.

By the time that the final details of the steel structure, like the fixings for the cladding and the modules, were frozen, it was October 1982. Barely 10 per cent of the steelwork remained the same as it had been at the time of the tender nearly fifteen months earlier. Without a full and detailed design audit it was, Archer reported, impossible to tell how much of the 'fine tuning' of the design was the result of architectural changes or structural requirements. He ought to have added: the design development carried out with BSC/DL. Several of the alterations were for the reasons suggested earlier: the increase for loadings at various levels in the building, the removal of the vierendeels at level one. In addition there had been impact from work elsewhere on the project. Development work on the modules taking place during the year now showed that the modules would be heavier than originally anticipated. Due to the extension of the basements, the masts had had to be lengthened. There was no disputing that the design development work by the BSC/DL engineers, which had centred on the connections in the structure, had made the joints simpler and eased fabrication, Archer noted; but it had also increased the amount of ingot steel used to make the building. In many places, the plate steel was no longer of such a high standard as had been specified in the tender; unfortunately, however, in many places, it had to be much thicker. Throughout the building more than 10,000 tonnes of steel had to be changed from concast to ingot; overall nearly 6,000 tonnes more steel was required to build the structure.[14]

Why had the steel contract changed so dramatically? No one really knew. The thing that personally enraged and frustrated Foster was that it was impossible to get a clear picture of the facts. Looking at the figures which Archer had produced it was simple to assume that those on the drawing board were oblivious of the impact of their decisions on the shop floor. To a certain extent they were. As Archer pointed out, the team of designers from Fosters, Arups and BSC/DL changed the joints in the structure to make it easier to fabricate and erect. The by-product of the decision to take out the complicated connection which Arups and Fosters had defined in the tender designs for the structure, and replace it with the single massive pin through thick plate steel which the BSC/DL engineers recommended, was that every truss member throughout the building had then to be changed from thin plate to thick plate steel to fit with the joint.

The structural engineers were perfectly aware that to change from thin to thicker steel would have ramifications. But they had to have the advice of the fabricators to get the full measure of the implications. The figures that MacGregor had produced in his August meeting with Archer did not tell the whole story. A decision to switch production from concast to ingot can occur at a whole variety of thicknesses in a range from 50 millimetres (2 inches) to over 80 millimetres (3 inches), depending on the quality of the plate specified. In November 1981 BSC/DL advised Ove Arup that drawings should be supplied two to three weeks ahead of their original programme, so that they could

14 October 1982. A 'Christmas tree' in production.

order supplies of ingot steel in time. But were Redpath Dorman Long fully aware of the problems of getting ingot steel? Did British Steel tell them? Were John Lok/Wimpey up in Middlesbrough monitoring the activities of the steel sub-contractors closely enough? To complicate the issue further, in early 1982 whole sections of the British steel industry were badly demoralised, changing hands and winding down.

Moreover, the project was vulnerable contractually. While the pre-qualification documents for the steel tender had stated that the successful sub-contractor would be expected 'to participate in consultations with the project team during the finalisation of the details'[15] – that is, to help develop the design – this fact was not reflected anywhere in the tender documents. Northcrofts, the quantity surveyors, believed that the steel contract, which was the first to be prepared on the project, was to be a conventional fixed-price tender based on drawings prepared by the structural engineers. They believed that the design was reasonably fixed; Arups and Fosters knew it was far from final. The tender went out in a tearing hurry. Even so, ultimately, it was not the actual costs of the steel that were to become so expensive, but the cost of the increased labour for the fabrication, the doubling of the amount of welding on site, and the costs of the acceleration.[16]

By November 1982 ingot steel to supply the contract had been bought in from Mitsui in Japan and from Krupp in Germany. Fabrication was taking place at twenty-two centres in Britain instead of the four originally envisaged. Machining was being done at twelve different companies, instead of the one originally intended. The scale of the settlement to be made to BSC/DL that John Lok/Wimpey now outlined to Munden was staggering.

Detailed analysis of the revised scope of the work showed that the cost of the steel package was worth HK$930 million at current prices, as compared with HK$608 million at 1980 prices, when the tender was let. But the potential cost of buying in the steel from outside sources, speeding up the production programme and providing an incentive to deliver the frame on time would be close to HK$1,370 million. Munden was appalled. The figure was nearly double the original contract sum and represented almost the entire published figure of HK$1,380 million for the shell cost of the building. Munden warned Archer that he could not begin to predict what the board's reaction to this news would be. 'You could all be out of a job,' he said. Archer urged Munden to persuade the board to relent on the deadline for the building's completion so that some kind of balance between time and costs could be achieved. On 9 November, Munden outlined the whole grim picture to the board.

It was not a good moment to put such a case. By the late summer of 1982, the Hong Kong property market was in deep trouble. Early in September, a run on the Hang Lung Bank, the first since the boom/bust days of 1965, showed the potential for hysteria bubbling just below the surface of the Hong Kong economy. Ten days later, Prime Minister Margaret Thatcher had arrived in the colony after three days of talks in Peking. She announced that negotiations on the future of Hong Kong after 1997 were to open between the British Foreign Office and the Chinese government. The announcement was blunt and heavy-handed. It did nothing to restore business confidence or quell the fears of the mass of the people who did not want to be handed back to China. The Hang Seng Index plunged. The value of the Hong Kong dollar was falling daily as thousands transferred their savings to US dollars.

The discussion in the Bank's boardroom that day was fierce and acrimonious. The board had been told in July that the steel contract was in trouble. At that time the cost of the overrun had been regarded as annoying, but it had looked manageable. As the true scale of the situation was revealed, the board was appalled. That a contract let at the already substantial figure of HK$608 million (£57.36 million) could now rise as high as HK$1,370 million – why the frame alone was going to cost more than any other single building in Hong Kong! The one clear change to the contract that everyone could identify was the unauthorised removal of the vierendeels at level one. Even though this change would in fact account for less than HK$64 million in the final settlement, it offered a simple example of why the contract had run into trouble. To the experienced Hong Kong property developers on the board, in particular, the story of continuing changes in the design needed no confirmation. They had all seen for themselves that at each board presentation details of the overall design and the models of the building had changed. They knew what kind of penalties such changes could attract. Foster was heavily indicted. The realities of 'developing design' with industry horrified them. The figures that John Lok/Wimpey were suggesting as the basis of a settlement with BSC/DL could not possibly be accepted. The project had to be brought under control.

There were suggestions that the architects be summarily dismissed. But Sandberg proposed that the first step should be for the board to nominate three of its members to examine the case of the steel contract in detail, negotiate a settlement and advise the Bank what to do next. His view was that none of them should be executive directors. He put forward the names of Li Ka-Shing, Trevor Bedford, managing director of Hong Kong Land, and Norman Thompson. Together these men possessed some of the toughest and most widespread expertise in building and property in the Far East. Munden had already approached Ron Mead, Norman Thompson's former engineering and project director on the MTR. They wasted no time in co-opting him. Then they summoned the management contractor and the quantity surveyors to go through the whole situation again in detail.

It was a lengthy meeting. Towards the end, they instructed Frank Archer to continue negotiations with BSC/DL to get the best settlement possible. Perhaps, before he left, he would also care to comment on the future control of the project? Archer did not mince his words. The Bank ought to introduce at once effective project management – with full authority – to control the design, construction and costs of the project. No more design should take place in London; the entire project team – Fosters, Ove Arup, J Roger Preston, John Lok/Wimpey, and the quantity surveyors on the job from Northcrofts – should be moved to Hong Kong without delay. Once there, design development on the project should be rigorously overseen.

Left to themselves the group considered the Bank's options. They could dismiss the architect, even the management contractor, and start again. Plainly this would be time-consuming; it would lead to a host of lawsuits and in the present atmosphere of Hong Kong the publicity would be exceptionally damaging. Moreover, the nature of the building and its concept were so complicated that it would be impossible for any other architect to step into Foster's shoes. If they decided to cut their losses now, no other headquarters they could commission would remotely compare with the originality of Foster's concept. They would have spent all that money without having anything to show for it. None the less threats of action could be useful, and privately the Bank should decide to reserve its legal rights.[17]

A series of telexes was despatched to the consultants in London. A task force of consultants was to be sent to Japan immediately, to ward off any overspending on the module contract. All consultants working full-time on the project were to move to Hong Kong as soon as possible: the transfer was to be complete by the end of January. No further design was to take place outside Hong Kong. 'The whole future of the project is hanging in the balance,' Roy Munden told them. 'Everyone's wholehearted co-operation – mere compliance is not sufficient – is essential.'[18]

In London, Norman Foster called the twelve architects in the office who had been working on the project into the model shop at the back of the basement. For the sake of the office – no, for the sake of the project – they would have to advance their plans for the move to Hong Kong and go by January. Ken Shuttleworth, who at home had spent months of spare time plastering his new flat, was instructed to hire a plasterer, to marshal a sixteen-man task force of consultants and get to Japan to start work on the module contract immediately. The rest were told to put their homes out to rent, and get ready to move. Graham Phillips and Chris Seddon flew over from Hong Kong to meet the enlarged team over dinner. Foster nominated Roy Fleetwood to be his representative in Hong Kong and be in charge of the office. Within a week of Munden's instructions, the task force had arrived in Japan. The remaining members of the design team would be in Hong Kong with their families in six weeks' time. (In all there would be twelve from Fosters and five from Ove Arup to boost their team already in Hong Kong, twenty four from J Roger Preston and nine from Northcroft, Neighbour & Nicholson.)

On 14 December, the board approved the establishment of a new Project Policy Co-ordination Committee (PPCC), to be in charge of all major decisions on design, finance and project management. The committee was to consist of the three men earlier seconded from the board: Li Ka-Shing, Norman Thompson and Trevor Bedford. In addition, the new committee co-opted a fourth board member, Hui Sai Fun, another seasoned Hong Kong developer. Bedford was invited to chair the committee and Munden was to serve as secretary. Both he and Ray Guy were removed from effective authority on the project. From now on, Ron Mead was to be the project co-ordinator, in charge of running it on a day-to-day basis.

Fosters were no longer to have any authority to instruct the contractors and consultants without the sanction of the PPCC or Ron Mead, and steps were considered to reduce John Lok/Wimpey's control over contracts with sub-contractors. At the same meeting the board ratified further steps to get to grips with the project, including preparation of a comprehensive cost plan and budget. A complete technical and financial audit of the project would take place. Munden had proposed such an idea to the consultants in London a few weeks earlier; its purpose would be to establish and freeze the state of the design. To this extent it had been welcomed by the consultant team. In fact, the audit was to prove a more sinister vehicle. Its underlying intention was to determine the viability of the project. Could it be completed by 1985? What was the worst in final potential costs? Where were the hidden dangers, the booby traps, that might mean that the Bank would be landed with a headquarters that could never be built? Depending on the result of the audit, the PPCC would decide whether or not the project should continue. Five days before Christmas, a telex was despatched to the London consultants. The future of the project would be decided in three months' time.[19]

For the sake of the project

Anxiety about the future of the project at once began to take its toll. It acted like a corrosive on relations between the Bank and the consultants. For the sake of the project Fosters, Arups and the rest of the consultants were determined to keep their heads down, do all they could to co-operate with the Bank's demands and try to work normally.

So far, Fosters' day-to-day relationships with Ray Guy and Munden had been good. But now they had been removed from effective responsibility on the project. When the board had launched its investigation into the steel overrun in November, Munden had warned Chris Seddon and Graham Phillips that the way costs on the project had been treated so far was likely to be changed. The question had been how? Would it be necessary to recover the costs of the steel overrun from other sub-contract packages? By cancelling items altogether?

After the meeting with Munden in November, Graham Phillips telexed the office in London to warn the rest of the Foster team that instead of specifying items for 'the best Bank building' they might well have to wind back the quality to 'good Hong Kong standards'. Fosters had been finalising a system of demountable partition walls which would be hung from the ceiling, a fundamental provision in the concept of internal flexibility. Now Munden told them that, instead of partition walls designed to be readily moved, they might have to use permanent wall construction in an attempt to compensate for the extra costs of the steel structure. Talk of building walls with concrete and plaster led logically to the subject of the gull-wing ceiling, then almost ready to tender. After considerable debate, Munden allowed the team to put the gull-wing out to tender, but told them to start work on a less expensive, conventional flat ceiling.[1] The whole concept of having a flexible building appeared to be in jeopardy.

By the time the team arrived in Hong Kong that January of 1983, the situation was much worse. When the news of the steel overrun had been outlined in the sanctum of the boardroom the previous November, one member had exclaimed with disgust that the Bank could have had a fine building for the price of the steel frame alone. This statement was repeated with relish to the design team. It reverberated round and around. Speculation was that the Bank would

14 October 1982. Production of the steel masts at BSC Middlesbrough.

197

sack the lot of them, throw away the steel for the frame and the Cupples cladding, and invite Palmer & Turner to build an ordinary tower on the foundations which were now being dug. 'Removal of the vierendeels' had become a shorthand cudgel with which to bludgeon the consultants.

If the Bank terminated its contracts the collapse of the project would cause grave difficulties for many of the sub-contractors, to say nothing of what it would do to the consultants. Cupples were in full production ('spread out all over the floor', as Bonzon put it), HMT Consort were completely geared up for the production of the modules. During the past year eight more substantial sub-contracts had been commissioned. Dozens of companies around the world were hugely committed to this project. In fact, the crisis in confidence that would follow such an announcement in Hong Kong itself would be disastrous. What was happening on the project was only one in a series of calamities that afflicted the financial community.

It was almost as if, having obliterated the traces of the 1935 building and disturbed the site to the very bedrock, the worst the geomancers could predict was starting to come true. Between the summer and the close of 1982, half the value of the shares on the Hang Seng Index had been wiped off. The price of land was falling alarmingly. The year-end results for Hong Kong Land, whose managing director, Trevor Bedford, was now chairman of the Project Policy Co-ordination Committee and in charge of the Bank project, showed debts totalling the staggering sum of HK$15.1 billion, some 40 per cent of its assets. He was soon to be replaced at Hong Kong Land. In January, shares were suspended in Carrian Holdings, the vast property company whose demise the Bank had been fighting to prevent for more than a year. Was it mere coincidence that the project's second fatality, that of a steel fixer foreman struck on the head by a baulk of timber, happened early that January? Work on site would cease while a ceremony of exorcism was carried out. The financial atmosphere in Hong Kong was decidedly jittery. It was essential that rumours of trouble on the Bank project should not be allowed to suggest trouble at the Bank.

In mid-January, Trevor Bedford, Roy Munden and Ron Mead paid a four-day visit to London. They summoned the principals of each of the consultant firms to the Bank's London headquarters. There Foster, Jack Zunz, Jim Abrahams for Northcrofts, and Deryck Thornley from J Roger Preston were handed the terms of reference of the new Project Management Committee that would be chaired by Ron Mead as project co-ordinator. Bedford outlined the new procedures for running the project. Henceforth, communication was to be carried out between the Bank and the consultants through Mead: officially, recorded on paper, submitted in reports, according to the needs of committees. The consultants would only meet the PPCC if they were invited to do so. A new body, the Building Users' Requirements Group (BURG), chaired by Munden's deputy, John Strickland, was to replace the steering committee to brief the architects on the details of the interior of the building. BURG would only take decisions on design proposals on the basis of written submissions, preferably on no more than a single side of A4 paper. The design team would no longer be asked to make personal presentations of plans. The architects had been gagged.

On this trip Bedford, Munden and Mead also interviewed seven London firms of consultants of varied expertise for the task of carrying out a technical and financial audit to establish the 'total extent, content and cost of the project'.[2] The commission was awarded to consulting engineers Pell Frischmann & Partners, a firm made famous for its investigation into the collapse of Ronan Point, a concrete tower block in the East End of London, after a gas explosion in one of the flats in the building in 1968. At the same time, it was announced that Gordon Graham had been asked by the Bank to return to Hong Kong as its architectural adviser once more, for the period of the audit.

Graham had never really left the project. From the time he was first appointed by the Bank in 1979, he had stayed on to keep a watching brief on the developing design for the Bank, and to translate aspects of technology and servicing for it. By early 1982, when most of the sub-contracts had been let and the final outlines of the design had been finalised, Graham's useful role had diminished. En route from Wanchai, where Fosters then had their small Hong Kong office, to a meeting with the Bank that February, Graham had shared a cab with Foster. They got on extremely well together. Graham told Foster that he would be sorry to leave it all. Foster did not hesitate. He was very much in need of a right-hand man, and of someone who had the authority to meet his clients at chairman level. 'Provided the Bank is happy,' he said as they went up in the lift to meet Sandberg, 'would you consider heading the project jointly with me?'

Graham was flattered. He was also elated at the opportunity to remain involved with the project. When they arrived in the chairman's office, Foster put the proposal to Sandberg.

'Delighted,' he said. 'At least,' he added, 'as long as I don't have to pay Gordon the same exorbitant fee as I do you.'

Foster was taken aback. 'No, no. Of course not.'

'You mean I won't have to pay Gordon anything?' he joked. 'Then I'm even more delighted.'

That had been nine months earlier. Now Graham was to work with Mead, and sit on BURG, advising them all on architectural matters; he was also to work with the rest of the consultant team, the management contractor and Frischmann, giving advice, explaining the background, speeding up design progress, easing the way. His position was inevitably invidious.

With the audit in train the architects, especially, felt besieged. Neither Fosters nor Arups had been given an opportunity to put their side of the case in the investigations into the steel contract, nor any part of the negotiations. It had been a commercial not a moral settlement that Munden had required. This rankled and it was pointless now to be asked to comment on the new supplementary agreement that had been negotiated between John Lok/Wimpey and British Steel/Dorman Long. With the project potentially up for grabs, it was inevitable that they should be suspicious of Frischmann and his investigating team. As for the younger members of the Foster office, if the project collapsed, where else would they get a job? They would never again have the opportunity to work on a job like this one. Working for anyone other than Foster would mean working for second-best. They felt unemployable. Morale was bitterly low.

Inevitably, news of these troubles began to leak. Rumour had it that the new headquarters would cost HK$6 billion. Two days before the PPCC had even sat down for its first official meeting on 6 January, *Target*, a local investigative news-sheet, ran a story on the steel contract overrun. As far as the press was concerned, the cost of the building was that which had been published in February 1981: HK$1,380 million. If what *Target* had to say was true, the costs of the project were clearly out of control. At first glance the men on the PPCC believed *Target*'s speculation to be dangerously close to the truth.

The cost of the building that the board had sanctioned in January 1981 had only covered items normally provided in a speculative block; the figure of HK$1,380 million represented the cost of constructing the shell of the building at November 1980 prices. A further HK$207 million was allocated to fees, and HK$76 million for contingencies. This basic building, costing HK$1,663 million was to be owned and operated by a wholly owned subsidiary of the Bank, 1 Queen's Road Central Ltd; 1QRC Ltd would rent the finished building to the Bank. It was therefore on the basis of these shell costs alone that the board had been requested to comment and give approval.

In the meantime, the fitting out of the building, and the costs of special banking equipment had been covered by a separate 'fit-out' budget. This was controlled by Munden and administered by HS Property Management, the Bank's property managing subsidiary, in accordance with the Bank's system for routine cost control: each executive responsible for a particular block of expenditure was required to recommend and approve it. Board approval was only required when the amount involved was over HK$25 million, or the purpose was considered unusual. Thus Munden and his steering committee exercised control over the 'fit-out' in the same way that they would do so over any routine conversion and furnishing of premises rented by the Bank.[3] In early 1981 figures for the fit-out were reckoned at HK$611 million – at November 1980 prices[4] – and based on an assumption that the Bank would only occupy 60 per cent of the building.

To this system of accounting was added a further layer of difficulty. The subject of how best to estimate inflation over the course of the project had been a serious issue of debate in the early days of the project. Although it was Levett & Bailey's responsibility to forecast and monitor every detail of the actual costs of the project, because so much of the building was to be manufactured overseas the Bank's view was that it was in a better position to estimate rates of inflation, especially outside Hong Kong. Soon after their appointment, Levett & Bailey were instructed by the Bank to exclude any figures for inflation from their cost reporting. Then, in the late spring of 1981, while work on establishing the estimated prime cost of the project for the management contract with John Lok/Wimpey (HK$2,217,171 at November 1980 prices) was in train, Munden commissioned a total costing of the building, including the expected inflation over the course of the construction. The figure that was arrived at was HK$4.3 billion, not including fees and contingencies. During this exercise, the Bank arrived at a series of inflation factors which were applied by HS Property Management to Levett & Bailey's monthly figures and provided the Bank with its own premium for inflation with which to negotiate each tender. It was only in February 1982, after nearly three-quarters of the sub-contracts had been let, and the Bank was confident of its inflation factors, that the quantity surveyors were for the first time permitted to apply the Bank's formula for inflation in their cost reports.[5]

Nevertheless, at the project level, it was Levett & Bailey's reports that were circulated monthly to the architects, John Lok/Wimpey, and HSPM – who used them as the basis for the Bank's own budgets. From the first days of the project Fosters and Levett & Bailey had warned Munden of the dangers of the Bank's desire to exclude figures for inflation from their cost reporting and to split the shell and fit-out figures for the building. But to the Bank's executives their cost-control system, with its emphasis on individual accountability, was sacrosanct. However artificial it might be in this case, or difficult to administer, the system was not to be compromised.

By early 1982, however, even the Bank was finding it difficult to apply the theory of differences between the shell and fit-out costs in the packages that were going to tender. Moreover, even now there was no fixed budget for the fit-out. No decision had yet been taken as to how much of the building was in fact to be occupied by the Bank; whatever was to be let was to be fitted out to the minimum standards necessary to obtain a Building Ordinance Office occupancy permit. As for the part of the building that the Bank was to occupy, this was constantly changing. In the meantime Munden and the steering committee's approach was to judge each item to be included in the building on the basis of its costs-in-use as well as its capital cost. This was the way the project had been conceived: the building was a long-term investment, and the Bank wanted the best that money could buy. At the monthly meeting of the steering committee in May 1982, Ray Guy stressed the need for a fixed budget for the fit-out within which the project costs could be controlled: the final total for the project, he reported, could be as high as HK$5.5 billion if they were to accept all of Foster's design elements for the building.[6] By June, when the overrun on the steel contract could no longer be discounted, another factor had also come into play. The project's books were kept in Hong Kong dollars. But by now the Hong Kong dollar was falling and the US dollar was strengthening. What no more than half a dozen people at the Bank knew was that the content of all sub-contracts incurred outside Hong Kong was in fact being paid for in US dollars which the Bank had been able to buy forward during 1981. The Hong Kong dollar cost of the foreign contracts had therefore been fixed. It was no wonder that many found the situation confusing. With all these uncertainties, was any budget realistic?

As far as the members of the board of the Bank were concerned, however, everything was going well. Each time a major sub-contract for the construction had been submitted for approval the cost of the contract had been presented in the context of the budget that the board had approved for the shell, with allowances made from the fit-out budget and additions for inflation. So far, however, the board had had only one real opportunity to put all the various figures for the large sub-contracts which it was asked to approve into context, from the time that the question of costs was first being seriously debated in the late autumn of 1980. In July 1982, by which time contracts for approximately 80 per cent of the shell cost had been committed, the board was told that the final total shell cost (including claims for the steel contract, which, the paper added, were disputed), was expected to be HK$2,486 million.[7] In addition, 'total Bank requirements would amount to HK$584 million and building extras to HK$935 million' – giving a final cost of HK$4,005 million. These figures were quickly qualified by the reassurance that 'no detailed justification of such large figures has yet been presented to the steering committee and it is not intended to recommend total expenditure of this size'. By the time the problem of the steel overrun was outlined in detail to the board there was indeed no simple answer to the obvious first question: 'What is it all going to cost?'

Making sure that costs did not run any higher was Ron Mead's primary task. Henceforth all Architect's Instructions (AIs) had to be inspected by the quantity surveyors and costed before they could be passed to the relevant sub-contractor. All contract payments had to be signed by him. Commonsense and expediency were the bywords of a new, draconian approach: it was known as control by cheque book.

At 9 am each day, Ron Mead now chaired a meeting of the Project Management Committee. Round the table were Frank Archer from John Lok/Wimpey, Roy Fleetwood, whom Foster had nominated to run the project in Hong Kong; and Ray Guy, wearing the Bank's property hat, who was henceforth to look out for those things that would affect how the Bank would operate in the building. Coming on to the scene was Gifford Carey, a dry and seasoned quantity surveyor from Levett & Bailey. From time to time other specialists, like Tony Fitzpatrick from Ove Arup, or Derek Tuddenham or David Rigg, service engineers from J Roger Preston, were brought in to deal with aspects of the job which concerned them. Mead was trying to get a grip on the current state of the project, and to keep it on target with the minimum of new expenditure. Every four weeks there was a meeting of BURG where Strickland, too, was keeping a sharp eye on the costs of any items being considered for the finishing of the interior. Once a month Norman Thompson took the chair as the main sub-contractors were ushered in to testify to their performance. The only things that counted in this forum were what it was going to cost and how long it was going to take. The whole of the programme was now utterly dependent on the speed of the steel erection. This was not going well.

By mid-February, the story of the steel overrun was making headlines round the world. 'How Not to Build a Masterpiece' was how the *Asian Wall Street Journal* put it.[8] The gist of the story was that there had been no clear brief for the building, that Foster was vain and irresponsible and had been allowed 'too much latitude in pushing ahead an advanced structure that fit his own philosophical notions of what a bank's headquarters should look like', and that now the Bank was trying belatedly to get the project under control, to halt extravagant spending on crazy items of architectural frivolity. The article was seriously damaging to Foster. In London, the story broke in time to coincide with the March announcement that Norman Foster was to be awarded the RIBA's Royal Gold Medal, Britain's highest architectural accolade. 'The Sky-high Costs of Building Sky High', trumpeted the *Sunday Times*.[9] *Engineering News Record*'s account of the 'Soaring Cost of Hong Kong Bank Eclipses Down-to-Earth Obstacles'[10] spread the news to construction sites around the world. By now, mention of the Bank's new headquarters carried an automatic label: 'The World's Most Expensive Building'. In Hong Kong, there was nothing that the Bank could say that would not sound defensive. Foster himself was in Hong Kong with his team for some of this time: there and in London, he had to remain silent or break confidence with his client.

In Hong Kong, the design team was becoming seriously demoralised. John Strickland's approach on BURG was draconian. BURG was strictly concerned with practicalities, and above all costs, going back to items approved in the original EPC of July 1981, and considering whether the facilities were still required and whether the costs seemed reasonable. In most cases they did not. Where costs could not be pruned, they were referred to the PPCC for sanction. If BURG's procedures were not complied with – for example, if proposals by the architects had not been endorsed by HS Property Management beforehand – papers were thrown out. The architects were not good at writing reports; they failed to follow the procedures; the costs they put forward always seemed exorbitant. However exorbitant they might

The RIBA's Royal Gold Medal.

203

have seemed, Levett & Bailey were later to testify that Fosters' cost predictions consistently, even uncannily, turned out to be accurate. Dealings with BURG were fraught with frustration on all sides, and generally ended in humiliation for the architects.

Meanwhile, Fosters were producing 100 drawings a week; it was not enough. With a staff of forty now, they were seriously under-resourced; a week before Easter, John Lok/Wimpey reported that 700 interface problems had been tabulated by HMT Consort. They must be resolved within the week.

It was clear to Fosters that unless they set about co-ordinating the drawings between the sub-contract packages, a job which they had believed was up to the management contractor, no one else would. Overnight, they faced dramatic expansion. They had to co-ordinate the whole design in 1:20 drawings. Fortunately, they were set to move into much larger offices three minutes' walk from the site, in a newly completed tower, Fairmount House, where they would be able to take more and more space. The brief was agreed, new drawing boards purchased. The immediate problem was draughtsmen. In Hong Kong, there was no comprehension of a prefabricated building. In addition, the Bank job now held definite associations with bad joss.

By the end of March it was clear to everyone on the project that deteriorating confidence was taking a serious toll. Sandberg telexed Foster and the rest of the London consultants. He was sending Norman Thompson to London because he was becoming increasingly concerned 'with the slow progress being made with the design, contract letting and manufacture of our new bank headquarters'.[11] Foster reacted at once, telling the chairman he could expect a new initiative from the consultants within the next fortnight.

It was Easter. Gordon Graham flew in to London from Hong Kong, ostensibly for a break. He reported the state of affairs in Hong Kong to Foster, and told him what he had told Sandberg, Munden and Norman Thompson in Hong Kong: that he believed the office was seriously under-resourced. Over the next few weeks Fosters launched an international recruitment drive that would build up their staff on the project to over 120 people that summer. Easter weekend, however, was devoted to meetings at Foster's London office with the heads of the consultant firms: Jack Zunz, Deryck Thornley from J Roger Preston, Jim Abrahams from Northcrofts, on the telephone to Dennis Levett and other senior members of the team in Hong Kong. Frank Archer and Leslie Sallabank from Wimpey's joined them. Together they drafted a manifesto on the operation of the project to put to the PPCC. All of them wanted to restore the confidence that had previously existed between themselves and the Bank; they wanted to put an end to confrontation and dissension – and get on with the business of delivering the building. They called for an overhaul of the organisation and methods controlling the project. They wanted better communication between the management contractor and the rest of the consultant team, within the Bank itself and between the Bank and the consultants. They would set up joint consultant teams amongst themselves and called for the appointment of a full-time BURG 'co-ordinator' and clear authority for the Project Management Committee as the prime decision-making body on the project. They urged a meeting with the chairman of the Bank and the PPCC.[12]

That weekend, over the drafting of the manifesto, the consultant team had finally become united with the management contractor. Three months of uncertainty during the audit had given them a common cause and cemented their relations. They had come to trust each other in a way they had not done before. But the PPCC turned a deaf ear to the consultants' pleas. Persuaded by Sandberg and Munden, Trevor Bedford, Norman Thompson and Ron Mead eventually agreed to meet the consultants towards the end of April. Gordon Graham had been nominated their joint spokesman. But the meeting failed to heal the breach. Graham, in the role of interrogator, had earlier rehearsed the consultants before the meeting. On the day, he spoke first. As he came to the end of what he had to say, he turned to Bedford, who was in the chair. Both were former rugby players.

'Trevor,' he said, 'you know that when the team is on the field you have to let them play the game. You can't run it from the sidelines.'

It was the soccer player, Thompson, on Bedford's right who replied balefully, 'If you'd been playing my game, you would not qualify for the fourth division.'

It was inevitable that Gordon Graham's role as the Bank's architectural adviser was becoming more and more untenable. His direct and easy access to the chairman and Munden had seriously offended the members of the PPCC. At the end of May, Graham would retire from his roles with the Bank, and rejoin Foster, who then asked him to stay in Hong Kong at the head of the team.

Meanwhile the bad publicity was rolling on. By May the price tag was reported to be soaring over the HK$8 billion mark, and several shareholders wrote to the Bank to say that they hoped that the stories they were reading were not true. Between the end of February and early June, no fewer than five firms of management consultants wrote to the Bank to offer to come to their rescue with the project. As a final blow, in Hong Kong in June, an unnumbered copy (only seven, numbered, copies had been sent to the Bank) of the two-volume technical and financial audit which had been commissioned by the PPCC from Pell Frischmann in mid-January was delivered to *Target*. The source of the leak was never discovered.

Fortunately for the Bank, and Fosters, reputable newspapers hesitated to follow up *Target*'s revelations. The report represented a massive and alarming condemnation of the entire project. Frischmann warned that should one of the hangers used to support the building's floors fail, the whole structure would become liable to progressive collapse, a term which he himself had coined in his investigation of the Ronan Point disaster in 1968. Frischmann and his colleagues condemned the amount of heavy welding that was going to be needed in the steel frame, and were suspicious of the corrosion protection. They condemned the seawater tunnel as expensive and inefficient, and were highly critical of many details of the cladding system. Air-conditioning supplied from the floor was likely to blow cool air up trouser legs and ladies' skirts, and how was the space beneath the raised floors to be cleaned? Pell Frischmann thought the idea of using both lifts and escalators to transport people around the building anything but efficient; larger capacity lifts alone would be much more satisfactory. Such items were mere headlines in the technical section of the report; Frischmann and his colleagues' criticism of the costing, organisation and management of the project was fierce.

Inevitably, a number of the interested parties thought that Frischmann had gone too far. He was a volatile personality. His reported views about the technical inadequacies of the building infuriated and alarmed the consultants; a fortnight before his final report was delivered to the Bank, a meeting of the PPCC concluded that Frischmann was going beyond his brief.[13]

In addition, the consultants had rallied their defences. As has been seen, Ove Arup had already conducted rigorous tests to ensure that the strength of the structure and all its components would be able to withstand the consequences of any accidental loading such as explosions, even the removal of a portion of a mast, which might endanger the stability of the structure. They had been at pains to take account of the most up-to-date research on the dynamic response of buildings; that is, their behaviour under wind-induced vibration. Hence the extensive wind-tunnel testing to make sure that the occupants of the building would be comfortable.

By the time the PPCC had sent Jack Zunz copies of parts of the Frischmann report for comment he had secured eminent opinions which satisfactorily countered Frischmann's views on the strength and dynamic response of the structure. 'My present opinion,' wrote Dr AR Flint, a distinguished UK structural engineer (and another of those who had been considered for the job of performing the audit),[14]

'is that the design of the building is such as to provide robustness against accidental damage at least as great as that of most tall prestige buildings and that in certain important respects it is less vulnerable to malicious damage than the majority of buildings in Hong Kong (or, indeed, elsewhere). It is unlikely that, given the same brief, we would have approached the question of robustness in a more conservative or rigorous way than that of the designers.'

Elsewhere, Fosters replied citing 'the combined experience and expertise of design and production engineers engaged in engineering the current proposals' for the cladding as being 'without equal. The thoroughness of prototype testing, evaluation and independent certification could not be bettered'. Not only were the team's responses to Frischmann's points judged to be reasonable,[15] but by the late spring, when they were presented, the atmosphere on the project had subtly changed.

After a rough introduction, the PPCC was beginning to feel in control of the project. Ron Mead had found that he could not exercise the degree of absolute control that he had first imposed. This had included a ruling that all Architect's Instructions had to be costed by the quantity surveyors and signed by him before they were to be passed to the relevant sub-contractor. With over 2,000 AIs being processed a month, he quickly discovered that this procedure was stopping the job. Instead, small items were now to be covered by a budget for contingencies; and only the big ones would have to go to the PPCC.

More and more, too, everyone's attention was becoming focused on the real business of the project: the work on site, the need to get down to developing details of the interior with Bank staff, finalising the design, and putting the rest of the work on the building out to tender. During April and May negotiations on the final budget for the building were intense. Fosters were fighting to retain the vestiges of their original ideas for the interior. The gull-wing ceiling had been despatched at the beginning of the year. BURG had established a new budget to provide a standard flat ceiling and had substantially cut the furniture budget. By May, the Bank had recommended an internal investigation into how much of its existing stock of furniture could be re-used in the new building. At risk too were the sunscoop, reckoned then to be costing HK$10.1 million, crucial for the interior lighting of the atrium; the glazed floor of the plaza (a change to marble would save HK$14 million) and the glass underbelly of the building. These were the items that Foster intended to fight for: items like the gull-wing ceiling and the furniture were not. Through Mead, the PPCC was insisting that the consultants reduce the cost of the project to below HK$5 billion. If they did so, Fleetwood told Mead, they would have to redesign many parts of the building. By mid-May, the provisional budget before the PPCC remained stubbornly above the line, at HK$5.295 billion.[16] For this figure, at his first meeting with the whole board in nearly a year, Norman Foster told the Bank it could have the building as it had been designed: but not for less. By early July, the cost of the project remained resolutely over the HK$5 billion figure. The PPCC and Fosters remained at loggerheads. Privately, however, the PPCC had by now decided to accept that the budget could not be driven any lower, although it would continue to keep this knowledge from the architects. The crucial board meeting on the future of the project was to take place on 12 July.

Norman Thompson

**Trevor Bedford, chairman of
the Project Policy Co-ordination
Committee.**

Afterwards, the board issued a statement announcing the conclusion of the Pell Frischmann evaluation of the project. As a result, they said, no significant changes would be made to the design of their new headquarters, but certain organisational changes, which would ensure strict cost control, would take place. The cost of the basic building would be HK$3,189 million. 'In addition, the costs special to the banking operation would be HK$1,800 million, giving a total of just under HK$5,000 million.'[17]

To Foster, Sandberg wrote privately the next day. The project was not to be abandoned. It would proceed, as at present, under the control of the PPCC. Even though the quantity surveyors had said that the construction would cost approximately HK$5.33 billion, he was not prepared to discuss any costs over HK$5 billion. The tone softened. Foster had offered to meet him in Hong Kong. Sandberg agreed that this would be beneficial.[18] Good relations were to be resumed.

Had the Pell Frischmann audit shown up some unsurmountable obstacle to the completion of the building, the Bank's decision might well have been different. But, the audit had shown that *if* no major problems occurred, the job could be done for HK$5.8 billion, and would take eighteen months longer than the Bank planned. With the formal acknowledgment that the project was to continue, each member of the PPCC, and Ron Mead, now laid his personal reputation, with those of the consultants, on the line.

Sandberg had been astute in his nominees for the PPCC. Bedford and Thompson's roles in the Hong Kong property field were prominent and well known, but Li Ka-Shing and Hui Sai Fun lent the committee an exceptional degree of authority and local prestige. Both were attentive, financially astute, persuasive and tough. With less time to spare, they would leave Bedford and Thompson to take on the leading roles within the PPCC; nevertheless, however, together they would ensure that no problems arose to jeopardise the completion of the building. As far as the PPCC and Ron Mead were concerned, the most expensive commodity on a job like this was time: every day that went by added more costs, from consultants' fees to site crew wages, to the bill. It was to be finished as fast as possible. Thompson and Mead's philosophy, arrived at on the Mass Transit Railway, was that once you gave people the chance to ask questions, you lost time. The job was to be kept under hard, aggressive, tough control.

At the same time, having committed themselves, they now showed that they backed the job wholeheartedly. Henceforth Bedford, chairman of the PPCC, would play the nice guy. With a childhood spent in India and as a former Hong Kong government officer, Bedford had lived in the Far East for over forty years; unusually for an Englishman he spoke Cantonese. Bedford was charming, ebullient, one of the boys. 'Failure?' he would say when told of difficulties: 'Impossible. Use your best endeavours.' 'It's equal misery for everyone,' he would commiserate.

Ron Mead

'Don't trouble me with the details, get the job done.' By contrast, Thompson was a man of few words and dry humour. His work on the Mass Transit Railway had earned him much respect in Hong Kong, and the CBE. He was used to being in charge, and getting people to perform. Thompson never raised his voice.

Like Bedford and Thompson, Mead too was uninterested in hearing excuses. This gave him a heartless reputation but he was a large, affable man. Intellectually, he had sympathy with the project: the precision they were trying to achieve was familiar from his early experience in building nuclear power plants. In future, Mead's technique would be to keep himself in the background in dealings with sub-contractors. He made a habit of being inaccessible, coming forward only to apply extra clout; Frank Archer was to become the front man. As time went by, he and Archer were to work increasingly well together. Archer knew Mead was right behind him. The Bank was fortunate in the sheer size of the sub-contracts on the job. Most were the largest going through a company at the time. It was to give them extra leverage, which would be fully exploited, to make sub-contractors perform.

From now on, they were all in this together: Thompson, Bedford, Mead, John Lok/Wimpey, Fosters, Arups, J Roger Preston, Levett & Bailey. Up until now, Thompson had been fond of consoling the consultants: 'You will all swing together when you go.' In Foster's office Paraguay was where the team had agreed they would go for good. If they did not complete the building on time, Thompson, Mead and the rest of the PPCC would join them.

It was against this background that the physical construction of the superstructure had begun. Back on 3 January 1983, as originally programmed, the site had been officially handed over to the steel contractors: BSC/DL and their Hong Kong sub-contractor Argos, the company who would handle the physical erection. It must have seemed miraculous, in view of all the negotiations and recriminations with BSC/DL, that two weeks later the first shipment of steel arrived in Hong Kong from Teesside: forty-two mast assemblies, thirty-two slab bases, 197 secondary beams, one case of levelling screws and one case of rearing brackets.

Frank Archer of John Lok/Wimpey had succeeded in negotiating a supplemental agreement to the original steel contract just before the Christmas of 1982. Other changes had occurred. BSC had withdrawn from the management of the BSC/DL British Joint Venture, which was now in the hands of Trafalgar House, and confined itself to the supply of steel and shipment to Hong Kong. Late in January the supplemental agreement had been sanctioned by the board. The total settlement was £89 million (approximately HK$947 million) plus a maximum bonus of £2 million (approximately HK$21.28 million) for erection of the frame on time. In addition, there remained a figure of £12.9 million (approximately HK$137.26) for provisional sums.[19] The financial terms, however, were only one part of the new agreement. The other granted BSC/DL a twenty-week extension of time. This meant that the completion of the whole building, originally scheduled for June 1985, had now to be put back. The new target date for handing over the completed building to the Bank was to be revised to 17 November 1985.

This was the date to which those in charge– Michael Sandberg, Norman Foster, Frank Archer, Norman Thompson, Trevor Bedford, Ron Mead – now personally, and publicly, committed themselves in the summer of 1983. It was abundantly clear that no excuse would be remotely adequate if they failed to meet this date. Time was extremely tight. Nowhere was it proving more so than down on the site.

Programming the construction had been complicated. Right at the beginning of the project, Foster had planned that the superstructure of the building would be completed in sequence, one sub-contractor following another, in a series of zones up the building. First, zone three, the bottom eleven storeys, up to the level of the first trusses containing the atrium (zones one and two covered the basements underground and were not dependent upon the others); second, zone four up to level nineteen, and the second set of trusses. As soon as the steel frame had been completed in one zone, the sub-contractors for the modules and the cladding were to arrive. While the cladding and the modules were being slotted into place, the erection of the steel frame was to continue in the zone above. As the cladding and module contractors followed the steel erectors into the zone above, the sub-floor services people would follow them in the zone below. So on then, up the building to zones five, six, seven and, finally, zone eight, which embraced level forty-one and the top of the building. No one could afford to fabricate, ship, or erect any part of the building in the wrong order. The position of each component section of the steel frame – at any point in time – had been laid out in diagrams. Any delays anywhere would knock on to the next sub-contract.

In the construction programme, account had been taken of progress on each contract package in production. How long would it take to ship the materials to Hong Kong and how far away would they be stored when they arrived? What kinds of preparation (like the cleaning and the spraying of the structural steel with corrosion protection) were needed in Hong Kong before components could be delivered to the site? What types of container would they arrive in? The dates of arrival and erection of the glass for the cathedral walls of the atrium, in zone three, for example, had to marry up with the completion of the steel frame, the concreting of the floors and the arrival of the modules and risers for that section of the building. As the mechanics for the construction were assembled on site, each hoist, lift and crane had to be tested and certified by the authorities before work could commence; special licences had to be obtained to work at night. Blasting could only take place after a government licence had been issued; explosives were only obtainable from the Mines Division of the Labour Department.

Ten metres in diameter; eighteen metres below ground. The bottom of one of the eight main caissons awaiting delivery of the first section of steel mast.

Propitiation for the local earth god: altar at basement level, underground on site, 4 June 1983.

June 1983, basement level 2: the masts and basement columns become exposed as excavation continues.

They could only be applied for twenty-four hours in advance. If, for any reason, a blast had to be cancelled, a further application for explosives had to be made. Countless, myriad regulations, had to be complied with.

Physically, the organisation of the site was also extremely complex. Because of the way the construction of the basement had had to be reorganised to counter the delay to the diaphragm wall, for the first year at least excavation of the basements would go on at the same time as the construction of the superstructure. This brand of up/down construction was unprecedented. By early January, a massive works platform had been built to support the top of the diaphragm wall and serve as working space for men, materials and lorries. The plan was that, as the steel frame came out of the ground, tons of excavated 'muck and bullets' were to be hoisted up from the excavation below and dumped into waiting lorries on the work platform. Here, vehicle movements were to be strictly regulated to prevent congestion and time on the cranes would be rationed between sub-contractors depending on the priority of their work. By 22 January, five of six gigantic red cranes which would hoist the superstructure into place had been mounted in the bottom of the caissons, which were now ready, prepared for the masts.

Then, on 9 February, the first of the steelwork, a massive 'Christmas tree', was positioned in a caisson by Argos, the Hong Kong sub-contractor in charge of the erection of the steel. But it was to take almost ten days to align it accurately, down the shaft of the 18-metre (60 foot) caisson, before welding could begin. This was far too long. One month later, on 8 March 1983, Frank Archer told the Project Management Committee that site progress was not satisfactory. Argos had twenty certified welders. They needed ninety. Problems on aligning the steel masts needed the agreement of Ove Arup to be overcome. At the same time, John Lok/Wimpey's monitoring of the BSC/DL fabrication centres in England indicated some programme slippages on critical items. The weather on site was appalling.

Two weeks after that, the news on progress was little better: 700 interface problems on the modules had been claimed by HMT. The sixteen-man task force from the quantity surveyors, John Lok/Wimpey, J Roger Preston, Ove Arup and Fosters, which had been despatched from London to Japan at the end of the previous November, had signed off the first drawings for the modules in February. Production on the steel frames for the modules had begun. But design development was running into problems, especially on the risers.

The kinds of prefabricated riser which were common in Japan were slotted into conventional service shafts, next to the lifts inside the building. The risers for the Bank, however, were designed to be located on the outside of the building, where they had to support the cladding

that would protect them. Furthermore, they were to be connected to a structure of steel – which would move – while all the joints of the risers had to remain watertight. This was only part of the problem. At the end of May, eleven days after the modules had originally been due to arrive on site in Hong Kong, the Project Management Committee learnt that HMT Consort were insisting on using Japanese materials in the modules. The Hong Kong building authorities were refusing to approve them. The Fire Services Department was holding up clearance of the fire-control systems, and the Building Ordinance Office had rejected materials that were being proposed for making the water storage tanks. In terms of progress, delayed approvals and design changes to the modules could spell catastrophe to the construction. It was perhaps just as well, therefore, that the steel frame, which by the end of April had only just emerged from the caissons at ground level, was also well behind programme.

The first phase of the steel erection was proving phenomenally difficult. In the UK production had been slipping, shipping schedules missed. But the main headache was the sheer physical battle to achieve the minute tolerances required in their erection.

As Arups had done at the design stage of the structure, back in England BSC/DL had plotted the entire sequence of steel erection, step by step, on a computer, so that at the end the final geometry of the frame would be accurate. They knew that during construction the whole building would tend to sway progressively towards the west as loads on the structure increased. Therefore, the steelwork would have to be built in such a way that when all the loads were applied it would sway to the correct vertical position. Thus the vertical and horizontal movement of each piece of steel was predicted so that the best position for it could be set up in advance. The first of these to arrive on site were the massive sections of the masts, each made up of a dozen pieces of steel, known as Christmas trees. At the base of the building the tube sections of the Christmas trees were 100 millimetres (4 inches) thick. Four Christmas trees went to make up a two-storey section of each mast. More complex than the Christmas trees, but not as huge, were the thirteen-piece nodes designed to join the trusses to the masts, which had also been conceived to reduce welding on site and be efficient in erection. Many of these steel elements, however, were just within the limits of handling by the cranes. It was one thing to manipulate a forty-six-tonne Christmas tree on to its base within 2 millimetres of true on a computer (0.08 inch); quite another to perform the operation with it swinging from a crane.

The main operations had to take place after midnight. A fleet of huge, specially adapted flat-bed lorries loaded with mast sections would arrive in Bank Street from the Cargo Handling Basin in Wanchai. A round padeye (temporary lifting lug) at the top of a Christmas tree would then be hooked to the cables from two cranes, high above. The mast section was reared up, then lifted high, up and over the site, and

Early February 1983: steel 'Christmas trees' on site ready for lifting into the caissons.

Overleaf:

Hoisting up and over the site.

213

Lowering into position.

Aligning the tree as it is lowered on to the mast.

Welding the base of the mast.

gradually lowered on to its base on the mast. A spigot at the bottom plugged into the section of the mast beneath. Long bolts made a secure temporary fixing of the section until it could be wedged and eased into accurate alignment. The next night, when the warmth of the day had diminished, and the movement of the cranes had ceased, the positions of the new Christmas trees were surveyed.

It was not possible to align a section of the mast with the column beneath. In order to counterbalance the tendency of the structure to sway towards the west, each piece of the mast had to be surveyed in relation to a grid at the base of the building. The process was called 'setting out to the Indian rope'. As the steel erection progressed higher up the building, the mast sections had to be aligned as much as 10 millimetres (0.39 inch) east of the zone below. It was the extreme accuracy demanded in the erection of these huge pieces of the steel frame that was causing most of the problems at this initial stage. The 2 millimetre (0.08 inch) tolerances between the mast sections could only be marginally relaxed; otherwise the rest of the pieces of the building – the mast cladding, the curtain walls, the modules, the staircases – would not fit. Then, patiently, the work would begin on turning, jacking, correcting the alignment of the mast sections.

It was a job that was not made easier by the necessity to match up the arms of the vierendeels. Some of the steel had 'relaxed' in transit, causing a mismatch at the tips of the arms. It took days and days, much longer than the steel erectors had anticipated, to correct the position of each mast section on the first zone of the building, before welding, which took twenty-two hours for these sections of the bottom of the building, could begin.

By July John Lok/Wimpey had reprogrammed the construction. In St Louis, Cupples were recruiting their American supervisors for the erection of the cladding; in Japan, HMT Consort had overcome their problems with the specifications for the modules and had gone into full production; modules were now in store ready for shipping. Their new date to start on site was 18 September. Incredibly, however, by late summer the delivery of the steel was still not proceeding as planned. The basement was progressing satisfactorily, on programme. By early September the steel-frame erectors had reached the first level of suspension trusses at the top of zone three but the more intricate work – the installation of the flooring, link bridges and staircases – had yet to begin. The target date for completing the steel frame for zone three was rescheduled as 7 October. This, too, was receding fast.

On Monday, 5 September, after one of his routine visits to the site, Sandberg called for a meeting with the steel contractors to see what could be done to speed up progress. It was taking six days, not the two originally planned, to hoist and weld each of the mast sections. There were six cranes on the site, but only two steel erection gangs. John Lok/Wimpey had reported that they could see only one team engaged in surveying the masts as they were erected. Eight masts should have eight survey teams. It was a good but somewhat glib argument. The fact was that there was not room on site for everything to happen at once. The application of the cementitious barrier coat was very slow. They were falling further and further behind every day. Two days later, warnings that Hong Kong was in the path of a typhoon were signalled. All work on site stood down.

The full force of Typhoon Ellen struck the territory at 2 am on the morning of 9 September. Damage in Hong Kong, especially to vegetation, was extensive. The largest trees in Statue Square were brought down. But mercifully the site escaped with some flooding. The greatest relief was that the giant steel 'sails' attached to the arms of the cranes high above the steelwork had succeeded in preventing collisions by ensuring that they all pointed in the same direction. They had weathered their first major storm.

9 September 1983: the aftermath of Typhoon Ellen. The two-storey-high 'typhoon sails' fixed to the jib of each crane prevented them from colliding in the high winds.

On 26 September the meeting called by Sandberg was held with representatives from Trafalgar House in an attempt to cut through the morass of problems afflicting the steel. Yes, more welders, working more time must be employed. But the main problem affecting progress was the same as before: the stunning difficulty of matching the steel to the tolerances specified by Arups. As if this problem were not challenging enough, sixty-two steel floor beams had now arrived on site. BSC/DL claimed that they had 'relaxed' in transit, many millimetres out of true. During the erection of the building, the beams would be alternately propped up by the hangers until the trusses in each zone had been completed, and then jacked down until they were suspended from the trusses; then they would be spanned with steel-ribbed deck shuttering and covered in concrete. When finished, the floors were required to be level to within $\pm$ 10 millimetres (0.4 inch). The recalcitrant floor beams would have to be corrected on site. Trafalgar House begged for the tolerances, especially for the floors, to be relaxed without delay.

It was too late to do anything about zone three. In Arup's view, since the entire building was manufactured, and not built up using wet trades, physically, it had to fit. If two faces of the mast steelwork did not match up within a millimetre, the mast section itself would have to be built up, or cut down, before it could be welded. Even more of a problem was the fact that different degrees of tolerance had now been specified and built into every sub-contract on the project. But Norman Thompson agreed that the team would investigate the practicalities of relaxing the tolerances on the floors. At Fosters, David Nelson and Ken Shuttleworth were given twenty-four hours to come up with a statement on the major implications. As always on the design, it was easy to identify one potential problem area: changing the floors meant changing the ceilings. The difficulty was checking the same item consistently right through the building, seeing where it impacted – not only physically, but also contractually – on work which had already been manufactured. Fortunately, Cupples had specified a 50-millimetre (2-inch) tolerance in any direction on all of their work. In many areas of the floors, BSC/DL would be able to grind down the concrete screed to make the floor beams fit. The main problems would come on some of the brackets on the masts, which would have to be repositioned in Hong Kong. After three weeks of extensive discussions the floor tolerances would be conceded. They could be erected within a $+10/-25$-millimetre (0.39/1-inch) band of true for above zone three.

By now Cupples were renting over 50,000 square feet of covered warehousing in the United States to store the acres of finished cladding. The company had moved twenty-four supervisors and their families to Hong Kong and set up a training rig for the site erectors, so that once they started to put the cladding up on site there would be as few problems as possible. The installation of the escalators for the building had already missed two commencement dates. They were now rescheduled for the end of February the following year. Everyone would have to be compensated for the expenses incurred during the delay and then paid extra to do the work in half the time. Thompson to Archer: 'There must be somewhere along the line where we come back on programme!'

It was a question of persuading the sub-contractors to keep to the revised schedule. At the end of September the PPCC announced the introduction of a new procedural weapon. The concept of a quarterly review, attended by the chairman or managing director of every sub-contractor, major supplier and consultant on the project, had been used by Thompson and Mead with success on the Mass Transit Railway. The purpose was to get everyone round the table and, for three days, talk progress. Into this forum (it would later be referred to as the Star Chamber) would be injected all the current problems that were holding up progress on the project, and discussion would then take place on how they were to be solved. Any criticism or congratulation was understood to be purely objective; but the seat opposite the chairman of the PPCC, Trevor Bedford, would always be reserved for the sub-contractor who was in the greatest trouble. The first review was scheduled for 12 December.

By 20 October five days out of the preceding three-week period had been lost due to typhoons. The next day, a steel rigger jumped from a beam on to a vierendeel. He had no safety belt, there was no safety net. It was the third death on site. It must be exorcised. Arups wanted a meeting to discuss underground water levels in the seawater tunnel in the region of the MTR tunnel and the Bank of China building. These had reduced by one metre and could affect the Courts of Justice. One month earlier the seawater tunnel had flooded; as a result the concourse at the Star Ferry had settled and had to be cordoned off. Conflicting surveys now indicated that the seawater tunnel might be 800 millimetres (31.5 inches) out of alignment. BSC/DL had put up a spare crane in Junk Bay to carry out trial erections of the masts so that,

Above and overleaf:

Wrenching the giant trusses into alignment.

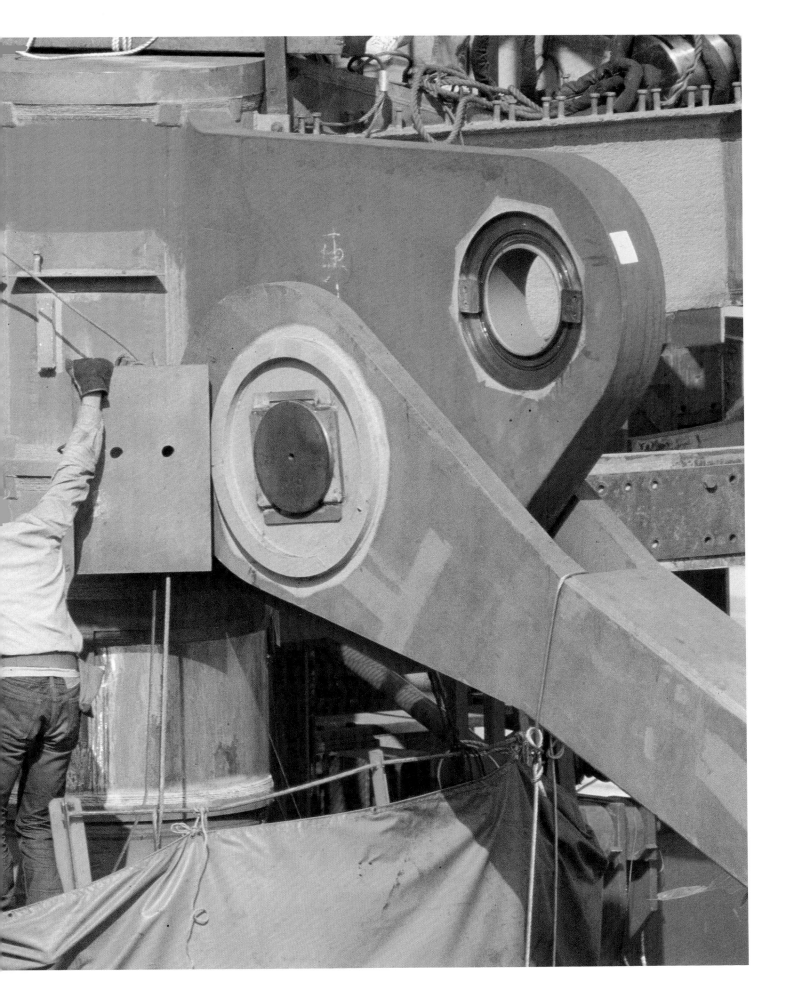

once on site, the job would run more easily. With the relaxation of tolerances, the actual steel erection was coming off the critical path. Now it was the application of the cementitious barrier coat – CBC – to the steel that was becoming the new threat to progress.

Three parts sand, one part cement, mixed with aggregate, a polymer and water, CBC had to be sprayed on to the steel in two 6 millimetre (0.25 inch)-thick layers to provide corrosion protection. The whole process was extremely messy. Before the CBC could be applied the steel had to be grit-blasted clean. CBC got in the eyes and in the hair. It caught up lumps and trapped dirt on to the steel, and it was extremely difficult to control on corners and in tight intersections.

The problems with CBC had already been responsible for many of BSC/DL's difficulties in zone three. It was impossible to erect steel, or to weld, while CBC was being applied near by. For reasons which remain obscure, the sub-contract for CBC had not been let until February 1983, seven months late, and a month after BSC/DL had started on site. Actual applications had not begun until 1 April. Consequently, there had been no time for the sub-contractor to carry out a second stage of development trials before CBC had to be applied in full production – and in enormous haste – on the job. It was only now that standards of quality control and acceptance were being determined. When the idea for CBC was conceived, it was envisaged that the vast bulk of the steel for the building would be sprayed before it was delivered to the site. Now it was not only around the joints (welded on site and needing corrosion protection) that CBC had to be applied on site, there and then, under plastic shrouds, but to many other areas of the structure as well. How could Cupples possibly start putting their pristine cladding on the building, with all this dirt and muck flying around?

Then a glimmer of light. Sometime after midnight on 12 November, the first module was lifted into position. A gleaming sealed stainless steel container, it came in under police escort, on a specially developed low trailer from Oklahoma, along a route where all the overhanging signs had been removed. At the factory, they had only experimented with slings to lift the modules. Now the first one was slotted into the structure within an hour. There were problems of course. The next day Fleetwood reported that twenty items of contention existed, on flushing water, pipework and fans.

Five days later, Archer is hoping that the modules for zone three will be installed by the second week of December. There are problems with service connections which are out of level. But looking again at the critical path, could Cupples be persuaded to accelerate their start on site from 1 February by almost a month? 'Whatever the new programme,' Thompson says, looking around the table at the members of the Project Management Committee, 'this is IT. Completion date is two years from today.'

26 October 1983: the excavation of the seawater tunnel that will bring water from the harbour to cool the air-conditioning system.

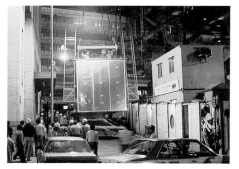

12 November 1983: the first module is hoisted up on to the site.

Monday, 12 December 1983: the first quarterly review assembles in the Bank's temporary boardroom, a huge room high in the Admiralty Centre, overlooking the harbour. Over the weekend, Norman Foster, Jack Zunz, Deryck Thornley from J Roger Preston and Leslie Sallabank from Wimpey International had flown into Hong Kong from London: so too had senior vice-presidents from Cupples, directors from BSC/DL and John Fletcher, a young, energetic third-generation steelman from Trafalgar House. Others came from Dragages, HMT Consort and Otis. They arrived at the meeting accompanied by their Hong Kong heads of operation.

That day it was the steel contractors who were seated opposite Trevor Bedford. Not over the erection – they were working twenty-four hours a day, seven days a week and making up time – but over the application of CBC. It was taking far longer than anyone had anticipated; if Morceau, the fire protection people, could not get on site to wrap the masts in ceramic fibre blanket soon, they would stop Cupples dead in their tracks. In any case, Cupples dared not start on site because of the mess. HMT dared not open the modules to correct faulty connections for fear that the expensive internal finishes would be ruined. As Frank Archer put it, half of Central District was covered in grit blast and CBC.

The three days of the review were conducted using basic interrogatory techniques; one by one, the assembled sub-contractors were called upon to answer for their progress. In front of the assembled company, those from BSC/DL were asked to explain the reasons for their deficiencies.

'I'm not really interested in difficulty,' Thompson said slowly to Fletcher from Trafalgar House after he had heard what they had to say. 'As the client, I'm interested in overcoming problems. At the moment access for Cupples is a problem and a potential danger. How will you ensure – without excuses – that financial claims from Cupples will not be forthcoming?'

'We'll keep a photographic record,' said Fletcher.

Archer interrupted. The intervention was deliberately challenging, and delivered with characteristic heat: 'It will be a record of failure. Total failure! Every programme ever submitted is behind – sometimes they're behind even before they're submitted!'

'Rubbish!' exploded Fletcher. 'We will keep a photographic record that *will show* exactly where Cupples are able to work on site!'

Archer was calling for an alternative to CBC to provide corrosion protection for the steel. At a meeting the next day with Ove Arup and BSC/DL, the alternatives were rehearsed. There were none. They had to resolve the problem by the end of the week? By now it was Wednesday. BSC/DL put more men on the job.

Protecting the steel against corrosion. Spraying the cementitious barrier coat (CBC) on site under shrouds.

221

Shortly before the quarterly review, Mead had realised that according to the current programme zone three of the building ought to be finished by September 1985. The installation of the modules was running smoothly at the rate of two every night. Cupples had agreed to accelerate their start on site. After a meeting of the PMC he took Archer aside. 'Come up to the office,' he said. Thompson went with them. 'Surely we can do something about a phased handover to the Bank,' Mead said.

'I think we can,' Archer conceded. 'So long as nobody screws it up.'

'What kind of date do you have in mind?'

'The date I'd like to see,' said Archer,' is July 1st, 1985 – because that's when we said we'd do it.'

A day or two before the quarterly review Mead put forward the proposal. 'We need to address the proposition of bringing the completion date forward,' he told the consultants. 'What about 1 July 1985?' In vain did someone point out that the lift motor rooms, fire pumps and standby turbines needed to run the building would be located at the top. Three-quarters of the building's plant would need to be operational. Additional fire protection would have to be built into the staircases and risers, and the whole security system which was to be housed in level twenty-seven of the finished building rewired to suit a new temporary location. It really meant considerable extra work and even more acceleration to the programme.

Bedford, Thompson and Mead were implacable. 'It would be criminal to have the building standing empty until it is totally completed,' said Bedford. At the quarterly review, Sandberg introduced the suggestion to the assembled company: 'It is normal in Hong Kong for buildings to be completed ahead of schedule. People in Hong Kong do not understand overruns. The Bank wishes to consider partial occupation, on a zone by zone basis, that is, before November 1985.' The new target date, July One 1985 for the occupation of the banking hall and atrium, had entered the programme.

By Christmas 1983, zone three of the steelwork had been erected. The modules, the floors and the staircases had been installed in the first twelve levels of the building. The second level of suspension trusses at level twenty/twenty-one had been completed. Every day 300 tonnes of steel were arriving on site. At Junk Bay thousands of different sections of steelwork were arriving from fabrication plants all over the UK and being identified and prepared for erection. But this was as far as they had got. There were only eighteen months left before first occupation. As far as the inside of the building was concerned, there were still no plans.

Michael Sandberg, chairman of the Bank, on site with Ron Mead, and Frank Archer, December 1983.

Roy Munden and John Strickland on site, December 1983.

The history of relations between the Building Users' Requirements Group and Foster Associates during 1983 was not a happy one. BURG was determined that the design team should relate its problems to the fit-out norms with which the Bank was familiar. But the design team seemed unable to provide BURG with the information it needed to be able to take decisions, and appeared inconsistent and irresponsible with cost information. During the year the two had scarcely met face to face; and when they did it was only to deal with specific issues, like viewing a mock-up of the glazing system for the building or the layout of the banking hall, items that could not be confined to 'one side of A4 paper'. At the end of May, Gordon Graham, whose role on BURG, in any case, had been no more than to hold a watching brief, had left the Bank's camp and returned to work for Fosters; by September, he had given up regular residence in Hong Kong and had begun a programme of commuting from London for one week in every four. Chris Seddon, who was in charge of preparing the papers for the monthly meetings and received the minutes afterwards, bore the full brunt of BURG's broadsides for the architects.

In July, Roy Munden stepped down as secretary to the Project Policy Co-ordination Committee and took over the chair of BURG. There was, however, no relaxation of BURG's procedures. BURG checked and double-checked whatever facts and figures the architects put forward; it repeatedly compared costings presented for the building with those of standard Hong Kong developers' blocks. It berated Fosters for obfuscation, it recommended reductions in budgets set by the PPCC if it thought they were unreasonably high, and appeared to begrudge any approval. BURG's remit was to make recommendations on all items that would affect the Bank's use of the building: from floor finishes to lighting, from fire protection systems to floor layouts, food hoists, communication systems, furniture, doors, locks, signs, lavatories. By the end of 1983, it had considered reports from the architects on eighty-three detailed aspects of the building. It went into them all in painstaking detail. Report after report was thrown out. Progress was despairingly slow.

There was still no agreement as to how the building as a whole should be arranged and used. For much of the year BURG and the architects operated on the basis that the Bank would occupy about 80 per cent of the building itself; but levels thirteen to nineteen in zone four of the building, some 18,600 square metres (200,000 square feet), were probably to be let. By the end of the year this had changed: Sandberg decided the Bank would take the whole building. Gradually some facilities had become agreed. BURG had settled, for example, the capacities of the kitchens and dining facilities, but not where it wanted them. A conference room had been located on level twenty. But until a stacking plan for the building could be agreed, dozens of decisions with unexpected implications for the construction programme remained to be taken.

In the summer, BURG had allocated the responsibility for procuring the furniture for the building to Group Methods Research (GMR). RJ Mead was to handle the letting of the contract; Fosters were not to be involved except to advise GMR on the technical aspects of its design. GMR had always been on the sidelines of the Bank's briefing of the architects; it was the department of the Bank that was traditionally responsible for O & M studies and for testing and advising the Bank on new equipment. By 1983, GMR had, for example, tested all the personal computers on the market to see which, if any, would suit the Bank. They were the people who would specify the telephone system for the building, and be intimately involved in the design of areas needing special equipment, like the foreign exchange dealers' room. Specifying furniture was, however, inextricably bound up with the planning of the layout of the building. Late in October BURG instructed Clint Marshall, the head of GMR, to set up a new working committee to work with the architects to determine the floor layouts of the new building and to sweep up the smaller items needed for the interior. By now Munden's good personal relationship with the Foster team was beginning to ease the tension between the design team and BURG. He went and had a long talk with Marshall. The creation of the new committee marked a turning point.

Talkative, a great enthusiast, Clint Marshall was hard-headed and thick-skinned. He held few illusions about either the Bank or Fosters. At the second meeting of the new 1 Queen's Road Central working committee in early November, discussion turned to an item on signs for the building. Chris Seddon had written to the Bank enclosing an outline budget for the sky-sign that was to be mounted at the top of the building. The figures totalled HK$5 million; HK$1.5 million of this was for the support of the external fascia. 'This is bloody amazing!' exploded Marshall as he stared at the figures. He sat back. 'Perhaps an alternative fixing method might be worth consideration and evaluation by a suitably qualified consultant?' His tone was mocking.

'Might I suggest a method I have used with success in the past? As a gesture of goodwill I will even pay for the necessary hardware out of my own pocket.' He held out his hand to Seddon. 'Allow me to present these two six-inch nails, at a total cost of fifty cents, to Foster Associates, with the compliments of GMR.'

The arrangement of the banking hall counters.

The layout of the banking hall back-up services.

That evening, the Foster team debated how they could make an adequate reply. Two weeks later, the meeting returned to the item on signs. Ian Davidson spoke for Fosters. 'The team have now completed their design solution, based on your goodwill gesture at the last meeting,' he said to Marshall. He handed him a Perspex cube. Inside was suspended one of the nails, now plated in gold. Marshall collapsed with laughter. When he recovered, he duly thanked Fosters for their extra '15 per cent'. It was the incident that broke the ice. Finally a team from the Bank had united with a team from the architects. From now on, whenever any member of the working party made a *faux-pas*, such as the time when Davidson tried to excuse an error by saying he had never designed a bank before 'although he felt confident he could probably manage it', he or she was awarded 'the nail'.

The composition of Marshall's committee changed over time, but generally consisted of Seddon, Nelson and Davidson from Fosters; Eddie Wang from Marshall's own department, who was put in charge of the office planning; Dick Watts, the building's new manager from HS Property Management; David Rigg from J Roger Preston; and representatives from the Bank's security department, the Hong Kong office and R J Mead. The committee quickly established itself as an intermediary between the architects and BURG; from now on no representations were to be made to BURG until they had been checked and dealt with in this forum. Away from the committees, the personnel from GMR and those at Fosters began to make real progress on the planning of the building. From now on, the papers presented to BURG gained much more ready acceptance; credibility and mutual respect began to be restored.

By now so much research had already been done into the workings of the Bank's departments, their space and furnishing requirements, that GMR had an uphill task gaining departmental co-operation. Planning a building at this level is intensely academic, detailed and dry. After the failure of Spencer de Grey's early attempt to arrive at a satisfactory stacking plan for the building, the Quickborner team had been brought back to Hong Kong in September 1982. The team analysed the Bank's existing workstations in terms of job functions (twenty-six different job categories from managers, to dealers, interviewers, clerical workers, tellers, etc., were identified) and had established space requirements, descending from 43.1 square metres (464 square feet) for an assistant general manager to 7.3 square metres (78.6 square feet) for a typist, for each role. These space requirements, but not the categorisation, had been accepted by the Bank. GMR now prepared its own set of 'integrated data sheets' to classify who among the 3,800 Bank staff did what. It took two months just to debate what information was required about each person, their relations within a department, and with other people in the building. This information was to lead them to decisions on how much, of which kinds of furniture they needed. By November, they had arrived at a preliminary brief for the furniture for each category of workplace.

As the detailed planning of the building began in earnest, the Bank began to discover that there were indeed limits to its flexibility. If, for example, a room in the building had to be specially fire-rated, say for computers or files, fire barriers had to be dropped down into the raised floors. Because of the arrangement of floor loadings, heavy cabinets could not be located near escalators, or near the edge of the atrium. In order to give everyone the maximum share of natural daylight and views, it was agreed that cellular offices should be sited 'inboard' in the building. The locations of the masts and the vierendeels affected the layout; so did the perimeter grilles in the floor, for the return of air into the air-conditioning system. At a more prosaic level, it was sensible to locate groups of female staff near female lavatories, and so on. Everything had to be laid out within the 1,200-millimetre (48-inch) grid used to plan the building – partition walls had to be hung from the ceilings, and services located according to this grid. All the time, however, Marshall, Wang and his team had to be aware of the dangers of putting huge numbers of staff into a vast 2,000-square metre (21,500-square foot) space – especially in the double-height floors – without making the layout look like that of a factory.

None of this could be achieved without general departmental uproar. It took a minimum of two weeks, and a dedicated series of meetings and consultations, to arrive at plans for a single department from which Fosters and J Roger Preston could produce working drawings for the sub-contractors. The process continued throughout 1984. They programmed a computer-aided design system. Eddie Wang set out one floor at a time. Plans would be presented to departments for comment. Departments would erupt in tumult. They would prepare their own plans, overriding the principles for planning the building, and specifying partitions where they could not be mounted. Munden would then intervene to tell GMR that departmental wishes must be accommodated, and remind managers that they must not be unreasonable. All the time, as they planned, the sizes of some departments kept growing, while in others the managers changed. It required endless patience, and they did not have much time.

BURG had been as taken aback as the design team at the PPCC's insistence that the occupation of the building should take place nearly six months earlier than anticipated. Now, as it continued to examine details of the interior it began to plan to release properties that the Bank had rented, and the practicalities of moving into the building.

Meanwhile, down on the site, the building appeared to have developed a life of its own. Men and their tools were dwarfed by the scale of the construction. The six giant red cranes mounted on the masts, alternately lifting and lowering, turned the structure into a kind of gigantic kinetic sculpture. One day, the tops of the masts would be seen to be so high. The next morning, they had risen further and two more modules had been slotted in. By the turn of 1984 the slow learning process on the first zone of the steelwork was beginning to pay benefits.

Late 1983: positioning a cross brace.

April 1984: fixing fire protection to a hanger.

The masts in 'turkey-wrap'.

Overleaf:

April 1984: the state of the seawater tunnel.

The erection teams had mastered their task. Welding on each mast was falling into a routine. The rate of production was superb, the quality exceptional. The application of the corrosion protection continued. They were making up time.

At night, beneath floodlights mounted on the underside of each crane, scenes of the site had the atmosphere of some kind of undercover operation. Outsize lorries flanked by police outriders delivered secret cargoes, which were hoisted silently on to the site, and bolted into place by men in hard hats. The sequence worked like clockwork. The programme for lifting the modules was slotted into the craneage times for the steel: two every night between midnight and 6 am, one zone every three weeks. During the day, the operations to fireproof the steel masts were becoming obvious. First a layer of stainless steel mesh was strapped tightly around the structure. Strands of the mesh were bent back and a thin, flexible layer of ceramic fire blanket was secured to them. Not long before Christmas, it had become clear that unless the blanket was protected it would be hopelessly damaged. A further wrapping of all steel members in a reinforced aluminium foil was specified. 'Turkey wrap' (in honour of the season) would provide temporary protection from construction damage; more importantly, it would also prevent any fibres in the blanket from breaking off and infiltrating the air-conditioning system: the gap between the cladding and the structure formed part of the return air system for the air-conditioning for the building.

Below ground, the seawater tunnel, 7 metres (23 feet) in diameter, that had been driven through solid bedrock for 350 metres, more than 1,000 feet, broke through beneath the site from the harbour. Now it could be lined with concrete, prior to taking the pipes that would bring the cooling seawater to the main refrigeration system. In the basement levels themselves, a concrete finish of exceptional quality, the result of more than two years' research and development, was being achieved. A year before, three months of trials had been carried out to secure the right proportions of its ingredients – Japanese cement, washed Pearl River sand, and Hong Kong aggregate – to arrive at just the degree of smoothness and uniform pale grey finish that would survive in the humidity of the Hong Kong climate. Fosters had wanted to mix the concrete on site, where they could monitor the quality control, but as there was no room they had settled on a location twenty minutes away. On site, the concrete was poured into plywood formwork made of beech and coated with resin, imported from Finland. Such care was taken to protect the smoothness of the formwork that the carpenters working on the ply were issued with plimsolls, and each area was covered with polystyrene, which was removed only just before concreting began.

Such was the public face of the progress on the construction of the Hongkong Bank. Behind the scenes, however, things moved fast and problems dominated, as the almost daily progress meetings showed:[1]

229

Tuesday, 10 January 1984: The weather on site has now been good for over two months. Substantial handover of zone three by the steel contractors is expected to take place immediately after Chinese New Year. But – the tenders received for the new ceiling system are HK$8 million over budget. Specifications will have to be reduced.

Frank Archer is hoping that Cupples will be able to start cladding the masts this week. But access is seriously restricted, and when it rains CBC [the cementitious barrier coat] streams down the modules. If the stainless steel of the modules is becoming streaked what is going to happen to the polymer finish on the cladding?

Monday, 16 January: Cupples arrive on site. They are having trouble with the fixing brackets; it is only the brackets that the Building Ordinance Office is worried about.

Monday, 13 February: Cupples have lost twelve days due to holidays. Since 16 January? They can't put all that time down to Chinese New Year. They have had problems accommodating the fire protection, and problems with the fixing brackets; there was a dimensional error during manufacture on the tapering mast sections at level four. CBC is still a mess. Archer wants to throw the sub-contractor off the job. The erectors from Cupples had to stop work because CBC was being sprayed on above their heads: it wasn't safe. 'Whenever it rains,' Archer says, 'we're dead.'

Thursday, 16 February: 31 out of 36 modules for zone four have been installed; 80 out of 140 risers are in. HMT Consort are ahead of programme. But the interface between the ductwork on the modules and risers is not working well; HMT's ducts are not in the right place to marry up with the sub-floor services now being installed! Incorrect ductwork is now being remanufactured in Hong Kong. J Roger Preston are having a terrible job redesigning, and amending; as a result of the same error, Fosters are having to redesign the floors.

The good weather is continuing. But cladding is now clearly on the critical path. The rainy season is coming. They have *got* to get the curtain wall up in zone three. Whatever happens, they are going to need temporary protection: more tarpaulins must be ordered.

Wednesday, 7 March: 08.30. Archer is determined to make the Project Management Committee consider alternatives to CBC, especially inside the building and at the top. A long, complex and depressing discussion about the relative merits and problems of the known fireproofing materials – Emaco, Carbomastic, and SBD, a kind of Italian concrete – ensues. Finally, one of the representatives from John Lok/Wimpey had had enough.

'If all the intelligence on this job cannot get us over this one,' he said, 'we have a problem.'

July 1984: cladding being mounted on a vierendeel.

The glass floor proposed for the plaza during lighting tests, November 1982.

'It's all the intelligence on the job that got us *into* the problem,' says Mead.

John Lok/Wimpey have to concede. CBC will be used on all external work.

Thursday, 8 March: Early completion of the building: the glass floor for the plaza is the problem. The Bank has decided that in addition to zone three it also wants to move into the first level of the basement, which has always been seen either as a lower banking hall, with a public concourse and access to the safe deposit vaults, or as a typical office floor. All is well, the glass for the floor passes all the tests, the chairman especially is very keen on it. But the joints are still not guaranteed 100 per cent against leaks. Technically, Foster Associates still have a further six months of development work to do. 'We did say that design should not prejudice the decision to hand over early,' says Mead.

'The problem is that if the Bank need BL 1,' says Archer, 'we will have to give them a floor slab on the plaza. The glass floor will not be ready in time.'

'Kill any ideas of temporary waterproofing as an option will you?' offers Fitzpatrick from Ove Arup. 'What about giving them access over the work platform?'

'You don't have much time,' warns Thompson. 'The chairman is talking about making a statement about July One next week. Maybe a press conference. Can we decide now?'

'You must warn the chairman about what the public will think,' says Fleetwood. 'Everyone will be able to look down from the banking hall into a work site.'

'The chairman', declares Thompson, 'is going to announce July One next week as sure as God made little apples – and tell everyone to work backwards to achieve a solution!'

Saturday, 10 March: The glass floor is out. Fosters say there is no reason why they cannot telescope the work that remains to be done in the time, but HS Property Management cannot afford to take the risk that it might not work. Three years of design work is thrown away in a day. Sandberg's own reaction, expressed to the PPCC, was equally bitter: 'Three years of design work and they *still* can't get it right!' The PPCC orders a stone ground floor.

Monday, 26 March: The good weather is holding. Site progress is satisfactory. The chairman has not issued a press release yet. It is going to be just possible to put down a stone slab floor in time for the advanced completion. HH Robertson, the sub-contractors for the raised floor system, are mobilised and training their crews, ready to start on site April 2nd.

Meanwhile, BURG has approved a block section of the building showing the size and location of each department, and samples of furniture supplied by tenderers are on view for comment in a godown in Quarry Bay. In February, work had begun on installing the main plant in the basement. The steel had been erected up to the level of the third suspension trusses, twenty-nine storeys above ground. By the end of the month, the first escalator had been lifted into position, on programme. By the middle of March, Dragages had reached the bottom of the basements and had completed the slab. Two weeks later, John Lok/Wimpey reported that approval of drawings by the design team was improving, but that the programmes remained extremely tight. Outstanding design items include carpets and floor finishes for the building, which have only just been approved by BURG. But decisions are awaited on surfaces for the refuge terraces before details can be finalised and – on the back-up wall, a subject with a long and complex history.

In the first designs for the curtain wall back in the summer of 1981, Fosters had specified reflective mirror glass for the building: it was the pragmatic answer to cutting down heat gain in a building with so much glazed walling, but not a concept that appealed to Foster. Six months later, inspection of a Cupples mock-up confirmed his dislike for the mirrored effect. The glass had been manufactured: but not yet coated. Talks with the Bank showed that they agreed. A clear glass wall would go on to the outside of the building.

22 September 1983: after the rejection of the Corning glass solution for the window glazing, testing venetian blinds at Tsing Yi island.

The architects' task was then to find a system to put behind the glass wall that would cut down heat gain to the point where it would not interfere with the levels of air-conditioning that had been specified for the building and which were then being built into the modules. Some kind of double-glazed zone, containing 'high performance solar-controlled louvres' or more simple blinds? They experimented with Koolshade, fine metal screening, like a miniature woven Venetian blind, used behind glass in display cases. The trouble was that in big areas looking through Koolshade was like looking through stockings. They considered vertical panels that were half clear glass, and half translucent shoji glass. At last the solution had seemed near at hand: Corning Glass were commissioned to develop a special translucent glass, along the lines of some 1950s samples in their glass museum, which allowed clear vision through at various angles. Just in case things went wrong, however, Cupples had been called. Did they still have that stock of uncoated mirror glass? Would they hang on to it, just in case?

Late in August 1983, Sandberg and the members of BURG and the PPCC had visited Tsing Yi Island, where Cupples had mounted their Hong Kong training rigs, to inspect a mock-up of the Corning glass wall. The delegates from the Bank did not like it. On 23 September, Corning glass had been removed from the specifications. Cupples were instructed to change the Corning glass to one with a mild grey tint to reduce glare, to stand behind the clear glass wall of the building. To further reduce heat gain they would use blinds inserted between the two layers of glazing to shade the interior. Now, in March 1984, the blinds are about to go out to tender. But, the members of the Project Management Committee wondered as they looked at the estimated cost: did the Bank really need them on the north face of the building? They took them out.

On Monday, 2 April, the chairman and executive directors were shown proposals for the treatment of the boardroom, chairman's office and other executive areas to be located on levels thirty-four and thirty-five. They did not like any of them; could they have alternatives from the team by the 6th? In the same week, members of the board attended a briefing at Fosters' office in Fairmount House to see the materials and colours to be used to finish the building – on the walls, and for the carpets. Foster was describing the lighting using a drawing of a cross-section of the atrium. As was his habit in the office, Foster referred to the glazed soffit of the plaza, as it had always been called in dealings with the Bank, as the glazed underbelly of the building. The cry went up: 'Glazed underbelly? What glazed underbelly?' In vain were drawings produced to show that this had been part of the design since 1982 and that it had been endorsed by BURG the previous June. If this was the solution for enclosing the bottom of the banking hall, the board now said, it would not do. Could they not glaze-in the plaza? As a result Mead now needed to see the Deed of Dedication, and three sketches showing three new options. Fosters warned that they would have to do a new wind study for any new option.

Spring 1983: 1:84 model showing the glass floor and an early version of the structure for the 'underbelly' of the building.

Thursday, 12 April: The good news is that two modules went up last night in zone five. Everything else is bad. Eight modules have been built to significantly different details from those approved. JR Preston are to go through it all 'with a practical eye'. Cupples are having trouble with zone four. The materials they need are not in Hong Kong because the warehouse is full of zone three material. 'This cannot be allowed to become a problem!' exclaims Mead. 'There are eight weeks to be recovered! Don't you realise we are living on borrowed time?'

Ryoden/Mitsubishi, the people who are supplying the sub-floor services, cannot get into the building for another two weeks because of the chaos. The mess in the building is something to behold: full of dust, full of rubbish. Twenty men won't touch it.

By Monday, 7 May, Mead has met the Public Works Department about the underbelly: any question of enclosing the plaza with glass is out. The glazed underbelly stays. By 9 May, the chairman had approved the boardroom plans, and the remainder of levels thirty-four and thirty-five. On site, they were still having problems making the building

weathertight so that the underfloor services could be installed. By 11 May the situation in zone two, the first basement level (BL1 and the rest of the underside of level three), was becoming critical. This was where all the pipes and tubes coming down from the risers met (or rather, at that time, were failing to meet) the main plant installation. Random piles inserted underneath the annexe to support it while the building was being erected had proved impossible to extract. As a result, the service risers on the west side of zone three could not be run straight down the side of the building into the basement to connect with the plant, but would have to turn an extra corner. Design information was required within the week. Meanwhile, Archer was in bed with pneumonia:

Monday, 14 May: Mead reports that he has informed the chairman that the last steel will leave England on the 1st of June, to arrive on 6 July. A task force, headed by Ken Shuttleworth, has been formed to deal with the servicing problems in zone two.

Monday, 11 June: 9 am In the Bank's boardroom in Admiralty Centre, the third quarterly review begins. Water has entered the modules. HMT are instructed to put the damage right, and weatherproof effectively. Otis are having labour problems on the high-rise escalator that will run up from the plaza to the banking hall, in Germany. The PPCC is very concerned about the amount of design still outstanding.

The site is a fire trap – it is horrendously dangerous. Foster protests that the building is not a shell to be fitted out. He castigates the sub-contractors. 'Finished work is being subject to the ravages of building work and weather. Protection is critical.' 'Norman's got it right,' says Archer.

Should a typhoon strike though, everyone knows it will be even worse. There is no way they can make the building watertight. Water will flood down the hoists, and damage finished work. The added danger is the amount of damage there could be all around the site. If someone is killed, it will stop the job. 'I hope to hell we're lucky,' mutters Bedford.

Ten days later two large sheets of glass shattered as they fell on to cross bracing. On Sunday, 24 June, they had their first close brush with a typhoon since finished materials started to go into the building. Fortunately only polythene and cardboard were blown into Queen's Road. Meanwhile, driving rain has been getting between the Cupples panels and the firewalls on the lift shafts. John Lok/Wimpey are looking for protection on both faces of the material, inside and outside the shafts. Decadex costs HK$97 a square metre – supply only(!). Can they use something else? Silicone epoxy? Bubblewrap? Cardboard? Foam? Quickly!

Monday, 2 July: Cupples now have 275 men on site. Confusion over the whereabouts of some of their materials is causing a hold-up. The outer sunscoop is threatened by a two-month delay. Levett & Bailey will not commit to a pre-tender estimate of its cost. If the PPCC wants an assurance on price information, they say, it will have to come from potential sub-contractors. Chris Seddon at Fosters is keen to start discussions with the authorities as soon as possible on the pavements and services work to be done by the government in Queen's and Des Voeux Roads, so that all the work can be finished by July One – in just one year's time.

Tuesday, 3 July: BURG is trying to clarify the procedure whereby the building will be handed over to HSPM. The layouts for level forty-three are disappointing and more private dining space is needed in the building. Munden tells GMR that the block layouts for the building are 'very tight'. With the expected expansion of some departments it might be necessary to extensively rearrange or relocate departments. This is clearly unacceptable. Can GMR investigate alternatives?

Monday, 9 July: The number 3 signal went up yesterday. This time the sub-contractors were better off the mark. At the Project Management Committee, Gifford Carey of Levett & Bailey presented the cost report. He said that delays this month had cost HK$40 million.

'Sounds cheap,' said Mead. 'So that means we're spending HK$100 million a month?'

Monday, 16 July: Dock strikes in Europe. A seamen's strike in Germany is threatening to delay the escalators by six to fourteen days. Okay, say John Lok/Wimpey, fly them out. In the UK, five containers of Otis equipment are stuck in Liverpool docks. Can they shift the lifts they already have around?

'You may well find things will be tied up for several months,' Thompson says. It is Thatcher versus the unions: a fight to the death.

Thursday, 19 July: The quarterly review. HMT's progress in checking thousands of small items has improved, but Cupples are four or five weeks late in zone four. After the day was over Thompson turned to Mead. 'Let's record it, Ron. We've all been in a state of tension. Now I'm getting into a state of alarm. The Bank will have to put things into the building after the opening.'

'I think it's the mechanics we have to deal with,' said Archer. 'What I need from you is the commitment to get the men and the money to complete on time. What does crisis management mean?'

'I've never said you shouldn't take action in a crisis,' said Mead with a grin. 'If something has to be done, it has to be done.'

'If that's the case,' said Archer, 'I think you've just given us a mandate to complete by July 1st.'

April 1984: fixing the glazing between double height truss mullions.

Overleaf:

July 1984.

237

26 June 1984: the highest excalator, the last of fifty, being lowered into the structure.

June 1984: connecting the final truss diagonal at the top of the building.

Laying concrete screed on the floors.

It was the end of the road for any more slippage on the programme. There was less than a year to go before the Bank wanted to move into its new headquarters. No more rearrangements of the programme would help. If the building was to be ready by July One, everyone on site would have to make up any delays they currently had. With the best will in the world, Cupples did not expect to be back on their programme until October. Trevor Bedford and Tony Braddon, the man at John Lok/Wimpey who was responsible for co-ordinating the worldwide production to meet the programme, now instigated a series of visits to the headquarters of the various sub-contractors around the world to check that progress was in fact being made to the Bank's requirements.

Braddon, dubbed the International Leg-Biter from similar visits he and Bedford had already made, was big and bluff, an ex-Sapper, well dressed, slightly lame. He carried a silver-topped cane. Bedford and Braddon's strategy was well rehearsed. Unwitting sub-contractors were sent a telex warning them to expect a visit from the chairman of the PPCC within the next twenty-four hours. Upon arrival Bedford would open the discussion. 'The chairman of the Bank, to whom I report, is very concerned about the state of this sub-contract,' he would say:

'This is the most prestigious building going up in the world today. Unless you want your name associated with the failure to deliver the building on time, it is of paramount importance that you do not let John Lok/Wimpey down on your performance. I am here to report on the situation I find to the next meeting of the Bank's board.'

Then he would hand over to Braddon. Braddon would then take the sub-contractors – Cupples, HMT Consort, Otis or any of the others – step by step through their programme, asking detailed questions about production and delivery, and giving them a list of requirements. The success of the process – it invariably produced results – was entirely due to the eye-to-eye confrontation at senior level. In the course of the next year Braddon would fly three-quarters of a million miles.

By now, the state of the site was massively complex, and alive with men. Over 2,500 people were working for up to thirty different sub-contractors. Inside, the atmosphere was hot, steamy, dusty; the light was dim. The spaces around the temporary latrines stank. Like the men, the metal surfaces glistened with sweat in the damp humidity. Crowds of workers jammed the hoists all day long; queues formed to take the rubbish down and out of the site. There were limits to the number of deliveries, skips and lorries that could be accommodated at the base of the site. Archer was calling for additional hoists, more shifts of clean-up gangs. Site safety was a major preoccupation. Regular safety meetings were held with each sub-contractor, inspections were carried out daily and a dedicated site safety crew was constantly on patrol. The measures were paying off. In July, severe tropical storm Betty was successfully weathered.

17/18 September 1984: the complexity of installing the plaza escalators.

September 1984: putting down the raised floor panels.

Towards the end of June the highest escalators had been craned up, and into level thirty-five. The structural steel was still being erected by the cranes at the top of the building. Below, staircases and floors were being installed. Cocoons of green tarpaulins disguised the CBC operations. Between the gleaming stacks of modules, scaffolds of bamboo served as temporary work platforms and green safety netting shrouded the sides of the building. But lower down, in zone three, where Cupples had clad the structure and installed the glass curtain wall, signs of the finished building were beginning to emerge.

By the end of July, Cupples had noticeably improved their performance. Zone three had been effectively sealed. Items like the canopies over the entrances to the lift lobbies on the plaza had now been designed in conjunction with Fosters. The next step was to prepare detailed drawings before manufacture. One hundred and thirty-two out of 139 modules were in. Otherwise, not a single floor of one riser was yet satisfactorily complete. HMT Consort's work was spread out all over the building. The ground and basement levels were proving astonishingly complex. There was a mass of detailed co-ordination work still to be done between the builders' work at plaza level and the sub-contractors' work below ground. Was it really feasible to complete this level by July One?

There was an even more alarming problem. Naka/C Itoh were the Japanese sub-contractors who had won the contract to supply most of the interior 'fit-out' of the building: the steel ceilings, wall panels, demountable partitions, face panels, doors and coverings for the internal beams. They were due to start on site in December, a little more than six months before the deadline of July One. Except that the joints between the components would not have to be watertight, the package rivalled that of Cupples in its scale and complexity. It required, for example, more than 78,000 square metres (840,000 square feet) of ceiling alone. Now, one of four prototypes that would be needed to test the ceiling system had failed to match the installation tolerances which had been specified. There would be no time to rectify such problems on site. It had to be rebuilt and approved again.

The Naka programme was impossibly tight. The contract had been let less than six months earlier, in March, a full fourteen months behind schedule. The delay was a casualty of the change in control of the project. The PPCC had taken over responsibility for the project shortly after tenders for the gull-wing ceiling system had been sent out. At the same time, Fosters had opened negotiations for the contract for the face panels, doors and demountable partitions which were to be integrated with the design of the gull-wing ceiling with HH Robertson, who were also manufacturing the raised floors in the building. When the tenders for the gull-wing ceiling came in at the end of 1982, however, they were not only judged to be too high, but, by this time, the Bank had decided that the grid decreed by the gull-wing for partitioning was on too large a scale. The gull-wing was out.

6 February 1984: the state of the basements.

By this time as well, the PPCC had issued instructions that future sub-contracts were to be neither negotiated nor let on the basis of design development. The architects were instructed to specify a conventional ceiling, preferably one out of a catalogue, and an integrated system for the walls, face panels, doors and demountable partitions that would be let on the basis of a lower budget, in a series of separate packages. Talks with HH Robertson, who now refused to tender, ceased. In the early spring of 1983, Fosters had begun to design a complete system, but the first of the packages had not been ready to tender until August, and the last not until November.

When the final bids came in, in the New Year of 1984, the three lowest figures nearly matched those for the gull-wing ceiling alone: they were more than 30 per cent over the PPCC's budget figure. Negotiations continued daily, as Fosters, John Lok/Wimpey and Levett & Bailey worked to simplify details, and reduce specifications. Competition between the three contenders was fierce. It had only been four months ago, in March, that the first package had been awarded to Naka/C Itoh, a consortium formed between Naka, manufacturers of custom-designed architectural components (they had, incidentally, supplied the WC components for the modules), and C Itoh, a house of financiers. The first ceilings were required in Hong Kong in December, the face panels and doors by early January. Now, they had to remake the ceiling prototype, prepare the others, finalise design details, get into production, train a site crew and get the stuff to Hong Kong. A task force under David Nelson was instructed to get to Japan and clear the design problems – fast.

Sunday, 26 August: Bad problems, all below ground. Basement blockwork is having to be demolished to accommodate the revised openings for the services descending from the risers on the west side of the building. The risers will not be finished for another month. Construction of structural blockwork in BL1 is delayed due to late design information. The heating and ventilation plant switchroom due to be handed to Hong Kong Electric on 1 July (last) is now being delayed until later this week, since the built design does not comply with Hong Kong Electric's requirements. HMT's overall progress has further deteriorated. There is still not one riser that is complete. Archer is warning that July One is in serious jeopardy.

Sunday, 9 September: Early in the morning, Gordon Graham and Frank Archer inspected the site. They worked from the top of the building down. At level ten, they walked into the atrium. The morning sun was shining in through the cathedral wall. The hoists had been removed, the scaffolding and green safety nets cleared away. The masts gleamed. For the first time it was possible actually to see what the atrium and the banking hall looked like. It was a fabulous moment. 'Look at it,' breathed Archer. 'Look at it. We've done it.' He was unable to keep down the enthusiasm. 'We've done it! We've done it! It looks just like the model! We've done it!'

The state of the atrium, spring 1984.

Sunday, 30 September: The main structural steelwork is finished. Fire protection is proceeding satisfactorily. Cladding is going well.

Zone two is beginning to recover. The structural work required has been finished, the services are starting to go in. But Drake & Scull, the basement service sub-contractors, are entitled to claim a fourteen-week extension of time, caused by delays. Here now is *the* critical package. If the building is to be functioning by July One, the basement equipment has to be in, *tested* and *commissioned*, according to the current programme – no revised one will do.

More bad news. HMT are in serious trouble. The installation of the mass of pipework to couple the modules to the risers, and the risers to the underfloor services, continues at fault. Archer spelt out the situation: only 55 per cent of the riser work is complete. HMT have been engaged for nine months in reaching this stage. They have approximately twelve weeks left to complete to programme. They show no clear idea of how they can resolve their problems.

Thursday, 18 October: Practical completion of all the steelwork is declared. Much sundry work remains but, now that all the steel, modules and concrete of the floors are in place, the top of the main steel frame is lying no more than 12 millimetres [0.5 inch] west of the theoretical position at a height of 170 metres [558 feet] – 5 millimetres [0.2 inch] less than Arups' specification. It is a remarkable, and formidable achievement.

Sunday, 28 October: Eight months to go before July One. John Lok/Wimpey cannot contain the delays. BL2 is running six weeks late. They complain that decisions by the Bank and designs by the architects for the building layouts are still outstanding; they cannot get on with the works with the flexibility they require. They need to know *finally* how BL 1 is to be laid out and finished.

The details of the plaza floor construction are extremely complex. The floor will have to be built in time with the phased removal of the work platform, restricting access at ground level even further. Are these plans really going to work? Will the floor be watertight? They will not know until March 1985.

Design information for all levels of the basement MUST be frozen. HMT remain desperately behind. Despite the presence of 330 men and 60 supervisors, delays on their work seem to get longer each week that goes by. As for the rest:

Air-conditioning outlets: information not finalised.
Public address system: finalisation of design detail critical.
Fire detection & alarm system: ditto
Luminaires: ditto
General services: ditto . . . etc. etc.

Exterior progress, Autumn 1984.

Thursday, 1 November: The layout of BL1 is confirmed as frozen.

Wednesday, 14 November: Marshall reports to BURG that GMR are still having problems obtaining final layout approvals. Munden rules that if target dates are missed without final signed agreement by department heads, GMR is authorised to issue layout plans without further reference.

Wednesday, 21 November: In Tokyo, Trevor Bedford and Tony Braddon meet the heads of HMT Consort, MELCO and Takenaka to complain about HMT's alarming shortfalls in performance. Completion of the modules and risers in 1984 was now recognised as impossible. Now, if pressure testing of the hydraulic systems (a particularly bad area of HMT performance) was not completed by January, the whole job would miss the critical dates of 11–17 February when electric power throughout the building had to be turned on.

Friday, 23 November: There are 150 claims for delay and disruption. But Bedford and Braddon have come away from the meeting in Tokyo convinced that HMT have at last realised the gravity of the situation. The heads of each of the companies, HMT, MELCO and Takenaka, had formally rededicated their companies to achieving the Bank's goals and promised to achieve the required dates. 'We shall be able to tell better by the quarterly review in December how they intend to do so,' Bedford remarked cynically. But he knew the Japanese did not make such commitments lightly. 'In the meantime', he instructed, 'HMT must not be held up on any aspect of their work or I will be personally embarrassed – and bloody annoyed!'

The Bank has so far failed to meet every deadline for the departmental planning of zone three, JR Preston are having trouble contacting the correct Bank staff to get servicing and cabling information. The delay is prejudicing the wiring programme for zone three; if this is not met, Naka (who are due on site imminently to start the installation of ceilings and partition walls) will be disrupted. The Bank is planning to define its total requirements on a week-per-floor basis. With fifty departments to accommodate, the task is stupendous.

On 1 December 1984 there were seven months remaining until July One. Up until now, Frank Archer had been bullish. Come what may, they would meet the deadline. Braddon had been air-freighting essential parts of the building into Hong Kong, taking decisions to speed up the works wherever possible. But by the beginning of December, they could no longer work against what Archer described as the tide of late information coming from the Bank on how the building should be laid out, and, consequently, changing instructions from the architects. In zone three, sub-contractors at work on the fit-out were getting the information they needed just as they were programmed to start, or even after they were scheduled to complete a floor. John Lok/Wimpey were prepared, as Archer put it, 'to firefight' their way out of zone three, which would cost money; but they could not finish the whole building that way. Something had to give.

Wednesday, 12 December marked the final quarterly review before July One – six and a half months away. Fosters were in the hot seat over outstanding design information. July One was receding fast. Despite all the efforts being made to get ahead, the detailed design problems continued to increase. So far, the vehicle for clearing outstanding items had been Mead's weekly management sub-committee meeting. They no longer had this kind of time in hand. What were their alternatives?

Archer proposed that they should demolish the traditional divide between the contractors and the designers and create a multi-disciplinary team with executive authority to take design decisions on site. Archer's suggestion was quickly taken up by Foster; but others prevaricated. The PPCC wanted its answer in a week.

Over a lunch of sandwiches at Fairmount House, Foster put Archer's suggestion to the team. 'I feel very positive about this,' he said. 'Frank's coming round at two o'clock. What we need to do between now and then is talk about how we're going to do it.'

He went round the table taking suggestions. Fleetwood was against the idea. But others were in favour. 'Who has experience of a task force?'

Only two of the team: Ken Shuttleworth, who had headed the task force on the modules and zone two; and David Nelson, during the summer, in Japan on the Naka contract. Both had been taking charge of co-ordination problems with the management contractor and Arup for some time. Both knew Fosters' credibility was at stake. They put their hands up.

Foster turned to Fleetwood. 'Roy,' he said, 'I once said to you that you could have anything you liked to build this project.' He looked at Shuttleworth. 'Ken, I'm now saying to you: what do you need to build this project?'

'I need Nelson,' said Shuttleworth.

When Archer came round at the close of the lunch, he said to Foster, 'You know what we need here. It's people with enough guts, balls and clout to pull this thing off.'

'We're totally positive about it,' said Foster. 'We're going on site.'

'Good,' said Archer. 'I want pictures, not words. I want instant decisions on site, and people to deliver.'

Within half an hour two men each from John Lok/Wimpey, Arups, Prestons, R J Mead, and Shuttleworth and David Nelson from Fosters, had been given total authority by their organisations to run the job on site. At 2.30 pm these decisions were endorsed by the PPCC.

Ken Shuttleworth

David Nelson

April 1985: the installation of the interior sunscoop.

The task force was at work on site by 8 am the next morning. Archer got the construction headlines from three of his men: Don O'Neill, Richard Holyoak and Mansell Evans. Shuttleworth from Fosters compiled the list of items to be tackled, and allocated the tasks in an abstruse shorthand:[1]

'Palm tree holes for flag pole lights – OAP [Ove Arup & Partners] drawing to be issued . . . HK Telephone manhole. Action JRP and sort out . . . RJM to confirm night safe requirements . . . PA speaker for ceiling – Phillips to produce a workable speaker . . . riser panel support steelwork doesn't fit . . . sort out problems today.'

On the first day, the list came to forty items to be cleared. All verbal instructions were confirmed to the rest of the task force by telex – which now became (apart from the Architect's Instructions) the main form of communication on the project. Henceforth each Monday morning the list would be revised; items accomplished were crossed off, more jobs to do were added on.

All the members of the task force were determined to perform. Now that Foster's authority had been sanctioned by the PPCC, David Nelson and Ken Shuttleworth felt they had the power to get the job done. Absolute expediency was the order of the day. Shuttleworth and Nelson were the two members of the task force who had to sign every form and instruction. Because their knowledge of the project was complementary, their double act was highly competent and difficult to overrule. Shuttleworth and Nelson now wrote instructions without going to anyone, and put them directly into the hands of the contractors. They could order up, say, 300 metres of cable, three or four brackets, and temporary labour for scaffolding. They did drawings as the contractors stood there, signed them, and the work proceeded. Within a week, Shuttleworth's first list had doubled in length. 'JRP to produce scheme for TV aerial system . . . Ceiling sequence – setting out problem . . . currently all zone three sprinklers out of position . . .'[2] Hundreds of details needed attention. By the end of December, however, Archer was recording that 'very meaningful progress has been made'. The task was formidable, especially in the time. But there was no doubt that the task force was providing 'the necessary answers on a priority basis'.[3]

These priorities were safety first, and maintenance second. Any change for aesthetic reasons was crossed out. In honour of Archer's quarterly review appeal, they adopted the initials GBC (Guts, Balls and Clout) to distinguish their task force from others that had been formed on the project. They meant it. A split was widening in the Foster office. Up until now, all the stress had been put on achieving quality above all else; but those on the task force felt that some of the design team were now trying to achieve perfection in ridiculous places. The priority now, as Foster kept saying, was completion – not details like the colour of gaskets. A clear division was developing between those who were prepared to don boots and hard hats, go on site and sort out solutions there and then, and those who remained aloof at the drawing board, deploring these activities, which they said meant they were butchering the building.

Typical of the kind of problems they faced were clashes between items from one sub-contract package and another ('transformer room doors may be too small'), unfinished details ('details of concrete landings to stairs'), making up omissions ('level thirty-five canopy additional gyproc'), and preparations of instructions on further details ('FA to set up meetings on vault entrance locks'). Frequently decisions affected two or even three sub-contractors. The project's strict cost-control procedures were inevitably being compromised. Two categories of instructions were established. Those which had significant cost or programme effects were labelled category A and were considered daily and in detail by Levett & Bailey. The others had to be picked up later. In fact, it would soon be shown that 95 per cent of the task force's instructions had little cost effect.[4]

With the turn of the year, the construction programme had entered the period when the building would begin to be subjected to scrutiny by the authorities; services would begin to be commissioned and a series of staged handovers to the Bank planned. After the handover of zones one, two and three on July One, the rest of the building would be occupied floor by floor by the Bank. To meet these deadlines, it was to be handed over in four phases: zone four on 9 September, zone five on 7 October, zones six and seven on 28 October and the remainder of the building on 18 November. A presentation showing the staged withdrawal of the external contractor hoardings, temporary hoardings, hoists and reinstatement of the plaza between July One and 17 November was prepared.

For the past year, HS Property Management had been building up a staff of more than 100 people who would manage the building when it was completed. Dick Watts, the building manager, had been to Japan to be in on the testing of the gas-turbine generators for the building. He and others had visited Naka to understand the erection of the demountable partitions; they had kept a close eye on the construction. It was imperative, as Munden reiterated, that HSPM should be suitably trained and competent to operate the building when it was finished.

250

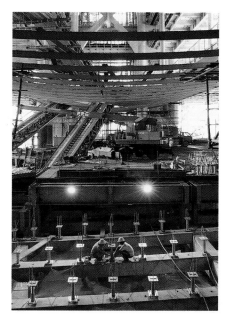

As details of the building's design were being finalised, BURG was renamed the 1QRC Relocation Committee in recognition of its changing role. Plans were made for 'someone senior' to fly to Turin to sign-off the production prototype for the banking hall counters so that production could begin. Talks commenced with *fung-shui* advisers on the most propitious dates to move the lions back to the front of the new Bank, and when to open for business. The opening date for banking operations had to dovetail with the state of the building, the *fung-shui* requirements and the practicalities of moving in. A programme for notifying customers of changes in the Bank's location was drawn up. The endless discussion and minutiae were exhausting. At its meeting on 10 January, a sample telephone handset was produced for the committee's review. A chorus of disgust was raised. 'The telephone was then thrown across the room,' the minutes recorded, 'but it failed to break.'[5]

On Thursday, 17 January 1985, the Fire Services Department (FSD) held an inspection to see whether the electric power could be turned on in the building. 'Now, are you absolutely relaxed about July 1st?' Norman Thompson asked Frank Archer. 'Not exactly relaxed,' Archer replied. 'The task force is operating successfully – we are getting the absolute co-operation of the design team, and they *are* clearing the information. The problem is BL1.'[6] Naka's production drawings for the face panels for the basement had still not been signed off. It was clear that all the BL1 face panels and beam cladding would not be in place on 19 May when the final FSD inspection was to be made. Fit-out was going to have to continue right up to 1 July and – beyond.[7]

By the end of January, the task force list covered 232 items. Nelson and Shuttleworth had signed nearly 1,500 site instructions. Their methods were evoking outcries from sub-contractors. Archer protested: 'We clearly cannot continue to absorb the issue of variations at this rate and expect to achieve our completion objectives.'[8] From now on, he said, no Architect's Instructions were to be issued other than those *absolutely essential* to making the existing design workable or operational. At the end of almost every day, Shuttleworth relayed progress to either Foster or Gordon Graham in London; daily bulletins were directed to the rest of the task force:[9]

Thursday, 7 February: Heavy rain. It is coming in through the refuge terraces, down the lift shaft openings, and from the top of the building. Water is streaming down hoist five, and the bus ducts (lengths of copper plate carrying electric current up the building) in the risers. Seventy men are putting up temporary roofs, tarpaulin covers, and manufacturing bamboo chutes to drain the top of the building. Polythene is being taped over openings, timber plugs are going into the holes in the floors, and they are building brick walls on level thirty-five around the lift shafts and escalator opening to keep the water from flooding down the building. They need even more protection now that they are trying to 'liven up the building'.

Friday, 8 February: The downpour continues. 'Water worlds' and bund walls, tarpaulins, sumps, etc., are proving effective where built. Unfortunately, the situation is worse than they understood last night. Rain is getting into zones three and four on the west side cantilevers, risers, and lift shafts; supposedly complete refuge terraces above levels ten and nineteen are leaking and work on the edges of zone five is being soaked. Is it safe to keep the power on?

Monday, 11 February: Water has damaged 95 per cent of the bus-ducts in the risers. Drying out estimated to take 7–10 days.

Sunday, 24 February: Cupples have been ordered off their programme of floor-by-floor completion, and instructed to close in the top of the building. Literally hundreds and hundreds of architect's instructions are now being issued, says Archer. Nothing is being helped by the fact that over 80 per cent of Naka door frames in zones three cannot be installed without being modified due to the mismatch of designed openings and erected works.

Tuesday, 5 March: John Lok/Wimpey are to increase site supervisory staff by four. JR Preston are to increase site staff from three or four to seven or eight. Fosters are to dedicate three more site architects. Task force teams are to buy walkie-talkies and set up an office on level fifteen. Drake & Scull, in charge of the basement services and the protection systems, are being instructed to increase site staff from 80 to 200. HMT remedial work progressing well, Cupples committed to programme: total completion of cladding due 19 May. Naka remain committed to programme although they will make it by double shifting and air-freighting doors.

Thursday, 28 March: More heavy rain.

Sunday, 31 March: Failure to meet target date (today) for completion of BL1 services. Attempts to connect the foul and stormwater outlets into the public system have been disastrous. Highway Department have been digging holes all over Des Voeux Road for three months, in an attempt to identify viable routes for these connections. Potential solutions have now finally been identified . . . but this doesn't help the current problem of getting all the water off site.

Tuesday, 2 April: 3,000 boxes of furniture for zone three have arrived in Hong Kong and will start being unloaded into the building, through the atrium underbelly, in a month's time. Shuttleworth to Foster:[10]

'Generally zone three in terms of July 1 is looking good . . . However, Naka are now of major concern in terms of zone four and up . . . they display a great deal of confusion about whether they have, or have not, got materials in Hong Kong to build with. For example, Naka announced only three days ago that the basement doors will be one month later (beyond FSD). This came as a big surprise to JLW despite

April 1985: lowering the maintenance crane into position.

the fact they have a guy in Japan to monitor progress. Frank has sent an additional team to Japan today to see what's going on . . . It seems that Mitsui doors have closed the factory down to stocktake as they have been taken over. If worse comes to worst we will put in temporary fire doors for FSD – so it's not a show stopper. We will report when we hear from Japan.

'Also having approved a major increase in Naka's staffing plan (L&B cost – HK$25 million for half a jumbo-jet load of Japanese fixers) – it is madness if they haven't got the materials to fix. So generally Naka is a mess, with Frank feeling rather exposed about his own people being on the spot, and still it's seemingly off the rails.

'Probably of even more concern, is Drake & Scull in the basement. . . . they do not appear committed to finishing on time. They seem to lack the direct drive on site to go 'balls out' (to quote Frank today) for July 1, and even more importantly for FSD, now only six and a half weeks away. We now have 8.30 daily meetings . . . Frank did a lot of table banging today with D&S – they have 24 hours to respond.

'Temporary weather protection continues to be an issue and we are daily pestering JLW to ensure devices are in position (sub-contractors keep moving them) and they did get the busducts wet again – but JLW don't consider it to affect the live energisation programme . . .'

Wednesday, 3 April: Drake & Scull have responded and the response is good. They are shipping more engineers out from England and will meet daily to clear the problem. Shuttleworth to Foster:[11]

'. . . the Naka situation seems to have improved . . . the doors – Mitsui have agreed to meet the programme – but neither myself or Richard [Holyoak, from John Lok/Wimpey] are prepared to accept this.

'There is no float at all [in the programme] and we would be at severe risk to take 'yes' for an answer. Hence Richard will leave two guys in the Mitsui factory on camp beds over next three weeks to tick off each door and telex us in HK each day to monitor progress.

'The most interesting development has been on the Naka erection side. We now realise that there is a major problem with the relationship between Naka and Aoki [the installers]. This came to a head yesterday with a riot on site, with Naka supervisors and Aoki fitters fighting each other with hammers and iron bars. The police arrived and thirty people were handcuffed and carted off in the Black Maria. . . .

'Other issues today include the much debated, highly problematic stormwater drainage connection into the main sewers is finally resolved and work is proceeding with great haste . . . Unfortunately the first door to be installed in the basement B2 didn't fit (because of pipes going through the door opening) – hopefully not an omen of things to come . . .'

By now there are 3,500 workers on site: John Lok/Wimpey had hoped never to have more than 2,000. Parts of the site are more congested than ever. Punch-ups in the hoists become daily more frequent; safety, and the potential for damage to the now finished areas was a continual worry. Among the throngs of Hong Kong Chinese wearing little more than shorts and singlets the stream of uniformed Japanese installers flown in by Naka looked immaculate and organised. They began each day on site with exercises, then a talk about their aims for the day, before beginning work on the installation. In Japan, however, the consequences of the time lost on letting the Naka contract so late on the job were beginning to prove expensive. From September the previous year, Fosters had based a team of eight architects in Japan to sign off Naka's fabrication drawings for the ceilings, door frames, partitions and cladding panels. The great bulk of the contract – for the ceilings – had been cleared and had gone into production rapidly. But, once more, it was the endless details which had to be co-ordinated with other contracts which made the task, especially in terms of time, a nightmare. Now, one of the casualties of the pressure, and the inaccurate setting out of parts of the basement, was a batch of 200 doors for that section of the building. Production of the replacement doors was going to take six weeks of twenty-four-hour shiftwork in factories across the country. Some of them weighed over a tonne. They were to be air-freighted to Hong Kong straight off the production line.

On site, the erection of the Naka ceilings, walls and wall panels, doors and demountable partitions throughout the building was now dominating the programme. The sheer variety of the components, together with the varying range of their dimensions, had led to a system of components that was virtually custom made. If anything, the installation of the Naka package was proving even more complex than the Cupples one had been.

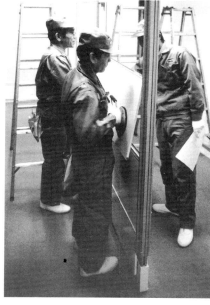

January 1985: Naka workers erecting demountable partition walls.

The erection sequence for many parts of the package was highly complicated and needed to be extremely accurate: the design had allowed for tolerances of only ± 3 millimetres (0.1 inch) between each component. Now wall panels, in the lift lobbies, for example, were being mounted on top of gypsum fire panels, conduits for security, fire alarms and lighting, and around items like lift call buttons and fire hydrants. If anything behind the panel had not been put in place within the limits of its tolerance, a panel on top would not fit. Clashes could be caused by any of half a dozen faults, from a problem with the size of the hole in the wall, to the possibility that they were trying to put the panel into the wrong place altogether. 'It is the inevitable and now unavoidable fact', wrote Archer in his monthly progress report to the PPCC at the end of April,[12] 'that almost every interface between the installed work of one package and completion of another's work, whether it be a service or an item of fit-out, involves an insurmountable clash, requiring discussion, analysis and remedial instructions...'

It seemed a never-ending task.

Monday, 13 May: (Fire Service Department inspection is the 20th). Chris Seddon rehearsed the walk through for the fire authority's inspection. The rest of the task force are on ahead, using the walkie-talkies to clear people out of the way, checking all the installations and mending any last-minute faults. 'Radio Ron' Young, a Geordie from Wimpeys, was testing the sprinklers. He called over, firmly, deliberately. 'I'm turning the pump on now. Yes . . . and it's leaking!'

Then a pause – for celebration? On Monday, 20 May, Cupples reached the top of the building. It was a blazing hot day. Before a large crowd and rolling television cameras, the final piece of cladding was lowered into position. In a traditional Oriental gesture of good luck, Sandberg led up senior officers from the Bank and Cupples to touch it. Champagne corks popped. The building had been topped out.

By Saturday, 1 June, twenty-five working days remained before the handover of the base of the building on July One. At 4 am on that day, the lions had been moved from Statue Square, where they had been placed following the demolition of the annexe, to their new positions on the edge of the plaza at the base of the new Bank. A formal ceremony to welcome them back would take place the following week. By now the number of site instructions issued by Nelson and Shuttleworth in the preceding month had risen to 2,500. The big issue was no longer whether they could hand over levels three, four, five, six or seven in time (the furniture was already being laid out on levels five, six and seven and the counters for the banking hall were en route from Italy), but whether they would be finished in BL1, with its public banking facilities. The level below the plaza was still a mess. Archer was no longer confident they would get over all the problems in time. 'So,' he said, 'I'm giving you guys two weeks. At the end of that time I want to clear this basement up so that I can have a trial as to what it will look like on the opening date.'

On Saturday, 15 June, Archer and Gordon Graham toured the building. As usual, they started at the top, and worked their way down. They went down the stairs beside the plaza into BL1. Before their eyes unfolded a scene of comparative tranquillity. The rubbish had gone. The lights were turned on. The wall panels were in place. The basement was finished, immaculate and clean.

Graham was amazed. 'Frank,' he said, 'I can't believe it.'

'Gordon,' said Archer, 'to be honest, neither can I.'

All that day, the members of the task force prowled over the basement, looking for the trouble spots, listing the faults to put right over the next two weeks. By the evening, they had torn it apart.

Sunday, Monday, 23/24 June: Typhoon signal number 8. All work on site stands down.

Monday, 20 May 1985: Cupples lower the last piece of cladding into place. The building is topped out.

Michael Sandberg, chairman of the Bank, at the topping out ceremony.

Tuesday, 25 June: Shuttleworth: 'There is six feet of water down on BL1. You call that a basement! It can't even keep out water!'

Thursday, 27 June: An unspecified crisis in the Bank today. A plane-load of journalists from London being flown in by John Lok/Wimpey to tour the finished building is due in tomorrow. Around 11.30 the phone rang at Fleetwood's desk in Fairmount House. 'This is *not* April Fool's Day,' he said. 'Tell me it isn't true.' He put the phone down: 'The building's on fire!'

In his section of the office, Chris Seddon was waiting for a call from the Building Ordinance Office to say that signatures had been put to the all-important temporary occupation permit. He looked out of the window to see a wide column of thick black smoke rising out of the side of the Bank. Inside the building, Shuttleworth, Archer and Mansell Evans were on the fifteenth floor. Choking black smoke poured up from the firestair. Pandemonium broke out in the building. Glass was exploding out of the sides of the building. It was terrifying. A fibreglass toilet on level thirteen had caught fire, and flames were spreading into the escape staircase in the north-east corner of the building. Fire pumps were activated in the basement; hydrants came on. The fire department arrived: the fire was not going to get the whole building.

Suddenly a bore of water raced out of the bottom of the south-east escape staircase. Trevor Farnfield, an engineer with JR Preston, tore up the stairs, water cascading over him. Someone had left a valve open on the fortieth floor. Farnfield found it, turned it off, and nearly threw a workman who was standing next to it off the top of the building. Downstairs, Archer nearly cried. The damage from the fire had been slight, but they had flooded the whole of the staircase and the basement. The task force retreated to the fifteenth floor, soaked. On Seddon's desk, the phone rang. It was the Director of Public Works. The occupation permit was ready for collection.

Later that day, it was as if work had never been interrupted. Upstairs, on level eight the foreign exchange dealers' room stood clean and ready with clear glass walls and fabulous views overlooking the harbour. The product of nearly eighteen months' painstaking work, the room was furnished with elegant matt-black workstations, each equipped with computer screens and telephones, immaculately laid out, ready and silent. The banking hall was lined with counters of black marble and stainless steel, wrapped in layers of bubblepack, which had just arrived, apparently safely, from Turin. Elsewhere the site was awash with litter from packing cases, polythene and paper, light fittings going in, carpet being trimmed. Fosters could not issue a Certificate of Practical Completion until they were completely satisfied that the work had been finished. The moment the certificate was issued, payments were to be made and sub-contractors would pack up to leave the site. Despite the political pressures to complete on time, the necessary signatures from Fosters were not a foregone conclusion.

June 1985: unwrapping the tellers' desks and banking hall furniture.

April 1985: preparing for completion of zone three.

On Monday, 1 July 1985 representatives from the Bank, Ron Mead, the architects and John Lok/Wimpey toured the building from level eleven down, checking the services, looking at details, searching for problems, down into BL1 and the rest of the basement levels. It was a tense inspection. At the end of the tour, the men returned to level fifteen. They crowded into the timber plywood room which served as Fosters' site office. As Roy Fleetwood and Graham Phillips put their names to the Certificate of Practical Completion for zones one, two and three of the new headquarters a great cheer went up. Champagne was broken out; they had done it. That night John Lok/Wimpey threw a great celebratory party.

The relief for the task force was palpable. But Archer's only recorded comment to the PPCC was dry. 'We are not in the miracle business on a permanent basis,' he said. On Sunday, 7 July, the first Bank department, 'Trade and Credit Information', moved into level eight. 'The impression of the space is generally good,' Shuttleworth reported to Foster; 'and although it's too early to judge, the user reaction seems positive.'[13] At 9 am on Tuesday, 30 July, after a brief ceremony to mark the occasion, the banking hall opened for business.

It had taken a long time for anyone to realise quite how big this building really was. Forty-seven storeys, another three levels below ground: over 90,000 square metres, a million square feet. Many buildings are far bigger. What made the Bank different was the building process. Unlike a conventional high-rise building, the steel frame of the Bank was not buried under layers of concrete which could be built up, coated and filled to flesh out its imperfections. The frame was like a skeleton; it defined the building's whole appearance and dictated the position of each of its other components. Most of the interior of the building had to be capable of being taken apart and put back together in a different arrangement. It had to be made of a kit of solid, lightweight, movable parts. Partition walls, for example, were suspended from a channel in the ceiling, their skirtings designed to disguise discrepancies at floor level when changes in floor loadings caused movement. They were intended to be easily demounted and shifted; they could not be fixed, made of plaster, moulded at the edges to disguise discrepancies; and, afterwards, covered in wallpaper to disguise the joints. The only wet trades used on the Bank had been in the basement, the concrete that was poured into the steel frames of the floors and on the plaza paving.

It took a long time, in some cases too long, for the sub-contractors, even John Lok/Wimpey, to begin to understand the complexity of the animal they were dealing with. The Bank was in fact the modern equivalent of a hand-made building. Its components were machine-tooled, but – and this is where it broke new ground – almost every one was different. On the Bank, Foster had shown that mechanisation and industrial production need no longer mean standardisation. The highest quality precision engineering, the most stringent quality

257

control, and the latest industrial technology, had been applied in the quest for something as old-fashioned as craftsmanship. It would not have been possible to make the pieces of the Bank without sophisticated, computerised machine-cutting and processing, or the Cupples robots and the Trumpf machine which could be programmed to specific requirements in individual areas. On the Naka package, technology had not been so advanced, but advantage was taken of the character of Japanese industry. There any major contract is broken up and handled by many different sub-suppliers, who rely on small production runs.

Once made, however, the setting out of the whole building, in particular the interior, had required enormous discipline. When all the pieces of the building came together, they had to lock together with the precision of a well-made car door. As construction neared completion it was the sheer quantity of the detailed engineering problems which almost threatened to overwhelm the design team and the contractors.

By the late summer of 1985, the task force was engaged in meeting the next deadlines for completing the construction: zone four, 16 September; zone five, 7 October; zones six and seven, 28 October; zone eight – 18 November. Each handover required separate Fire Services Department and Building Ordinance inspections. On 17 July, Shuttle-worth telexed Foster:[14]

'. . . I have been through all the critical programmes above zone four and it is not a pretty picture . . . GIG (internal cladding and kitchenettes) are now a major risk to completion. They are quoting dates on all items that are totally unsatisfactory. The situation is serious. Braddon was doing his usual flying 'lunchtime' visit to GIG next week but . . . it needs more than this. This means a delegation going to Austria next week . . . JLW propose to put one or two people in Austria full-time to expedite the works. If all this doesn't work we'll have to redesign to meet the dates with local sub-contractors . . .

Zone eight (occupation scheduled 18 November) frightens the daylights out of me. GIG are quoting 3 Nov ETD Austria for all zone eight works. Naka have still to submit initial door drawings for approval and we are still marking up face panel drawings – only submitted last Friday. Naka are due on site in three and a half weeks with door frames and face panel sub-frames. They are obviously not going to make it or anything close to it without more off-shore acceleration which we were trying to avoid. Zone eight is also the zone with a lot of outstanding design details . . . Living hell is an apt description.'

The Bank had begun a programme of closing down half a dozen 'mini banks' which it had opened in Central District for the period of the redevelopment. In spite of the task force's near despair, zone four, levels 13–19, was proceeding as planned for handover to the Bank on 16

Fung-shui ceremony to mark the blessing of the entrance escalators.

Overleaf:

Mounting the exterior sunscoop took place in November 1985.

259

September. On that day, GMR moved into the new building; from then until the end of September, one department per day moved in. The task force was becoming more and more preoccupied with the finishing details of the building: boardroom blinds, trim to Philips speakers, waste bins on the plaza, conference room lights, dimmer panels, the boardroom table. It was now areas like the chairman's and executive office area on level thirty-four, the boardroom and conference facilities, that were running behind. On a typical day there were around 120 men from seventeen different sub-contractors working on level thirty-five. As the floors at the top of the building were smaller, and the hoists had been removed, working conditions were as congested as they had ever been. But by late October zones one, two, three, four and five had been handed over; over the weekend of 2 and 3 November, the chairman's and senior executives' offices were moved into the building. All but the top three per cent of the building had been occupied.

The final Fire Services Department/Building Ordinance Office inspection took place, as scheduled, on the morning of Monday, 4 November 1985. On Sunday, 17 November, there was a complete tour of the building. This inspection was more formal than it had been on 1 July. Roy Munden was the senior representative from the Bank, Leslie Sallabank from Wimpey's London office had flown in to be there. The works were declared complete. The next morning, in a glass-enclosed dining room looking high over Hong Kong from the top of the Bank, the final Certificate of Practical Completion was formally presented by Foster Associates and the Works were accepted by the Bank. It was two years and eleven months from the day that the superstructure for the building had begun on site. It was a formidable achievement.

Level 34. Reception area for executive offices.

Outside the boardroom, level 36.

The job, of course, was not over yet. For another year Fosters and John Lok/Wimpey would keep their offices open and Arups and J Roger Preston would maintain their personnel in Hong Kong to oversee the clearing of defects and make any changes the Bank might require. Just before Christmas 1985, the 'Current List of Bangers' included, for example, dropping luminaires, falling ceiling tiles, missing sprinkler-cover plates and migrating silicone on laminated glass. Inevitably, some of the Naka panels had been delayed, and had to be fitted in after completion; the partitions for the executive dining room had been held up by a strike in the USA. The aim was to tie up all the last-minute details by the end of March 1986, ready for the formal opening of the building on the evening of Monday, 7 April 1986.

Walking by the Bank at lunchtime that day, passers-by could see rolls of red carpet being unloaded from a huge lorry and laid over the plaza. Flags were hung from the typhoon screen inside the plaza, floral tributes lined the walls. The opening was to be an event in true Hong Kong style. 'Cast of thousands of course, everybody asking everyone else if they'd been invited, Queen's Road closed for the night (where else would a major city street be closed for the opening of a bank?) and synchronised screening of the whole shebang at Happy Valley and Shatin,' as one observer commented privately later. The ceremony in the Bank itself took place before nearly 2,500 guests from around the world; as music played by the Coldstream Corps of Pipes and Drums in scarlet tunics and bearskins faded, the banging of Chinese drums and gongs heralded the arrival of a magnificent multicoloured dragon, operated – to mark the auspiciousness of the occasion – by forty-four men. Champagne and lobster were served. At Hong Kong's two racecourses giant monitoring screens simultaneously relayed the ceremony to the staff of the Bank and their families. That night His Excellency the Governor of Hong Kong, Sir Edward Youde, declared the new headquarters of The Hongkong and Shanghai Banking Corporation officially open. Eight years of effort on the part of hundreds of Bank staff, architects, engineers, specialist consultants, contractors and manufacturers from all over the world was formally brought to an end.

They had brought it off. The controversies over the costs of the construction had not been forgotten, but the building itself was hailed

Hongkong Bank

Under the masts: the entrance to the corner of the plaza from Queen's Road.

The Bank from Statue Square.

as a triumph. Those who had studied the models of the building in its early days walked into the atrium above the banking hall for the first time and, as Frank Archer and Gordon Graham had done in the late summer of 1984, were amazed to see that the architectural conception that Foster had proposed had been so exactly realised. Journalists and visitors from all over the world flocked to the building. In England, America, Japan, Italy, France and Germany major architectural periodicals devoted whole issues to studies of the Bank. In London, the editor of the *Architectural Review* confessed that he had never before felt so inadequate as when he had tried to translate his experience of the Bank into mere words and photographs. In Paris, *Le Monde* described the building as 'astonishing'. *Newsweek* described the building's 'visual panache' but suggested its most significant innovation lay in 'its attempt to redesign the huge, impersonal office building on a more human scale'. A building had never received international coverage like this before. In June 1986, Norman Foster was awarded the RS Reynolds Memorial Award for distinguished architecture, one of the most coveted prizes awarded by the American Institute of Architects, for an unprecedented third time.

For most of the construction period, some four years, work on site had taken place twenty-four hours a day, seven days a week. At its peak, the workforce on site alone was 3,500. An additional 480 staff were employed by Fosters, J Roger Preston, Ove Arup & Partners, Levett & Bailey, John Lok/Wimpey and R J Mead. The miles flown on behalf of the project are incalculable. In Fosters' office, the average working day was twelve hours, six days a week. During the year of the task force, Nelson and Shuttleworth put in ten hours on site before coming back to the office to deal with paperwork at night. On all the members of the consultant team the project took its personal toll. In the office itself, the decision to go on site, to abandon the architect's conventional position, remote at the drawing board, has had a profound and lasting effect.

Against the bad times were balanced priceless moments of hilarity. The project produced over 120,000 drawings. It spawned its own language. Besides the gull-wings, the Christmas trees, the vierendeels, there were the bow-ties, the butterfly nodes, the Nell Gwynn struts of the steel structure and the ostrich grilles of the air-conditioning system. They took pains to eliminate the Marilyn Monroe effect from the up-draught of the air-conditioning and that of the Burning Bush when the module generators were fired. The team picked up endless arcane pieces of information. The list of studies, new materials, techniques and systems developed for the project ranged from the wind studies to the welding robots, from the top-down method of construction to the sunscoop, from CBC to the flooring system, and beyond. For the first time research, precision engineering and computerised production techniques normally reserved for the aircraft, nuclear and defence industries had been applied in a major commercial building – and had ended by producing a work of art.

Reception area, level 12.

The boardroom.

The banking hall.

How had they done it? When the Bank first briefed Foster it had asked him to give it the best bank building in the world. Apart from its appearance, the new building had, above all, to provide flexibility. For the first few months of the commission, costs were not even mentioned. The commission had about it a flavour of old-fashioned patronage. The Bank wanted a fine building; it took considerable trouble to find an architect; once it had done so, it let him get on with the job. Providing more specific details for the brief frequently left the Bank at a loss: its growth over the period was dramatic; and for that very reason it had to have the flexibility Foster had offered to provide.

Between 1979 and 1985, The Hongkong and Shanghai Banking Corporation changed from a regional bank to a major international financial institution. By the end of 1980 profits were 38 per cent higher than when Norman Foster was commissioned in 1979. During the next five years the Bank's assets more than doubled; the number of its offices worldwide rose from 800 to over 1,200. During that time the Bank bought a majority shareholding in Marine Midland Bank, the largest bank in upstate New York. Towards the end of it, the Bank purchased James Capel, a major London stockbroking firm, and not long after the official opening of the new building the Bank opened in Australia and took over the Bank of British Columbia in Canada.

Time and again Foster requested more detailed input into the plans for the building from the Bank. As has been seen, planning of the building's interior came, in some cases, only months before completion. The Bank was always diffident about making aesthetic judgments. Even when at its most draconian, the members of BURG, for example, forbore to comment on aesthetic aspects of the design, leaving it to the architects, or to the board of the Bank, to make decisions on matters of taste. Although they had to justify everything, the architects had an astoundingly free hand.

As for the other professionals and contractors who were approached to build the Bank, the project captured their imagination. However difficult or unpredictable Foster was known to be, however impossible to see, he was also a brilliant architect. They admired him and they respected the lengths to which he would go to insist on the highest standards of precision and quality. Foster was in his element discussing methods and details with men on the shop-floor. His commitment to design extended from the largest scale to the smallest minutiae. For many of those who were approached to contribute to the project, Foster's design for the Bank was brave, provocative, inspiring. It was in a sense the consummate challenge. The building would be extremely difficult, almost impossible, to put together in the time. But here was the opportunity for a radical departure, the chance to build something rare. Men with years of experience in the building industry – like Jack Zunz, Frank Archer, Gordon Graham, Ron Mead and Phil Bonzon – repeated the same thing. It was the project of a lifetime. They committed themselves to bringing it off.

267

Hongkong Bank

The Queen's Road front.

Today, the Bank has settled into the building. People are more comfortable than when they had first moved in over the late summer and early autumn of 1985. There is paper about, fresh flowers on reception desks, and many more clumps of plants. Earlier, the perfect regimentation of the matt-black furniture in the huge, uncluttered floors of the double-height spaces was disturbingly Kafka-esque; now, with people about, the surfaces of their desks and belongings arranged to suit them, that feeling has disappeared. They come in across the plaza in the morning, through curved glass doors which slide back automatically to the lift lobbies on the west side of the building. Others take the long, high escalator ride, surfacing, as if from a pool, up through the glass 'underbelly' of the building, into the space of the banking halls in the vast atrium above. The staff have mastered their routes to their desks in the morning, up a lift to level twenty for example, down an escalator to level seventeen, and worked out the quickest route to, say, the chairman's office on level thirty-four. Against the scepticism of the planning stages, the combination of lifts and escalators is proving highly efficient. Otis carried out a study in December 1986: during the morning peak period the average waiting time for a lift was just over twelve seconds.

In Hong Kong today, over 4,000 people work in the new Bank headquarters. Around 22,000 cross the plaza beneath the building every working day. About a third of these come up into the banking hall. Standing on the edge of a floor, looking over the glass sides of the atrium, down into the banking hall and the plaza below, it is the life inside the building, more than the architecture, which commands the attention. The giant cross braces of the atrium and the bridges between the floors are there; but the floors themselves, the partition walls of glass and the external curtain wall of the building far in the distance are all as if held by nothing and appear, as in a reflection seen in a pair of angled mirrors, to repeat themselves and disappear.

It is the vast scale of the place that is impressive. Nothing quite prepares you for it. From one side to the other it is like looking into a giant layered dolls' house: on each floor are assembled different aspects of the Bank's existence. You can look from one floor, or one room, into the next. There is the intermittent rustle of paper, the dulled tapping of electric typewriter keys, the burr of telephones, the hum of the escalators. The handrails of the bridges vibrate gently as you walk across; on the west wall, usually shrouded in black shadow, there are shimmers of light and shade as the lifts, their passengers screened from view by translucent shoji glass, race up or down. It is like being in a hive, at the heart of a major industry.

Level ten, at the top of the atrium, is where the Hong Kong management office is located. As you stand in the waiting area outside the general manager's office, there is a magnificent floor-to-ceiling view of the harbour. But look back, over the bridge of the atrium, towards the Peak. Through pools of light and shadow, the distant view of

Over Easter 1985 the Bank sponsored a second competition of the Bank as seen by children, this time through paintings.

greenery is framed by the vierendeel structure of the masts: formal, symmetrical, beautifully proportioned; it offers, for a moment, a glimpse of the sublime. There are dozens of others like it, in other corners of other floors.

The diversity of spaces, and plays of light, and views out from the building, are rich and rewarding. The mood of the building is largely dependent on the weather and the day. On a June day in damp and low cloud it is like some alien battleship, brooding and grey. As you move up the building on the long ride on the escalators, each floor is different. Some, full of computers, are completely screened behind blank walls; on others, the view from the escalators is through a series of clear glass offices, to an open-plan office area and the harbour beyond; on others, however, there will be empty space, waiting for people to move in. Odd things catch the eye: a clock at a peculiar angle, a row of brightly painted Thai owls ranged along the back of a black air-conditioning unit in the foreign exchange dealers' room, a Ming bowl full of aggressive goldfish who are meant to indicate the character of visitors to an office by their reaction.

Level thirty-four, where the chairman and senior executives have their offices, is one of the finest. It is a serene haven of peace and tranquillity. The offices, arranged around the outer walls, are walled with translucent shoji glass; thick carpets of pale turquoise with borders of silver threads, are laid on the grey marble floors. Light filters through from the offices into the central reception area where a series of elegant glass display cases houses collections of coins and drawings from the archives. The solid walls are hung with the Bank's collection of pictures from the China sea trade; their colours, and the texture of the oils, made richer by the contrast with the metallic monochromes of the walls. Pictures are hung, too, on the floor above, where the boardroom is located. Here the impact is startlingly different. Near the top of the building, the set-backs of the building dramatically reduce the amount of floorspace. As the building scales down, so the true massiveness of the steel structure becomes aggressively apparent. Outside the boardroom, a gigantic, massive cross brace is stretched before the double-height bronzed aluminium doors at the entrance, as if to mark the forbidden entrance to some long-lost tomb of the Pharaohs. Outside the building at high level there is much more going on than the restraint down below has led one to expect: flying braces, massive trusses, great stacks of masts and maintenance cranes. It is enough to make you ask, is this the same Bank?

Today, many things have changed in Hong Kong since the Bank first commissioned Norman Foster. Michael Sandberg, chairman of the Bank, was knighted in the Queen's birthday honours in 1986 and retired from the Bank not long after the new headquarters was graced by a visit from the Queen, at the end of that year. Roy Munden had left a year earlier; he now writes books in the New Territories. The Hong Kong office of Foster Associates closed at Christmas 1986. During the

269

year, the team of draughtsmen and architects, engineers and quantity surveyors amassed for the project had dispersed. The joint venture between John Lok and Wimpey came to an end. Frank Archer is now in charge of the Great Man-Made River Project in Libya. Foster himself has received many new commissions.

With 1997 less than ten years away, the depression which dominated the Hong Kong economy during much of the course of this story has ended; confidence has returned. Next door to the Bank, the Chartered Bank redeveloped to designs by Palmer & Turner. To the east, a new headquarters for the Bank of China designed by IM Pei has risen. Across the road, six or seven new fifty-storey towers are going up. There is talk of reclaiming the waterfront from Central District to Wanchai, and of a new airport in Lantau. Height restrictions on building in Central have been abandoned. The streets are cleaner, the standards of architecture are improving. Signs at the airport now say, 'These doors are closed for energy saving'.

In banking, too, the changes do not stop. In eighteen months after the first stage of the Bank was completed twenty-four floors – 60 per cent of the workplaces – were changed. Moves of a whole floor are accomplished over a weekend; a new, enclosed office is assembled in a couple of hours. The cost of this is roughly HK\$28.80 per square metre (HK\$3.50 per square foot), in comparison with what the Bank had to pay for similar moves in 1982 (HK\$183.80 per square metre: HK\$67 per square foot). The foreign exchange dealers' room on level seven, for example, has been completely re-equipped with a new information system. Its operations could not cease. Had the department been functioning in a conventional building, new space would have had to be found for it first, and would then have had to be wired, furnished and equipped before the department could be moved. As it was, the dealers were moved just outside their room with their furniture and existing system for a month, while a new environment was created for them in the original space.

I last saw the Bank at lunchtime on a sparkling day of winter sunshine in February 1987. The sky was azure blue, the sea of the harbour somewhat darker. As Roy Munden and I walked across the plaza I was struck by the simple elegance of the lines of the slope beneath the building, and the clean grey of the granite paving. Bright sunlight from the sunscoop – the brightest Roy or I had yet seen – fell across the centre of the plaza. People, I noticed, favoured two routes across it: diagonally from north to south; or up on the west side, through the broad vaulted passage beneath the vierendeels of the masts – a space which echoes, with an uncanny sense of *déjà vu*, Foster's early slides of the Galleria at Milan.

By then it was a considerable time since the Bank had opened for business in its new headquarters, but many people had obviously come for no reason other than to look at the building. There were the familiar groups of people clustered about the lions on the Des Voeux Road side; a child was having his photograph taken astride one of them. People were taking pictures of themselves and the Bank, and riding the long, high escalators up and down from the banking hall. The Bank and the gold; good fortune and *fung-shui*. Foster's building was on the back of their banknotes. It had become a new symbol of prosperity and a part of their daily lives.

Following pages:

Norman Foster's finished masterpiece.

Hongkong Bank

These figures represent the construction and fit-out costs. They do not include preliminaries and insurances, demolition costs, miscellaneous contracts for temporary works, minor labour and service contracts, and various special items such as security and foreign exchange dealing systems, which were held by the Bank directly. Neither do they include professional fees, nor the fee of the management contractor.

Although expressed in Hong Kong dollars the figures incorporate a substantial foreign currency element which has been translated at the actual exchange rates used. Most foreign exchange expenditure was covered by forward exchange contracts fixed at rates prevailing during the early part of the project before the devaluation of the Hong Kong dollar in relation to the US dollar in October 1983.

Significant parts of this expenditure were financed under export credit schemes offered by countries of manufacture and the bulk of the heavy plant to run the building was leased, not purchased. Final payments under these arrangements will not fall due until the early part of the twenty-first century.

The construction costs

The following figures have been provided by the Hongkong and Shanghai Banking Corporation.

Item	HK$000
Seawater intake system	140,786
Substructure	341,437
Steelwork	1,203,228
Walkway	8,252
Corrosion protection	69,279
Fire protection	141,343
External cladding & glazing	1,112,874
Refuge terraces & plaza	21,960
Sunscoop	9,023
Basement plant	179,004
Subfloor services	229,975
Modules & risers	632,397
Lifts & escalators	143,291
Fire detection & defence	41,482
Internal cladding, partitions & doors	323,864
Floors	178,796
Ceilings & lighting	102,389
Furniture	69,636
Signage	12,275
Security systems	33,119
Toilet & utility room fitout	14,372
Telephone system & wiring	8,545
Banking hall furniture & fitout	34,600
Computer room plant	7,653
Safe deposit boxes	20,485
Building management system	41,303
Public address system	1,998
Document handling system	6,392
	5,129,758

Photographic credits

A case of modern patronage

The Bank and its context

1 Maurice Collis, *Wayfoong: The Hongkong and Shanghai Banking Corporation* (Faber, 1978).

2 See Frank M Tamagna, *Banking and Finance in China* (New York: Institute of Pacific Relations, 1942), p 92; quoted in *ibid.*, p 28.

3 Christopher Wood, 'Strategy for Survival', *Far Eastern Economic Review*, 20 September 1984. In 1981, when the Bank bid to take over the Royal Bank of Scotland, 73 per cent of shares in the Bank were held by Hong Kong addressees. However, beneficial owners of shares who are outside Hong Kong often have registered addresses in the Territory.

4 *Ibid.*

5 *Ibid.*

6 See Christopher Yip, 'Four Major Buildings in the Architectural History of the Hongkong and Shanghai Banking Corporation' in Frank HH King, ed., *Eastern Building: Essays in the History of the Hong Kong and Shanghai Banking Corporation* (Athlone Press, 1983).

7 'Shanghai Premises' in the archives of The Hongkong and Shanghai Banking Corporation, quoted in *ibid*.

8 'The Hongkong and Shanghai Bank Building', *Journal of the Royal Institute of British Architects*, vol 43, no 3, 21 March 1936, pp 527–33.

9 The Hongkong and Shanghai Banking Corporation, board paper, 14 November 1978.

10 Hong Kong Census and Statistics Department, *Hong Kong 1981 Census* (Hong Kong Government Printer, 1982). Tokyo's density was 12,332 persons per square kilometre (*Japan Statistical Yearbook*, 1981). In the mid-1960s, Hong Kong's density was ten times that of Manhattan.

11 Hong Kong Department of Rating and Valuation, Property Review 1971 (Hong Kong Government Printer, 1971).

12 Joe England, *Hong Kong: Britain's Responsibility* (Fabian Society, 1976).

13 Keith Hopkins, 'Housing the Poor' in Keith Hopkins, ed., *Hong Kong: The Industrial Colony* (Oxford University Press, 1971).

14 Hong Kong Department of Public Works, Annual Report 1963/1964 (Hong Kong Government Printer, 1964).

15 *South China Morning Post*, 10 March 1958.

16 GW Skinner, *The City in Late Imperial China* (Stanford University Press, 1977).

17 See Section 16(1), Hong Kong Building Ordinance, quoted in
P J Roberts, *Valuation of Development Land* (Hong Kong University
Press, 1975), p 20.
18 Alan J Hill, 'The Hong Kong Property Market', paper delivered to the
Asian Property Conference in Hong Kong, December 1980.
19 Hong Kong Department of Rating and Valuation, Property Review
1982 (Hong Kong Government Printer, 1982).
20 Hill, *op. cit.*

The choice of an architect

1 The Hongkong and Shanghai Banking Corporation, board paper, 14
November 1978.
2 HKBC, board paper, 23 January 1979, and correspondence between
R V Munden and PA Management in late autumn 1978.
3 PA Management to R V Munden, 22 December 1978.
4 HKBC, board paper, 23 March 1979.
5 Minutes of HKBC board meeting, 10 April 1979.
6 A Caplan to R V Munden, 29 November 1978.
7 HKBC, 'Notes on the Selection of the Architect for the Feasibility
Study', January 1979 (unsigned).
8 HKBC, board paper, 12 June 1979.
9 HKBC, 'Redevelopment of 1 Queen's Road Central, Hong Kong.
Request for proposals', June 1979.
10 *Ibid*.
11 R V Munden, notes of trip made between 24 September and 4 October
1979.
12 R V Munden, notes on Foster Associates submission, October 1979.
13 G Graham to R V Munden, 12 October 1979.

The Foster factor

1 Norman Foster, 'The Design Philosophy of the Willis Faber + Dumas
Building in Ipswich', *Architectural Design*, vol 9, October 1977,
pp 614–25.
2 Robert Maxwell, 'Purity and Danger – The Foster Method', *A + U: A
Monthly Journal of World Architecture and Urbanism*, no 57, Tokyo,
1975.
3 Reyner Banham, 'LL/LF/LE v Foster', *New Society*, 9 November 1972.
4 Maxwell, *op. cit.*
5 Norman Foster, in 'Questionnaire to Norman Foster', *A + U*, no 57.
6 'SCSD Project, USA', *Architectural Design*, vol 35, July 1965,
pp 324–39.
7 Norman Foster, Arthur Batchelor Lecture to the University of East
Anglia, 7 February 1978 (unpublished).
8 'SCSD Project', *loc cit.*, p 326.
9 Foster, in 'Questionnaire to Norman Foster'.
10 Norman Foster, 'Links', in *Foster Associates 1963–79* (RIBA
Publications, 1979).
11 Norman Foster, 'Exploring the Client's Range of Options', *RIBA*

Journal, June 1970, p 246.

12 Norman Foster, in a lecture delivered to the American Institute of Architects' Conference, October 1977 (unpublished).

13 Maxwell, *op. cit.*

14 Foster, AIA Conference lecture.

15 Kenneth Frampton, *Modern Architecture: A Critical History* (Thames & Hudson, 1980).

16 Norman Foster, 'The Design Philosophy of the Willis Faber + Dumas Building in Ipswich'.

17 *Ibid.*

18 Conversation with author.

The concept

1 Foster Associates, 'Hongkong and Shanghai Banking Corporation: Proposals for 1 Queen's Road, Hong Kong', October 1979. This chapter is based entirely on that submission.

Foundations of the project

1 Norman Foster, notes of meeting held 14 November 1979.
2 R V Munden to S de Grey and L Butt, 15 November 1979.
3 G Phillips to R V Munden, 29 February 1980. *See also* Foster Associates, 'Proposals for an Integrated Management Structure', January 1980.
4 R V Munden to Norman Foster, 13 December 1979; *ibid.*, 22 February 1980.
5 R V Munden, notes of trip made between 24 September and 4 October 1979.
6 The Hongkong and Shanghai Banking Corporation, board paper, 28 October 1980.
7 The plot ratio for a commercial building was 1:15; for a residential building it was 1:10.
8 J A Hamilton, manager, communications to R V Munden, 12 January 1980.
9 HKBC, board paper, 25 November 1980.
10 R V Munden to Norman Foster, 9 October 1980.
11 Quickborner team, Quickborner Report, January 1981.
12 HKBC, board paper, 9 December 1980.
13 Memo from D Brown to R V Munden, 8 December 1980.
14 HKBC, board paper, 23 December 1980.
15 HKBC, board paper, 9 December 1980; see also HKBC, board paper, 23 March 1982.
16 R V Munden to Norman Foster, 24 December 1980.

Strategic designing

1 Memo from R V Munden to Ray Guy, 9 February 1981.
2 Peter Bolingbroke, unpublished, undated paper on project programming; Ove Arup & Partners, 'Project Planning', *Arup Journal*, vol 20, no 4, Winter 1985; Levett & Bailey, conversation with the

author, November 1985; GD Phillips to Ray Guy, 16 March 1981.

3 RV Munden to Chen Hung, Bank of China, 30 November 1979.
4 N Keith to G Phillips, 6 October 1980.
5 *Engineering News Record, c.* January 1981; quoted, without date, in John Lok/Wimpey, 'Report and Recommendation of the Negotiations for the Main Cladding Subcontract', 3 April 1981.

Going to tender

1 John Lok/Wimpey, Report of the Assessment of the Prequalification Submissions, 24 February 1981, in 'Notes on Meetings and Negotiations Leading up to the Final Award for Package 5000 Structural Steelwork', October 1981.
2 Memo from RA Guy to RV Munden, 7 March 1981.
3 John Lok/Wimpey, *op. cit. See also* The Hongkong and Shanghai Banking Corporation, board paper, 13 October 1981.
4 HKBC, board paper, 24 March 1981.
5 John Lok/Wimpey, 'Report and Recommendation of the Negotiations for the Main Cladding Subcontract', 3 April 1981. These figures referred only to the costs that were to be allocated to the basic shell cost of the building. A further HK$90 million was to be applied to fit-out costs (RA Guy to John Lok/Wimpey, 21 April 1981).
6 John Lok/Wimpey, 'Report on the Negotiated Agreement Between the Management Contractor and HH Robertson HK Ltd for the Design, Supply, Manufacture and Construction of Cladding and Curtain Walling Package 5100', 17 September 1981.
7 John Lok/Wimpey, 'Instructions for the First Stage Prequalification for Service Modules', 16 March 1981.
8 *Ibid.*
9 John Lok/Wimpey, 'Second Interim Report and Recommendations Leading to the Award of the Subcontract for Services Modules and Risers for the Redevelopment of 1 Queen's Road Central, Hong Kong', 23 November 1981.

Testing and development: the steel and the cladding

1 In 1896 a Belgian, Professor A Vierendeel, constructed an open-web truss relying only upon vertical rather than the conventional diagonal members between the top and bottom booms. This kind of rigid frame is known as a vierendeel truss.
2 AG Davenport to Norman Foster, 16 November 1981.
3 GJ Zunz, MJ Glover, and AJ Fitzpatrick, 'The Structure of the New Headquarters for the Hongkong and Shanghai Banking Corporation, Hong Kong', *Structural Engineer*, vol 63 A, no 9, September 1985, pp 255–84.

Of client and architect

1 Levett & Bailey to the author, 6 January 1986.
2 GA Talley to Foster Associates, 26 November 1980.

3 GA Talley to Foster Associates, 16 September 1980.

4 HS Property Management to Foster Associates Hong Kong, 3 October 1981.

5 'Errors in Lions' New Habitation', *Hong Kong Economic Journal*, 23 June 1981.

6 H McAteer, Office of the Building Authority, to CR Seddon, Foster Associates, 2 December 1980.

7 RV Munden to Norman Foster, telex, 22 January 1982.

8 Norman Foster to RV Munden, 8 February 1982.

9 RV Munden to Norman Foster, notes of telephone conversation, 27 January 1981.

10 The Honkong and Shanghai Banking Corporation, minutes of HS Property Management, 14 January 1982.

11 HKBC, minutes of the 1QRC Development Steering Committee, 8 February 1982.

12 RV Munden to Norman Foster, 13 May 1982.

13 HKBC, board minutes, 25 January 1983.

14 Foster Associates Hong Kong to Foster Associates London, 10 February 1982.

The project in peril 1982/83

The Year of the Dog

1 The totals for the contracts were approximately as follows: structural steel HK\$608 million; cladding HK\$646 million; modules and risers HK\$405 million; lifts and escalators HK\$93 million. The average variation between these and the November 1980 costs was 11.5 per cent. *See* The Hongkong & Shanghai Banking Corporation, board paper, 23 March 1981.

2 RA Guy to RV Munden, 11 March 1982.

3 Foster Associates, client progress report, 23 February 1982.

4 RA Guy to Foster Associates Hong Kong, 28 December 1981.

5 Christopher Wood, 'Wardley Takes Cover', *Far Eastern Economic Review*, 17 March 1983, p 104.

6 G Phillips to RA Guy, 14 May 1982.

7 Ove Arup & Partners, notes of a meeting 19 October 1981 regarding material supply; E Blower, project manager BSC/Dorman Long British Joint Venture, to John Lok/Wimpey 23 November 1981.

8 John Lok/Wimpey, 'Package 5000, Structural Steel Summary of BSC/DL Programme and Claim Position 19 July 1982'.

9 The Hongkong and Shanghai Banking Corporation, minutes of 1QRC Development Steering Committee meeting, 21 May 1982.

10 HKBC, 1QRC, 'Development Steering Committee report: Summary of Present Position with BSC/DL', undated (end June/early July 1982).

11 John Lok/Wimpey, *op. cit.*

12 *Ibid.*

13 John Lok/Wimpey, notes of a meeting held 3 August 1982 at the BSC offices, 9 Albert Embankment, London.

14 John Lok/Wimpey, 'Comparison of Tender and Developed Design Requirements for Major Structural Elements', 6 November 1982. In

the final account the gross tonnage – which included wastage and
was therefore not included in Bills of Quantities – had increased
from 22,242 tonnes (21,890 tons) at tender stage to 29,952 tonnes.
The amount of concast steel used in the fabrication dropped from
19,672 tonnes to 15,031 tonnes; ingot steel rose from 4,841 to 14,921
tonnes. According to Frank Archer (letter to author, 29 April 1986),
the actual fabricated steel erection rose from 21,676 at tender to
26,230 tonnes on completion.

Northcroft, Neighbour & Nicholson's Schedule of Weights on 9
December 1982 for the nett tonnage (the only figures which count
for cost purposes, however) show tonnages of 22,080 at tender and
25,082 on completion of the structure. Of the final figure, 2,500
tonnes had been attached to the tender as a provisional sum; a
further 500 tonnes was used at the top of the building, which was
not designed at the time of the tender. The discrepancy between the
John Lok/Wimpey and the Northcroft figures can be explained by
the differences in definition of temporary works, fittings and
fastenings which are normally excluded for accounting purposes.

15 John Lok/Wimpey, 'Instructions for Prequalification for the
Structural Steelwork Tender', undated.

16 FH Archer to the author, 29 April 1986.

17 HKBC, board paper, 23 November 1982: 'Report of the meeting of
the sub-committee of the board held on Monday, 15 November
1982'.

18 RV Munden to Norman Foster, 17 November 1982.

19 RV Munden to all consultants, 20 December 1982.

For the sake of the project

1 The Hongkong and Shanghai Banking Corporation, minutes of the
1QRC Steering Committee, 18 November 1982; telex Foster
Associates Hong Kong to Foster Associates London, 18 November
1982.

2 RJ Mead, 31 December 1982, to the engineers WS Atkins &
Partners Overseas, Scott Wilson Kirkpatrick, Pell Frischmann and
Flint & Neill; and the quantity surveyors Monk & Dunstone,
Dearle & Henderson and James Nisbet.

3 HKBC, board papers, 9 and 23 December 1980; *see also* board
papers, 23 January 1981, 23 March 1982.

4 R Guy to G Phillips, 28 March 1981. In March 1981, two months
after the board had originally sanctioned the basic shell cost of the
building, HS Property Management estimated the extra fit-out costs
to be around HK$611,000,000 but noted that no firm figure had yet
been agreed.

5 Levett & Bailey to the author, 6 January 1986.

6 HKBC, minutes of the meeting of the 1QRC Steering Committee, 25
May 1982.

7 HKBC, board paper, 27 July 1982.

8 *Asian Wall Street Journal*, 22 February 1983.

9 *Sunday Times*, 13 March 1983.

10 *Engineering News Record*, 7 April 1983.

11 MGR Sandberg to John Lok/Wimpey, Ove Arup & Partners, Foster Associates, Trafalgar House, J Roger Preston, 31 March 1983.

12 'Project Organisation', 13 April 1983, signed by Leslie Sallabank and Frank Archer (John Lok/Wimpey), Norman Foster and Roy Fleetwood (Foster Associates Hong Kong), Jack Zunz and Peter Ayres (Ove Arup & Partners Hong Kong), Deryck Thornley and D Tuddenham (J Roger Preston), D Levett and J Abrahams (Levett & Bailey).

13 HKBC, minutes of the meeting of the Project Policy Co-ordination Committee, 25 April 1983.

14 HKBC, board paper, 12 July 1983.

15 *Ibid*.

16 CR Seddon to R J Mead, 12 May 1983.

17 HKBC, press release, 12 July 1983.

18 MGR Sandberg to Norman Foster, 14 July 1983.

19 HKBC, board paper, 25 January 1983.

The battle for July One   1984/85

Under siege

1 The diary account in this chapter is based on the minutes of the meetings of the Project Management Committee and other progress meetings kept by Foster Associates from January to December 1984; and from executive summaries of the monthly 'PPCC Construction Progress and Unlet Packages Reports', prepared by the management contractor/consultants January–December 1984.

Task force

1 Foster Associates Hong Kong, 'Report of 1QRC Redevelopment Task Force Meeting GBC', 13 December 1984.

2 Foster Associates Hong Kong, 'Report of 1QRC Redevelopment Task Force Meeting GBC 3', 19 December 1984.

3 John Lok/Wimpey, 'Redevelopment 1QRC Hong Kong PPCC Construction Progress and Unlet Packages Report', 30 November 1984.

4 K Shuttleworth in conversation with the author, 12 February 1987.

5 The Hongkong and Shanghai Banking Corporation, minutes of 1QRC Relocation Committee, 10 January 1985.

6 Foster Associates Hong Kong, notes of 'Progress Review', 17 January 1985.

7 B Simmonds, John Lok/Wimpey to CR Seddon, Foster Associates Hong Kong, 15 January 1985.

8 FH Archer to R J Mead, telex, 2 February 1985.

9 Abstracted from 'Task Force GBC' correspondence, 7 December 1984–16 May 1986 and PPCC 'Construction Progress and Unlet Packages Reports', February 1985 – December 1985.

10 K Shuttleworth to Norman Foster and G Graham, telex, 2 April 1985.

11 *Ibid*, 3 April 1985.

12 John Lok/Wimpey, 'PPCC Construction Progress and Unlet Packages Report', 30 April 1985.

13 K Shuttleworth to Norman Foster and G Graham, unsent telex (report by telephone), 10 July 1985.

14 K Shuttleworth to Norman Foster and G Graham, telex, 17 July 1985.

Bibliography

This book is based on the correspondence and papers of Foster Associates, the private papers of Roy V Munden, before his retirement as director of the Hongkong and Shanghai Banking Corporation, the minutes and papers of the board of the Hongkong and Shanghai Banking Corporation and those of the main committees formed for the redevelopment of 1 Queen's Road Central, Hong Kong between 1978 and 1986. John Lok/Wimpey, the management contracting consortium formed for the job, have provided me with the material cited below. Ove Arup and Partners have provided me with sight of relevant correspondence, and Levett & Bailey with much cost information. In addition, I conducted more than 125 interviews with those who worked on the project.

Private papers: Foster Associates

Foster Associates:

Minutes of the meetings of the Project Management Committee and Daily Action Notes, January 1983–30 January 1985.

Series 501 (Hongkong and Shanghai Banking Corporation) Files consisting of 166 vols of material dated between June 1979 and January 1983, including 7 vols of client correspondence, from 2 June 1979 to 10 Jan. 1983; 3 vols client meetings 14 Nov 1979–2 June 1980.

Task Force GBC Papers and Correspondence, 12 December 1984–16 May 1986.

Reports for the Hongkong and Shanghai Banking Corporation (HKBC):

'Interiors Masterplan', Hongkong Bank, New Headquarters Building, One Queen's Road Central, Hong Kong, December 1986.

'Office Areas, Internal Concept Report', June 1981.

'Preliminary Concept Report', May 1980.

'Proposals for 1 Queen's Road, Hong Kong', October 1979.

'Proposals for an Integrated Management Structure', January 1980.

'Proposals for Project Organisation', October 1979.

'Special Areas – Schedule of Briefing Information', June 1982.

'Vertical Movement: A Comparison of Two Systems', March 1982.

Client Progress Reports nos 1–33, February 1980–December 1982.

HS Property Management Company, Redevelopment of One Queen's Road Central, 'Summary of Key Client Decisions', October 1981.

The Hongkong and Shanghai Banking Corporation, Redevelopment of One Queen's Road Central: Preliminary Submission to Building Ordinance Office, October 1980.

Hongkong and Shanghai Banking Corporation

Hongkong and Shanghai Banking Corporation:

'Financial Services Worldwide', 1985.

'Hongkong Bank News', Special Edition, April 1986.

'Hongkong Bank News', Special Edition, June 1984.

'Hongkong Bank News', Special Edition, June 1985.

'Redevelopment of 1 Queen's Road Central, Hong Kong. Request for proposals', June 1979.

'The headquarters buildings of Hongkong Bank', catalogue of exhibition held at City Hall, Hong Kong, January 1985.

'The Hongkong Bank Group: Background Briefing', June 1981.

'The Official Opening of the New Building', commissioned to commemorate the official opening of its new headquarters, 10 October 1935.

1 Queen's Road Central Redevelopment General Files containing letters and papers of RV Munden from May 1978–1985.

Annual Reports, 1984, 1985.

Minutes and Papers of 1 QRC Steering Committee, 24 February 1982–13 December 1982.

Minutes and Papers of the board of the Hongkong and Shanghai Banking Corporation relating to Bank Property at 1 Queen's Road Central, between 14 November 1978 and 28 May 1985.

Minutes and Papers of the Project Policy Co-ordination Committee, January–June 1983.

Minutes of 1 QRC Building Users Requirements Group (BURG) 1 March 1983–6 November 1984.

Minutes of 1 QRC Relocation Committee, 4 December 1984–4 June 1985.

Minutes of 1 QRC Working Committee, 3 vols, 9 November 1983–26 February 1985.

Report on the Management of Client Relations arising from the 1 QRC Redevelopment Project, no date (1984).

Research on Attitudes to HongKong Bank and the New Bank Building Report, prepared by AGB McNair Hongkong Ltd, October 1984.

John Lok/Wimpey

Archer, Frank/Executive Project Director, John Lok/Wimpey:

Letters to the author, with enclosures of 17 March 1985, 29 April 1986, 1 May 1986, 14 May 1986, and 6 June 1986 including correspondence and notes on meetings held between John Lok/Wimpey and various parties including BSC/DL, Foster Associates and HSBC on 7 and 8 January, 3 and 23 August, 8, 9, 11, and 15 November, and 10 and 15 December 1982.

John Lok/Wimpey:

'Comparison of Tender and Developed Design Requirements for Major Structural Elements', 6 November 1982.

'Identification of Structural Changes and Comparative Analysis of Tender and Reimbursable Cost Estimate', 8 November 1982.

'Instructions for Prequalification for the Structural Steelwork Tender', no date.

'Instructions for the First Stage Prequalification for Service Modules', 16 March 1981.

'Interim Report and Recommendations Leading to the Award of the Subcontract for Service Modules and Risers for the Redevelopment of 1 Queen's Road Central, Hong Kong', 30 October 1981.

'Management Contractor Proposals for Redevelopment of Bank Head Office at 1 Queen's Road Central, Hong Kong', 4 vols, 1980.

'Notes on Meetings and Negotiations Leading up to the Final Award for Package 5000 Structural Steelwork', no date (1981).

'Package 5000, Structural Steel Summary of BSC/DL Programme and Claim Position', 19 July 1982.

'Quality Assurance and Quality Control for Structural Steelwork Package 5000', June 1981.

'Report and Recommendation of the Negotiations for the Main Cladding Subcontract', 3 April 1981.

'Report on First Stage Prequalification for Service Modules Tender for Redevelopment of 1 Queen's Road Central, Hong Kong', no date.

'Report on Second Stage Prequalification for Services Modules Tender for Redevelopment of 1 Queen's Road Central, Hong Kong', no date.

'Report on the Negotiated Agreement Between the Management Contractor and HH Robertson HK Ltd for the Design, Supply, Manufacture and Construction of Cladding and Curtain Walling, Package 5100', 17 September 1981.

'Report to the Clients on the Continuing Negotiations with BSC/DL', 6 October 1982.

'Redevelopment 1 QRC Hong Kong PPCC Construction Progress and Unlet Package Reports', Volume 1, Executive Summaries, nos 34–65, January 1983–November 1985.

'Management Contractor's Monthly Report to PPCC', January–June 1986.

'Second Interim Report and Recommendations Leading to the Award of the Subcontract for Service Modules and Risers for the Redevelopment of 1 Queen's Road Central, Hong Kong', 23 November 1981.

'Subcontract Appointment Key Date Schedule', Issue 46, 4 July 1985.

'Summary of Package Progress: Pre-construction', 6 July 1985.

'Tender Documents for Structural Steelworks at the Redevelopment of 1 Queen's Road Central, Hong Kong of 1 Queen's Road Central Limited', 22 June 1981.

Unpublished sources

Benning, Gerald:

'The First Fifty Years: J Roger Preston & Partners 1926–1976', no date.

Chambers, Gillian and Lambot, Ian:

'One Queen's Road Central', commissioned by the Hongkong Bank to commemorate the official opening of its new headquarters, 7 April 1986.

Cupples Products Division, HH Robertson Company:

'Perceptions', 1982.

'Cupples Fabrication Drawings', 2 vols, 1981/82.

Foster, Norman:

Arthur Batchelor Lecture to the University of East Anglia, 7 February 1978 (unpublished transcript).

Lecture delivered to the American Institute of Architects Conference, October 1977.

Guy, Ray, HS Property Management Co:

Notes for lecture delivered at the Burrell Gallery, Glasgow, March 1986.

Hill, Alan G:

'The Hong Kong Property Market', paper delivered to the Asian Property Conference in Hong Kong, December 1980.

Hongkong Land Company Ltd:

Annual Report, 1983.

Levett & Bailey:

Letter and enclosures to the author 24 December 1985, including a History of Cost Reporting of Package 5000, and 8 January 1986 including extracts from cost reports dated November 1980, July 1981, January 1982, July 1982, January 1983, August 1983, October 1984 and November 1985.

Otis Elevator Company:

Traffic Analysis of Hongkong Bank, 16 December 1986.

Ove Arup & Partners:

Notes of a meeting 19 October 1981 regarding material supply.

Palmer & Turner (Hong Kong):

'The Hongkong and Shanghai Banking Corporation: Redevelopment of 1 Queen's Road Central, Hong Kong', October 1979.

Pell Frischmann & Partners:

'Redevelopment of One Queen's Road Central, Hong Kong: Technical and Financial Audit Report', May 1983.

Preston, J Roger and Partners:

Hongkong Bank, New Headquarters, 'Building Services', prepared to commemorate the official opening of the new Hongkong Bank Headquarters on 7 April 1986.

Quickborner Team:

'Quickborner Report', January 1981.

Richardson, Tim:

'North Point Hong Kong: A Case Study of High Density', unpublished Hong Kong University thesis, 1977.

Ritchie, JA:

'Wafoong Memories', sent to Controller, Hongkong and Shanghai Bank Archives, 2 November 1979.

Sandberg, Michael:

Text of speech delivered to Foreign Correspondents' Club, Hong Kong, 8 March 1985.

Seidler, Harry & Associates:

'Redevelopment of 1 Queen's Road Central, Hong Kong for The Hongkong and Shanghai Banking Corporation', October 1979.

Skidmore Owings & Merrill:

'The Hongkong and Shanghai Banking Corporation: Redevelopment of 1 Queen's Road Central Hong Kong', 3 vols, October 1979.

Stubbins, Hugh & Associates Inc:

'The Hongkong and Shanghai Banking Corporation', October 1979.

YRM:

'The Hongkong and Shanghai Banking Corporation', October 1979.

Yuncken Freeman Pty Ltd:

'The Hongkong and Shanghai Banking Corporation Redevelopment of 1 Queen's Road Central Hong Kong', 4 vols, October 1979.

Hong Kong Going and Gone, Photographic Survey of Western Victoria, Royal Asiatic Society, Hong Kong, 1980.

Some Traditional Chinese Ideas and Conceptions in Hong Kong Social Life Today, Royal Asiatic Society, Hong Kong, 1967.

Published works

Appleyard, Bryan:

Richard Rogers, Faber, London, 1986.

Baker, Hugh:

Ancestral Images, South China Morning Post, Hong Kong, 1979.

Bonavia, David:

The Chinese, Allen Lane, London, 1981.

Cameron, Nigel:

The Hongkong Land Company Ltd: A brief history, Hongkong Land Co Ltd, Hong Kong, 1979.

Chaslin, François, Hervet, Frédérique, and Lavalou, Armelle:

Norman Foster, Electa Moniteur, Paris, 1986.

Collis, Maurice:

Wayfoong, The Hongkong and Shanghai Banking Corporation, Faber, London, 1965.

Constructional Steel Research and Development Organisation:

Steel Designers' Manual, Granada, London, 1978.

Drakakis-Smith, David:

High Society: Housing Provision in Metropolitan Hong Kong 1954 to 1979, Centre of Asian Studies, Hong Kong University, Hong Kong, 1979.

Drexler, Arthur:

Three New Skyscrapers, Museum of Modern Art, New York, 1983.

Dwyer, DJ, ed:

Asian Urbanization: A Hong Kong Case Book, Hong Kong University Press, Hong Kong, 1971.

The Changing Face of Hong Kong, Royal Asiatic Society, Hong Kong, 1971.

Dyer Ball, J:

Things Chinese, Oxford University Press, Hong Kong, 1982.

Eitel, Ernest J:

Fêng-shui, The Science of Sacred Landscape in Old China, 4th edition, Synergetic Press, London, 1984.

Endacott, GB:

A History of Hong Kong, Oxford University Press, Hong Kong, 1979.

England, Joe:

Hong Kong: Britain's Responsibility, Fabian Society, London, 1976.

Feuchtwang, Stephan DR:

An Anthropological Analysis of Chinese Geomancy, Vithagna, Vientiane, Laos, 1974.

Foster Associates:

Foster Associates 1963–79, RIBA Publications Ltd, London, 1979.

Frampton, Kenneth:

Modern Architecture: A Critical History, Thames

& Hudson, London, 1980.

Hong Kong Census & Statistics Department:

Hong Kong 1981 Census, Hong Kong Government Printer, Hong Kong 1982.

Hong Kong Commissioner for Resettlement:

Annual Report 1954, Hong Kong Government Printer, Hong Kong, 1955.

Hong Kong Department of Public Works:

Annual Report 1963–64, Hong Kong Government Printer, Hong Kong, 1964.

Hong Kong Department of Rating & Valuation:

Property Review 1971, Hong Kong Government Printer, Hong Kong, 1971.

Property Review 1982, Hong Kong Government Printer, Hong Kong, 1982.

Hong Kong Government:

Annual Report 1956, Hong Kong Government Printer, Hong Kong, 1956.

Hong Kong 1978, ...1979, ...1980, ...1981, ...1982, ...1983, ...1984, ...1985, Hong Kong Government Printer, Hong Kong, published annually.

Rural Architecture in Hong Kong, Hong Kong Government Printer, Hong Kong, 1978.

Hong Kong Housing Authority:

Annual Reports 1978–9; 1979–80; 1981–82; 82–83, Hong Kong Government Printer, Hong Kong, 1982.

The First Two Million, Hong Kong Government Printer, Hong Kong, no date.

Hopkins, Keith, ed:

Hong Kong: The Industrial Colony, Oxford University Press, Hong Kong, 1971.

Hughes, Richard:

Borrowed Place, Borrowed Time: Hong Kong and its many faces, André Deutsch, London, 1976.

Japan Statistical Yearbook:

Japan Statistical Association, Tokyo, 1981.

Jarvie, IC and Agassi, J, ed:

Hong Kong: A Society in Transition, Routledge & Kegan Paul, London, 1969.

King, Frank HH, ed:

Eastern Banking: Essays in the History of the Hongkong and Shanghai Banking Corporation, Athlone Press, London, 1983.

Lambot, Ian:

The New Headquarters for the Hongkong and Shanghai Banking Corporation, Ian Lambot, Hong Kong, 1986.

The New Headquarters for the Hongkong and Shanghai Banking Corporation: The Construction, Ian Lambot, Hong Kong, 1985.

Lasdun, Denys:

Architecture in an Age of Scepticism, Heinemann, London, 1984.

Leeming, Frank:

Street Studies in Hong Kong, Oxford University Press, Hong Kong, 1977.

Lethbridge, HJ:

Hong Kong: Stability and Change, Oxford University Press, Hong Kong, 1978.

Hard Graft in Hong Kong, Oxford University Press, Hong Kong, 1985.

Needham, Joseph:

The Shorter Science & Civilisation in China, vol 1, abridged, Cambridge University Press, Cambridge, 1978.

Pevsner, Nikolaus:

A History of Building Types, Thames & Hudson, London, 1979.

Purvis, Malcolm:

Tall Storeys, Palmer & Turner Ltd, Hong Kong, 1985.

Roberts, PJ:

Valuation of Development Land, Hong Kong University Press, Hong Kong, 1975.

Sayer, Geoffrey Robley:

Hong Kong: 1841–1862, Hong Kong University Press, Hong Kong, 1980.

Hong Kong: 1862–1919, Hong Kong University Press, Hong Kong, 1975.

Skinner, GW:

The City in Late Imperial China, Stanford University Press, Stanford, 1977.

Tamagna, Frank M:

Banking and Finance in China, Institute of Pacific Relations, New York, 1942.

Topley, Marjorie, ed:

Hong Kong: the Interaction of Traditions and Life in the Towns, Royal Asiatic Society, Hong Kong, 1975.

Tregear, TR and L Berry:

The Development of Hong Kong & Kowloon as told in Maps, Hong Kong University, Hong Kong, 1959.

Wong, Luke SK:

Housing in Hong Kong, Heinemann Educational Books (Asia) Ltd, Hong Kong, 1978.

Articles and periodicals (unattributed)

'Building, Development and Construction Review' (Supplement), *South China Morning Post*, Hong Kong, August 1982.

'Errors in Lions' New Habitation' (translated title), *Hong Kong Economic Journal*, Hong Kong, 23 June 1981.

'Foster Associates' (Special Issue), *A+U: A Monthly Journal of World Architecture and Urbanism*, no 57, Tokyo, September 1975.

'Foster Associates: Hongkong Bank' (Special Issue), *A+U: A Monthly Journal of World*

Architecture and Urbanism, no 189, Tokyo, June 1986.

'Foster Tower: Hongkong Bank, A Re-evaluation of Tall Buildings' (Special Issue), *Process: Architecture*, no 70, Tokyo, September 1986.

'HK & Shanghai Bank New Head Office', *South China Morning Post*, Hong Kong, 18 October 1934.

'Harry Seidler 1948–1980' (Special Issue), *SD: Space Design*, A Monthly Journal of Art and Architecture, no 187, Tokyo, February 1981.

'Hongkong Bank's New Headquarters', *The Times*, 9 October 1935.

'Investing in Hi-Tech', *Architects' Journal*, vol 173, no 8, 25 February 1981, pp 342–3.

'Jubilee President', *Building*, vol CCXXXIII, no 7007, 14 October 1977, pp 92–9.

'Lloyd's and the Bank' (Special Issues), *Architects' Journal*, vol 184, nos 43 and 44, 22 and 29 October 1986.

'Norman Foster: Projets. Réalisations. 1980–1986', *L'Architecture d'Aujourd'hui*, no 243, Brussels, February 1986, pp 5–67.

'Ove Arup's 90th Birthday Issue', *The Arup Journal*, vol 20, no 1, Ove Arup Partnership, Spring 1985.

'SCSD Project, USA', *Architectural Design*, vol 36, July 1965, pp 324–39.

'Soaring Cost of Hong Kong Bank eclipses down-to-earth obstacles', *Engineering News Record*, vol 210, no 14, New York, 7 April 1983, pp 28–32.

'Special Issue: Hongkong & Shanghai Bank', *Architectural Review*, vol CLXXIX, no 1070, April 1986.

'Sydney Opera House Special Issue', *The Arup Journal*, vol 8, no 3, Ove Arup Partnership, October 1983.

'The $HK 7 million Pell Frischmann report: How sweet it is!' *Target*, vol XX, no 127, Hong Kong, 7 July 1983.

'The $HK 7 million Pell Frischmann report: A concise costing of the Bank's monument', *Target*, vol XX, no 129, Hong Kong, 11 July 1983.

'The Changing Face of Hong Kong', *South China Morning Post*, Hong Kong, 10 March 1958.

'The Hongkong and Shanghai Bank Building', *Journal of the Royal Institute of British Architects*, vol 43, no 3, 21 March 1936, pp 527–33.

'The Hongkong Bank', *Progressive Architecture*, Cleveland, March 1986, pp. 67–110.

'The Hongkong Bank: The new headquarters', *The Arup Journal*, vol 20, no 4, Ove Arup Partnership, Winter 1985.

'The New Buildings of the Hongkong and Shanghai Bank', *The China Mail*, 9 August 1886.

'The Pell Frischmann Report on the Bank Building: It's a Scorcher', *Target*, vol XX, no 126, Hong

Kong, 6 July 1986.

'The Turn Key System in Architecture', *Process: Architecture*, no 45, Tokyo, March 1984.

Articles and periodicals (attributed)

Amery, Colin and Dodwell, David:

'Monument to money', *Financial Times*, 5 April 1986.

Banham, Reyner:

'LL/LF/LE v. Foster', *New Society*, vol 22, no 527, 9 November 1972, pp 344–5.

Baum, Dan:

'Bill rises on Colony Bank Complex', *Asian Wall Street Journal*, Hong Kong, 10 February 1983.

Bell, John:

'The Banker who wants to Shanghai Scotland', *Sunday Times*, 12 April 1981.

Bowring, Philip:

'Yesterday's men of property', *Far Eastern Economic Review*, 26 November 1982, pp 59–60.

Bowring, Philip and Lee, Mary:

'Tread softly, Iron Lady', *Far Eastern Economic Review*, Hong Kong, 17 September 1982, pp 23–8.

Champenois, Michèle:

'Norman Foster, l'Homme au Crayon d'Acier', *Le Monde*, Paris, 9/10 fev. 1986.

ERCO:

'The Hongkong and Shanghai Banking Corporation, New Headquarter', *Lichtbericht 24*, ERCO Leuchten GmbH, Lüdenscheid, April 1986.

Fanjas, Alain:

'Mon Building à Hong Kong', *Le Monde*, Paris, 9/10 fev. 1986.

Foster Associates:

'Hongkong Bank Headquarters', *Vision*, no 20, Hong Kong, 1985, pp 24–5.

Foster, Norman:

'Royal Gold Medal Address 1983', Royal Institute of British Architects: *Transactions 4*, vol 2, no 2, 1983.

'Exploring the client's range of options', *RIBA Journal*, vol 77, no 6, June 1970, pp 246–53.

'Foster Associates: Hongkong & Shanghai Banking Corporation Headquarters', *Architectural Design*, vol 51, no 3–4, March/April 1981, pp 18–27.

'Histoire d'un Gratte-ciel', *Architecture Intérieure—Crée*, no 185, Paris, October 1981, pp 78–94.

'Questionnaire to Norman Foster', *A + U: A Monthly Journal of World Architecture and Urbanism*, no 57, Tokyo, September 1975.

'The Design Philosophy of the Willis Faber + Dumas Building in Ipswich', *Architectural Design*, vol 47, no 9–10, Sept/Oct 1977, pp 614–25.

Futagawa, Yukio, ed:

'The Hongkong and Shanghai Banking Corporation', *GA Document*, no 16, Tokyo, November 1986.

Glancey, Jonathan:

'Hongkong Bank', *Architectural Review*, vol CLXIX, no 1011, May 1981, pp 268–72.

'Nîmes Schemes', *Architectural Review*, vol CLXXVII, no 1059, May 1985, pp 31–9.

Goldstein, Barbara:

'Foster Associates, Designing the Means to Social Ends', *RIBA Journal*, vol 85, no 1, January 1978, pp 7–22.

Hillman, Judy:

'Good Offices', *Guardian*, 3 August 1977.

Humpheson, C, Fitzpatrick, A J, and Anderson, JMD:

'The basements and substructure for the new headquarters of the Hongkong and Shanghai Banking Corporation, Hong Kong', *Proceedings of the Institution of Civil Engineers, Part 1*, vol 80, August 1986, pp 851–83.

Lee, Mary:

'Hong Kong '82', *Far Eastern Economic Review*, Hong Kong, 12 March 1982, pp 46–78.

Levett & Bailey and Northcroft Neighbour & Nicholson:

'The Bank in Hong Kong', *Chartered Quantity Surveyor*, vol 8, no 11, June 1986, pp 27–30.

Linklater, Magnus:

'The sky-high costs of building sky high', *Sunday Times*, 13 March 1983.

Maidment, Paul:

'Hongkong Bank: How Not to Build a Masterpiece', *Asian Wall Street Journal*, Hong Kong, 22 February 1983.

Maxwell, Robert:

'Purity and Danger—The Foster Method', *A + U: A Monthly Journal of World Architecture and Urbanism*, no 57, Tokyo, September 1975.

Ng Shiu Wai:

'Decorations and Ornamentations in Chinese Architecture', *Boletim do Instituto Luís Camões*, vol IV, nos 2 & 3, Macau, 1970.

Pawley, Martin:

'Final fling in the imperial twilight', *Guardian*, 8 April 1986.

'Norman Foster', *Blueprint*, no 7, May 1984, pp 10–13.

Press, Aric with McDaniel, Ann:

'Rising Against the Trend', *Newsweek*, 14 April 1986, pp 40–3.

Pryor, EG:

'A Historical Review of Housing Conditions in Hong Kong', *Journal Hong Kong Branch Royal Asiatic Society*, vol 12, Hong Kong, 1972, pp 89–129.

Sharma, Suresh:

'Hongkong Bank Headquarters: Fosters first skyscraper design', *Vision*, vol 1, no 1, Hong Kong, January 1983, pp 28–67.

Sterngold, James:

'Mediocrity—or daring designs where the sky's the limit', *Far Eastern Economic Review*, Hong Kong, 5 July 1984, pp 31–3.

Sudjic, Deyan:

'How London Transport came to miss the bus', *Guardian*, 28 November 1979.

'Re-inventing the Skyscraper', *Blueprint*, no 22, November 1985, pp 32–8.

Thorp, Richard C:

'The Supply and Erection of the Structural Steel Framework for the New Headquarters Building of the Hongkong and Shanghai Banking Corporation', paper delivered to the Canadian Structural Engineering Conference, Canadian Steel Construction Council, Willowdale, Ontario, 1986.

Waterhouse, Robert:

'People in Glass Houses', *Guardian*, 31 May 1977.

Williams, Stephanie:

'Summing up the Hong Kong Bank', *Building*, vol CCXLV, no 7322, 16 December 1983, pp 32–7.

'The Bank Headquarters: Old and New', *The Hongkong Bank Group Magazine*, no 16, Hong Kong, Summer 1981, pp 3–8.

Winter, John:

'Building Study: Dock buildings', *Architects' Journal*, vol 152, no 48, 2 December 1970, pp 1307–20.

Wood, Christopher:

'Strategy for Survival', *Far Eastern Economic Review*, Hong Kong, 20 September 1984, pp 67–80.

'Wardley Takes Cover', *Far Eastern Economic Review*, Hong Kong, 17 March 1983, p 104.

Yip, Christopher L:

'Four Major Buildings in the Architectural History of the Hongkong and Shanghai Banking Corporation', in King, ed., *Eastern Banking*, op.cit.

Zunz, GJ, Glover, MJ and Fitzpatrick, AJ:

'The Structure of the New Headquarters for the Hongkong and Shanghai Banking Corporation, Hong Kong', *The Structural Engineer*, vol 63A, no 9, September 1985, pp 255–84.

Zunz, Jack and Glover, Mike:

'The Hongkong and Shanghai Bank', *The Arup Journal*, vol 17, no 4, December 1982, pp 2–10.